Praise for
Dream, Girl

"Written with heartbreaking honesty and touches of humor, Holly Mayes's *Dream, Girl* reveals the price of fantasy and the power of a dream. . . .

"*Dream, Girl* casts aside the glamorized myths of stripper life and takes readers behind the stage and into the authentic lives of the club's found family of dancers, bouncers, managers, and DJs. On the stage, then off, . . . *Dream, Girl* takes readers from grit to glamour, from loneliness to acceptance, and from a high-cost fantasy life to a hard-earned authentic one.

"A life fueled by seduction, held together by secrets, and lived among a found family, Holly Mayes's *Dream, Girl* tells the story of a woman seeking the acceptance of others but finding the acceptance of herself."

—Melissa Ford Lucken, editor,
Washington Square Review, and podcaster,
Washington Square on Air

"*Dream, Girl* is a courageous retelling of Holly's journey into erotic dancing, drugs, and toxic relationships, with a strength that lifts her up and out of an almost certain tragic ending. *Dream, Girl* is an honest look into a world rarely spoken about in polite company."

—Alexandria Sure, author of
Mister Manhattan

"*Dream, Girl* is a great story. It gave me total flashbacks while I was reading it. It took me right back to the clubs and the time period in the late '90s when things were so different."
—Sheena Wild, former entertainer

"*Dream, Girl* is the raw story of a young woman's search for a safe place that she can only find within herself. I couldn't put it down."
—T. K. Parker

"*Dream, Girl* dives into the reality behind the fantasy of exotic dance, taking an unflinching look at a complex world of the male gaze, sexual power dynamics, substance use issues, and economic instability. At its core, this is a book about what it is to be a woman operating within structures of oppression and the war between two intense priorities: the desire to be a good mother (and a good person) and the desire to be free."
—Anne H. Putnam, author of *Navel Gazing: One Woman's Quest for a Size Normal*

"Told with bravery and clear-eyed honesty, Holly Mayes in *Dream, Girl* takes us on an adrenaline-fueled journey from a restrictive religious and family background through a kind of underworld filled with drugs and alcohol and friends and bad jobs, ultimately ending on the stage at various strip clubs. Here, that *Dream Girls* world of staying forever young sputters to a halt on a string of exotic stage names until the more compelling and truer human dream of affirmation and acceptance for who we are is fully realized. Beautifully written, Holly Mayes's *Dream, Girl* is a harrowing and uplifting tale of survival and determination not to be missed."

—Dennis Hinrichsen, poet, author of *Dominion + Selected Poems*

"Reading *Dream, Girl* was an eye-opening journey into a world many of us have not bothered to consider, even though we may drive past strip clubs every day. As a woman, I'm grateful for this glimpse into a world that too many women face. I was particularly struck by the economic trap exotic dancers find themselves in when other doors are shut to them due to poverty, abuse, drugs, or other circumstances. The author's story shows clearly that exotic dancers are also mothers, wives, girlfriends, and friends, juggling childcare, relationship, and self-discovery challenges like the rest of us. There's vivid detail, humor, and above all, brutal honesty throughout. In the end, *Dream, Girl* is about hope and the fierce determination that can turn hope into a better life."

—Amy Buttery

Dream, Girl
by Holly Mayes

© Copyright 2024 Holly Mayes

ISBN 979-8-88824-544-6

All rights reserved. No part of this publication may be reproduced, stored in a retrieval system, or transmitted in any form or by any means—electronic, mechanical, photocopy, recording, or any other—except for brief quotations in printed reviews, without the prior written permission of the author.

Published by

3705 Shore Drive
Virginia Beach, VA 23455
800-435-4811
www.koehlerbooks.com

DREAM, GIRL

HOLLY MAYES

VIRGINIA BEACH
CAPE CHARLES

To younger Holly:
I'm so proud of you. Continue to dream, girl.

Playlist

"Pony"
Ginuwine

"Queer"
Garbage

"Mary Jane's Last Dance"
Tom Petty and the Heartbreakers

"Nothing Else Matters"
Metallica

"Never Tear Us Apart"
INXS

"The Tide is High"
Blondie

"Black No. 1 (Little Miss Scare-All)"
Type O Negative

"Rock of Ages"
Def Leppard

"Cocaine"
Eric Clapton

"Suicide Blonde"
INXS

"Edge of the World"
Faith No More

"Girls, Girls, Girls"
Mötley Crüe

"You Sexy Thing"
Hot Chocolate

"Female of the Species"
Space

"Birthday"
The Beatles

"Living Dead Girl"
Rob Zombie

"Sober"
TOOL

"Voodoo"
Godsmack

"D'yer Mak'er"
Led Zeppelin

"No Diggity"
Blackstreet ft. Dr. Dre, Queen Pen

"Closer"
Nine Inch Nails

"Jungle Love"
Steve Miller Band

"Fool in the Rain"
Led Zeppelin

"Crash Into Me"
Dave Matthews Band

"Bette Davis Eyes"
Kim Carnes

"Kashmir"
Led Zeppelin

"Deuces Are Wild"
Aerosmith

"The Dope Show"
Marilyn Manson

"Mouth (The Stingray Mix)"
Bush

"Fred Bear"
Ted Nugent

"The Beautiful People"
Marilyn Manson

"Pour Some Sugar on Me"
Def Leppard

"Stranglehold"
Ted Nugent

"Save Yourself"
Stabbing Westward

"Last Resort"
Papa Roach

"Oops! . . . I Did It Again"
Britney Spears

"Any Man of Mine"
Shania Twain

"Godless"
U.P.O.

"We Belong"
Pat Benatar

"The Joker"
Steve Miller Band

"Slow Ride"
Foghat

"Iris"
Goo Goo Dolls

"Men in Black"
Will Smith

"Stinkfist"
TOOL

"Don't Come Around Here No More"
Tom Petty and the Heartbreakers

"Return of the Mack"
Mark Morrison

"Closing Time"
Semisonic

Contents

Prologue 9
Pony 12
Queer 21
Mary Jane's Last Dance 28
Nothing Else Matters 34
Never Tear Us Apart 42
The Tide is High 48
Black No. 1 (Little Miss Scare-All) 53
Rock of Ages 58
Cocaine 62
Suicide Blonde 70
Edge of the World 78
Girls, Girls, Girls 83
You Sexy Thing 89
Female of the Species 97
Birthday 105
Living Dead Girl 113
Sober 119
Voodoo 124
D'yer Mak'er 130
No Diggity 139
Closer 148
Jungle Love 154
Fool in the Rain 159
Crash Into Me 166
Bette Davis Eyes 171
Kashmir 175
Deuces Are Wild 182
The Dope Show 190

Mouth (The Stingray Mix) 197
Fred Bear 202
The Beautiful People 206
Pour Some Sugar on Me 211
Stranglehold 217
Save Yourself 222
Last Resort 227
Oops! . . . I Did It Again 231
Any Man of Mine 239
Godless 243
We Belong 247
The Joker 251
Slow Ride 257
Iris 264
Men in Black 270
Stinkfist 274
Don't Come Around Here No More 281
Return of the Mack 286
Closing Time 291
Epilogue 298
Acknowledgments 301

Everything in this memoir is one hundred percent true as I remember it. Names of people and businesses have been altered for privacy.

Prologue

"There is no greater agony than bearing an untold story inside you."
—Maya Angelou

My long-dead second skins hang in the least-used closet alongside my daughters' old prom dresses and our spare luggage. Tiny skirts, midriff tops, barely-there bikinis, and leg garters of various colors and materials dangle limply from the hangers, waiting for their moment to shine once again. They have traveled all over the state in strip clubs throughout Michigan. As far as clothes go, they're ancient—over twenty years old—and fit someone half my size.

Sometimes, after a glass of wine or two, I open the closet and touch them. I hold them to my face, wondering if I can recall the scent of the Victoria's Secret body spray and cigarettes that remind me of a time so long ago. In one of my braver moments, I attempted to try one of them on, but I couldn't fasten the front, and the bottoms never came above my knees. I kicked it off with shame, like the old football player recalling his glory days but can never play again due to bad knees and failing eyesight.

I drove by one of the old clubs years ago and sat in my car, staring at the battered windows and the faded red carpet that leads to the front door. It's aged now with an old roof and a torn-up parking lot. No gaiety and fun to be had there now.

I signed up for a pole dance class at a fitness studio once, hoping to capture some of those old feelings and bring them back to me. I wanted to remember that it was an actual life I once lived. I could never go back, but I wanted to see if I could feel any of those memories once again. The class was filled with women of all sizes and ages. It's different now—as it should be. I didn't tell anyone about my past life as a worker in the sex industry, and I'm not sure they'd believe me. But I knew the stage better than any of them.

When I showed up for my first class at the studio, I was middle-aged and fifty pounds heavier than the last time I'd been near a pole, with bad hips and cellulite, and still, it all came back to me as if a day hadn't passed. The metal of the pole was cool to my touch, my grip strong as if my hands remembered what to do, the muscle memory kicking in after all those years.

History is always there for me, quietly simmering in the shadows. Occasionally, the memories well up, like a knife slicing into the membrane of my mind. A song, a smell, or a phrase can bring it all to the surface and instantly transport me back in time. All of it is still there, no matter how deeply I've hidden it away. Because it's all me. Not just a former me, but it's me now, and all of it, the good and the bad, is still in there.

It's been close to twenty-five years since that life. Most people who know me now know nothing about that version of me. I am a copy-and-paste version of myself over and over until the original is merely a shadow, like an underexposed film photo. Having been raised in poverty under the heavy blanket of an accusatory cult, I met a "cool" guy and then turned to the strip club trying to find a sense of belonging that I had lost.

Shame had caused me to hide it all—from my children, coworkers, and classmates in college. I'd gotten good at hiding uncomfortable things. It seems I was born that way. And the more time that passed, the easier it became—until eventually, it was like it wasn't me any longer.

Pony

I grew up the oldest child in a family of five. I lived with my younger half siblings, Curt and Scarlett, our mother, and my stepfather in a run-down farmhouse that belonged to my grandmother, Clara. The house, built in the late 1800s, was covered with pale yellow chipped paint and battered windows, which rattled in high winds. The front porch leaned inward, and we eventually had to block it off so that visitors wouldn't try to use it. One knock could have crumbled the porch beneath them or shaken the sagging roof down on top of them. The entire house was always battling a barrage of unruly plant life that threatened to take it over. The homes surrounding ours were newer and much better maintained. Over the years, my stepfather fought many rounds with the township about our eyesore home.

My mother, who had never married my biological father, married my stepfather when I was around four years old. There are photos of me at their wedding in my grandparents' yard, shyly hiding behind my mother's dark blue dress while she and my stepfather cut the cake. Before she met my stepfather, she lived with my Grandma Clara, who helped care for me. Grandma Clara was a firm, loving figure in my life. I always felt I was special to her, and she made me feel loved. She didn't care for my mother's marriage to my stepfather, but she mostly held her tongue and remained supportive for the sake of her grandchildren. She eventually moved out and allowed us to live rent-free in her home after my mother got married. The arrangement constantly reminded my stepfather that he couldn't provide for his family, and I suspect my grandmother never let him forget he was beholden to her.

We were fortunate to have a home to live in, but it wasn't without issues. One main issue: our house had no running water a good share of the time. Once a week, on Sundays, we bathed at Grandma Clara's house. After bath time, we filled empty milk jugs with water and lugged them, one by one, to the trunk of our car so we would have water for the upcoming week. When my brother, sister, and I got ripe by midweek, especially in the sweltering summer heat, we bathed ourselves with sponge baths. We heated water on the stove, then poured it into a large plastic tote on the kitchen floor. We took turns bathing from the same "tub," moving fast so the water didn't cool too much for the next person. As the oldest, I always went first. Curt went last since he was inevitably dirtier, and I refused to bathe in the same water after him. Scarlett was small enough to fit inside the makeshift tub, fully immersed. After bath time, we saved the water in buckets and used it to flush the toilet. The house rule: only flush the toilet when we did number two. We hoped that only happened once a day for each of us. The water in the jugs didn't last long between drinking, bathing, cooking, and flushing, so we learned to use it sparingly.

There was always a motley assortment of dirty dishes stacked high in the kitchen sink, sometimes licked clean by a cat who climbed up to investigate. We only washed dishes when we ran out of clean ones. Once a week, my mother rolled up her sleeves and enlisted our help in a process that took over an hour of washing, rinsing, drying, and putting away every dish in the house. Sometimes, while we worked, she sang to us or told us Bible stories.

One small battered wood stove was expected to heat our entire house. On frigid winter nights, the rooms that were the farthest from the stove were as bitter cold as the outdoors. My fingers and toes were constantly cold and tingly. I'd lie in bed and blow my breath out in plumes of white, pretending I was an ice dragon. We'd often wake up to find the old, gray dish water that hadn't been dumped in the flush bucket frozen over in the kitchen sink. Summers weren't so bad, but the upstairs bedrooms grew extremely hot and uncomfortable.

My bedroom ceiling leaked. Whenever it rained, I had to push my bed away from the wall to avoid the dripping. I learned to immediately wake up at the first sound of raindrops hitting the roof. If I slept through it, or if I wasn't home, I had to sleep on a wet bed. One night, I slept through the rain and woke up to a soaked mattress. With nowhere else to go, I slept crouched in a ball on the corner until my bed dried out days later.

My stepfather was self-employed. He always said he didn't want anyone telling him what to do, and he enjoyed working only when he felt like it. He dug up railroad ties from old train tracks, dragged them home, and stacked them in our yard. People bought them for landscaping. My stepfather didn't make a lot of money, but when he did make a sale, he left for hours and came wandering in drunk at 2:30 a.m.

Once, he pulled up to the house in a new car and told us it was ours. Our usual rusty vehicle barely made it down the road and had gaping holes in the floorboard of the backseat. We had to be careful not to drop anything on the floor or risk losing it forever to the pavement speeding by below as the car raced down the road. Once, at the gas station, a concerned person warned my mother that her children's feet were hanging out the bottom of the car and she'd better be careful when she pulled away. We didn't get to keep the new car. He had only rented it.

"Well, it's ours for a day," he joked.

When my stepfather made even a nominal sale from railroad ties, he bought beer, my mother was cheerful, and the house was full of food. During the times he wasn't selling anything, we ate watery potato soup with tiny pieces of bacon, pale and peppery with spices.

I promised myself that in the New System, I'd never eat potato soup again.

As members of the Jehovah's Witnesses religion, my family considered the New System a sort of heaven on earth—at least as far as their beliefs were concerned. While we all waited for the New System to arrive, we abstained from celebrating holidays or birthdays, and we didn't participate in activities that other normal families took part in. Our main mission was to witness to other people so that they could join us as God's sheep. Once everyone knew about the true God, then Armageddon would come, the New System would arrive, and the world would be filled with righteous believers.

Everyone in my family, except my stepfather, went to congregation meetings two nights a week as well as on Sundays. My stepfather refused to subscribe to "religious bullshit," as he called it. We also went out each weekend "in service," which meant knocking on doors to tell worldly people (people not of our religion) the good news about God and the imminent New System. If diligent Jehovah's Witnesses reached a certain number of service hours each month, they were called Pioneers. My family wasn't the diligent sort, mostly because we were diligently trying to survive poverty in *this* system while we waited for the new one.

Before I was born, my pregnant mother—single, confused, and afraid—had converted to the religion. She'd answered the door when someone knocked in service and felt that was God's way of reaching out to her. Thus, I was born into it, and I never knew about holidays or birthday celebrations until I started school, and, from a young age, I understood the reasons why we didn't celebrate. Jehovah's Witnesses do not celebrate any holidays other than the Memorial, a commemoration of the Lord's Evening Meal.

My grade school teacher once caught me on the playground frightening a fellow student. I told my classmate in no uncertain terms that if she didn't convert, she and her family would die at the end of this system with the rest of the wicked people. The girl was in tears, parents were involved, and I was sent home. While my mother appreciated my zeal, she told me I needed to learn how to frame God's news in a more positive light. I didn't understand why scaring the shit out of people wasn't a great way to get the message across, because it had certainly worked for me.

Some of the worldly girls at school went to dance classes and wore fancy little costumes with beads and sparkles. Some practiced gymnastics in the schoolyard, doing backbends and walkovers. They seemed so confident, like they knew who they were. They had a purpose, and they were good at something. I wanted to be good at something and show off in the schoolyard, and I wanted to learn something, too.

I begged my mother to let me sign up for something, *anything*. But the classes inevitably fell on either Tuesdays or Thursdays, when my time could be better spent serving God.

"You know you can't sign up for something that lands on meeting nights," she reminded me. She didn't want the elders to find out she was letting her child join a worldly event when she should be at the meetings.

I quit asking after a while. Even if the event didn't land on a Tuesday or Thursday, money was always an issue. I was jealous of the kids who got to learn a skill like tap dance or gymnastics. I tried to remind myself I was going to make it through the end of this wicked system of things and into God's New System. In the New System, I vowed I would sign up for whatever classes I wanted, because then they would most certainly not fall on meeting nights.

My school friends also got to go to each other's homes and spend time together outside of school. I never wanted anyone to see my house, but it didn't matter. My mother refused to let me hang out with worldly kids who might be a bad influence. "Satan," she said, "puts roadblocks in our way to stop us from serving God."

I didn't want to be worldly, and I didn't want to die in Armageddon, so I continued to go to the meetings. I stopped bringing slips of paper home for after-school activities. I made excuses when someone asked me to come over. I dreamed of the New System when things would obviously be so much better and the only way to get there was to stay strong and remain on the true course.

I tried to be religious. I really did. I clenched my hands tightly in prayer during meals and at bedtime. I sang loudly (albeit poorly) during meetings to show God I was one of his true followers. Groups of us packed in a minivan and drove out in service on Sundays after the meetings. We made up a game and took turns claiming homes we wanted to live in when the New System arrived. "I want to live there in the New System. I mean, if those people don't come around." And everyone would "ooooh" and "ahhh" over the home, imagining what it would be like to live there. I never considered how morbid it was to think about the homeowners' impending deaths because their beliefs didn't match ours.

Gazing at those extravagant homes allowed me to daydream about what it would be like to have running water and take a bath whenever I wanted—not just on Sundays. Homes like those we saw in service would have been a dream come true to me in this system. While others in the van dreamed about in-ground swimming pools or vaulted ceilings, I dreamed about flushing a toilet with a handle.

My mother was an artist and loved to draw portraits. She discovered I loved writing and encouraged me to write short stories, while she drew the illustrations for them. Parenting three children in poverty under the wing of a strict religion was difficult for her. But she loved us in her own way.

One morning, I forgot it was my turn for kindergarten show-and-tell. I rushed to the bus stop, crying, while my mother followed behind with various toys in hand, asking if any of them would work. I sobbed and shook my head no. None of those toys were good enough for show-and-tell. I was going to lose my turn. I cried the entire bus ride to school, upset that I would disappoint the class with nothing to share. When I arrived, my mother was already there with my baby sister in her lap. She brought Scarlett, dressed in a pretty Sunday meeting dress, for me to share for show-and-tell. The kids adored my baby sister, and I got to speak in front of the class about the important job I had as a big sister. I loved my mother so much that day.

We went to the laundromat once every couple of weeks to wash all our clothes. Even though it was hard work, I liked laundromat day, especially in the winter when the large floor-to-ceiling windows would steam up with condensation. Curt, Scarlett, and I created murals with our fingers on the cold frosted windows until the owner caught us and made us stop.

We carried in black trash bags filled with dirty clothes and placed them in front of the machines. Curt carried the detergent since he couldn't carry a bag. My mother sorted the clothes while I kept an eye on my siblings. Curt raced around, trying to find coins that had fallen beneath the machines. My stepfather immediately left—embarrassed by the amount of laundry we'd hauled in. On some of the special laundromat days, he returned with a twenty-five cent Shasta for each of us and a single Hershey's candy bar. We felt special when we each got our own soda. He divided the chocolate bar between the three of us, giving "Her" to me, "she" to my sister, and "y's" to my brother. We savored our piece of chocolate and our soda, taking tiny sips and bites to make them last longer. I enjoyed the time at the laundromat, especially if we got soda and candy.

My stepfather had dreams and high hopes that we would one day be able to live in a nice house. He wasn't part of our religion, so he wanted *this* system to work out. He talked about his dreams freely when he had a drink in his hand, often cracking open a beer or two and deciding the best thing to go along with that beer was a car ride. The three of us kids piled into the back seat, and he and my mother sat in the front. He stayed on back roads to avoid the cops and drove slowly over the gravel, alternating between holding his beer and smoking a cigarette.

One summer evening, we cruised the back roads with the windows rolled down as the soft late afternoon sunlight and gentle summer breeze floated through our car. We came to a complete stop in front of an old farmhouse. There was a "For Sale" sign in the yard.

"We're going to get that," he proclaimed and pointed his beer bottle toward the house through the car window. It was a lovely two-story brick house with a barn.

I bounced up and down in the back seat. "It has a barn! Can we get horses, too?" I loved horses. I always wanted my own horse. That was another thing I wanted in the New System—my very own stable of horses to ride.

"We'll see, we'll see." He laughed. Talking to my mother, he pointed out features she might like. I watched her reaction closely and noticed she acted excited—but with reservations. She nodded as she gazed out the window, a wistful look in her eyes as she twisted her hair. That was a habit of hers—twisting the ends of her hair into knots if she was nervous. We used to laugh at her when she had tiny little knots shooting up from her hair during particularly stressful life events.

For days after that, I kept reminding my stepfather about the house, asking him questions about when we could go inside, when we could move, and what we planned on bringing with us.

"We'll see," he told me, edging away and fleeing outdoors to escape my persistence.

With each passing day, he grew more annoyed with my pestering. Soon, it wasn't discussed anymore. I learned to recognize his daydreams, which usually came out when he was drinking.

Queer

At the congregation meetings, the parents of kids my age forced them to be friends with me. I wasn't an unlikable child, but I was an oddball. As I grew older, I became more aware of my poverty, my alcoholic stepfather, and the general angst of becoming a teenager. I was at an odd age where everyone at the meetings was either a few years older than me, or quite a few years younger. When the older girls were in high school, they threw slumber parties, and I was invited as an afterthought. Usually, the parents were the ones to ask if I wanted to come over, or they pushed their children to ask me.

I remember crying to my mother in our kitchen once that I didn't know who I was and had no real friends. Occasionally she broke down and allowed me to go to worldly friends' homes so that I had someone my own age to hang out with.

I had a couple boyfriends in high school, but I kept them a secret because I wasn't allowed to date, especially not a worldly boy. When a guy showed interest in me, I instantly felt needed and loved despite knowing the relationships were doomed to fail. I couldn't bring them home or go to their homes, and school dances or other worldly events were out of the question. The relationships petered out when it became apparent that the only time we were going to see each other was in the school hallways between classes.

I became good at compartmentalizing my life. The person I was at school was completely different from who I was at the meetings or out in service. At school, sometimes I cussed and secretly celebrated a few holidays. If someone brought treats for their birthday, I'd eat one. I began to detest going out in service for fear I'd run into my classmates from school. I could think of nothing worse than knocking on a door and having someone from school answer on a Saturday morning. Then I felt guilty because I knew God could see me and knew who I was on the inside. He knew I wanted to be part of this world, and my mother said that made him sad.

When I was fifteen, I started babysitting the neighbors' kids to earn money. My school friends wore nice clothes, and I wanted nice clothes too. I desperately wanted to fit in and was growing weary of the New System's arrival to have a better life. My stepfather drove me back and forth to babysitting jobs. He never complained and didn't overdrink on the nights he had to give me a ride, for which I was thankful. He always showed up and waited in the driveway until the parents returned after 2:00 a.m. when the bars closed.

I learned early on not to let him borrow any of my earnings with an ambiguous payback date. I would never see it again. I had to hide my babysitting cash from him, especially when railroad tie sales were slow. He knew when I had money, and most of the time he found my hiding places, tearing apart my room while I was at school. If he was unusually cheerful (i.e. drinking) when I walked in the door, a feeling of dread welled up in my stomach. I raced upstairs, and sure enough, my money was gone.

"I'll pay you back," he promised, laughing, holding the beer up to toast me as I stormed back to confront him. I knew

I'd never see the money again and stomped upstairs, angry because I had nothing to show for my weekends of babysitting.

When I was sixteen, I got a job at a local pizza place in town. I bought a car and paid for my own insurance. Sometimes my car was the only running vehicle in the house, and I was the only one earning regular income. I loaned money to my stepfather and even his father. And while I refused to let anyone borrow my car, they occasionally guilted me into picking them up from the bar after it closed.

Despite my growing concerns about my religion, I ended up getting baptized—mostly because by that time, it was expected that I would want to dedicate my life to God. I studied under a woman named Renee who had married a man with five children from five different women. They bred Shar-Pei dogs, and there were always children and puppies of various ages underfoot. Renee's house was loud, tiny, and crowded, and she always seemed to be on the verge of a mental breakdown. When she found out I enjoyed writing, she told me I shouldn't write my feelings down because that was a direct way for the demons to know how to manipulate me. I stopped writing for a while after that, constantly fearful that the devil and his demons were watching me write my thoughts on paper.

The day of the baptism, I hoped for some sign—some sense I was making the right choice. I wanted to have faith that the New System was coming and that life would be much easier, but deep down, I had my doubts. After my baptism, amid the hugs and the celebratory congratulations, there was an emptiness inside me. A persistent feeling that maybe something was wrong with me and that maybe God had decided he didn't need someone like me in the New System. He didn't want a girl who lived a double life in his new world. I continued to attend the meetings, but my prayers became a little quieter, I didn't sing quite as loudly, and the New System seemed even further away.

My senior year in high school, I sat down with the guidance counselor to go over my career options after graduation. I was excited that the matches on my career assessment came back with creative jobs like writer, actress, and dancer. The school counselor, a pinched-off older lady with small glasses, reviewed my form with pursed lips. She sighed, slid the form across the desk to me, and told me I should do those things in my spare time and that creative-type careers weren't considered real jobs for real people who needed to earn a living. She knew I had taken some office block classes to teach me about typing and office work, so she suggested courses geared toward secretarial work that would lead to a stable job and guarantee me income.

As a Jehovah's Witness, I wasn't expected to plan for a future in this worldly system if the end was imminent. It didn't make sense to go to college or plan long term for a life in this world when it was doomed to fail in Armageddon. Any discussions about post-high school plans with someone in my congregation would ultimately lead to talk of becoming a Pioneer after graduation. Planning for college meant you thought this system would last, and that was a waste of time. No one my age at the meetings considered college, or at least no one talked about it.

College proved out of reach, anyway. My family had little to no income and refused to file taxes to prove our inability to pay, because, in my stepfather's words, "the government needs to stay outta my goddamned business."

After graduation, I moved to Alcoa with another girl from the congregation, and we allowed a third girl to move in and share the costs. I loved living with them. We became our own little family and took care of each other. For the first time,

I lived in a warm home with running water. I had my own bedroom and a ceiling that didn't leak when it rained. I had a sense of what life could be like in this world instead of waiting for the New System.

My meeting attendance began to suffer. Every time I saw my mother, she pressured me to come back to "the flock" before it was too late. She reminded me that Armageddon was about to happen—and that I barely had time to make it back if I decided to return right away. Although I realized I was no longer interested in that religion, I was still nervous about the end of this system. It frightened me to know I could die with the rest of the wicked people who turned away from God—but not enough to return to the meetings. Being away from my family and religion granted me a freedom I had never known before, but I also felt guilt and shame for wanting to be free.

Eventually, my roommates and I had a falling out. I moved in with Grandma Clara and my step-grandfather, Grandpa Warren, instead of going back home and found minimum wage jobs here and there. I wanted to do something with my life, but I had no direction and no encouragement.

When the Nancy Kerrigan and Tonya Harding drama hit the news in 1993, I became fascinated with figure skating. The graceful choreography, beautiful costumes, and music made me fall in love with becoming a skater. I decided to try it and visited the local ice rink to check it out. I no longer needed anyone's permission to sign up for lessons or worried which night classes fell on. I wanted to learn to skate.

When I arrived, the ice rink was filled with young children taking lessons. Most of them were confident and already skilled. I daydreamed that perhaps someday I could skate as well as they could, if not better.

I laced up my skates and was ready to try. Skating was difficult, but it was the first time I had set out to learn something new. I discovered freedom in experiencing something I had only dreamed about. It unleashed in me the ability to see a dream and reach for it. I knew I was creative, and this was my chance to discover myself.

But after a few lessons, I grew impatient with how long it would take me to become a competent skater. I was jealous of the children who were developing their skills at a young age. I wished I'd started younger and resented my religion, my parents, and my childhood. I was only nineteen and already felt like life had passed me by. I continued to skate, but the dream of competition, glittery costumes, and music began to fade away.

Around that same time, a middle-aged couple moved into the vacant home next to my parents' house. Joseph worked at a lumber yard, enjoyed smoking cigarettes, drinking beer after work, and tinkering around the house. Karen worked for a local school district. She was tall with reddish-blonde hair and bright blue eyes. They had two sons: Joey, who lived with them, and the older one, Allen, who was away at college.

Joey was six-foot-two and lanky with dark hair that formed a widow's peak on his forehead. He had a strong jawline and dark blue eyes with an intense stare. I was visiting my parents one day when I caught sight of him in their yard from the kitchen window. I wanted to know more about him. Now that I'd moved out of my apartment in Alcoa, I didn't have many friends and was lonely.

Eventually, I found a way to introduce myself, and he invited me over for iced tea. I discovered he had a great sense of humor. Even though he was only a little younger than me, he seemed older and wiser in ways I wasn't. He admitted he didn't have a driver's license because of some mistakes in his past. He felt misunderstood in a lot of ways. Deep down, he was a good person.

He just needed someone who understood him.

Mary Jane's Last Dance

Joey and I soon became inseparable. It helped that I not only had a driver's license, but also a car. Karen worked full-time at the school bus garage and up until that point had driven Joey everywhere he needed to go. I think she was grateful that our spending time together relieved her of the burden of taxiing him around. Joey hated living in Springfield, away from Alcoa and his friends. I began spending more evenings with him at his parents' house.

When I wasn't with him, I was thinking about when I would be with him again. I loved listening to him tell stories about his life, which seemed so much more worldly and exciting than my own sheltered existence. Even though he was only nineteen, he drank beer, and even more shockingly, Karen bought it for him. That was against the law and made him even more dangerous and reckless—and more attractive to me.

Joey smoked cigarettes, which also made him seem older and cooler than me. I was eighteen the first time I smoked a cigarette. One of my former roommates was a smoker, and I purchased a pack of Virginia Slims one night to try it out. I wanted to look cool and sophisticated with the long, thin cigarette, but secretly, I thought it tasted nasty. When I discovered that Joey smoked, I started up again, carefully hiding it from my parents, whose windows had a view of his house. I bought the same Marlboro Lights that Joey smoked. It was more convenient that way since, if he was out, he smoked mine and didn't want to be caught dead with a Virginia "Slime."

I still dabbled in ice skating, but only half-heartedly. I had to be around in case Joey needed me to drive him somewhere. When I did go to the rink, Joey had me drop him off at one of his friends' houses and pick him up when my class was finished.

One night, while we relaxed by a bonfire in his backyard, he asked me if I'd ever smoked pot.

"No," I quickly answered.

I had a nervous feeling in my stomach. I didn't want to think he did drugs. I also didn't want to consider that if I didn't do them, it would affect how he felt about me. I wasn't raised around drugs, and my mother made sure I never saw them. I could almost hear her voice in my head. *Satan will do anything to get you to be a part of this world, and drugs are a tool Satan uses.* I glanced uneasily toward the driveway, paranoid that she'd heard him ask me that question from her house.

"Really?" Joey asked, casually taking a swig of beer. His gaze never left the fire. "I used to smoke . . . a long time ago."

I nodded, taking a sip of iced tea. I recalled how, when I was in junior high, I watched a neighbor's house while they were on vacation. I checked their mail, watered their plants, fed their cat, and kept an eye on the place. I started snooping around and found a bong on an ironing board in their bedroom. I didn't know what it was, but deep down I knew it was bad and something that I shouldn't have seen. I rushed back home and described it to my mother, and she never let me house-sit for them again.

"Does that bother you?" His dark blue eyes turned toward me. My own face was warm, either from the fire or the embarrassment of being scrutinized by his gaze. In my wild imagination, the flames eerily framed his face. He looked like the devil, asking me what I thought about illegal drugs.

"No, not at all." I released my breath. I realized it didn't matter. He liked me. He wanted to be with me. And I liked being with him. What did our pasts matter?

A few nights later, sitting by the bonfire, he mentioned it again. This time, I was drinking a wine cooler and feeling relaxed. I leaned back in my chair and stared up at the stars in the cloudless night sky. The smell of wood smoke rose from the fire and mingled with our cigarette smoke.

"I was cleaning my room the other day and found an old joint in my drawer. Do you want to try it?" He spoke casually, with his long legs stretched out in front of him, holding the beer loosely in his hand. "I mean, if I didn't throw it out."

It was one time, to try it. I pushed the thoughts of Satan away, finding it's a lot easier to do that with a wine cooler in my hand. "Sure, I guess," I said. "I mean, if you still have it."

He leaped up from the lawn chair, leaned over to give me a kiss, and ran to the house. When he came back a few minutes later, he handed me a tiny filterless cigarette. It was no thicker than a pencil and looked like a tiny cigar with paper that had been dampened or aged yellow at some point. I turned it over in my hands. It was so small for the big fuss it raised in our Sunday meetings about how it could mislead people into the devil's doing.

"See how the paper is yellow? It's because I've had it so long, so it's probably really old," Joey said, taking it away from me.

Unlike a cigarette, he held the joint between his thumb and forefinger, then lit it with his lighter. He leaned his head sideways, brought the joint to his lips, and inhaled. He held the smoke inside his lungs for a few seconds before exhaling. A sweet, cloying scent hung in the air between us. He handed it to me. I inhaled it like he did, and he told me to hold it in. I exhaled and then coughed.

Once I did that, I stepped over a threshold. I was no longer the same person I was before. I implicitly trusted him to show me his world, and he was happy to be my teacher. I no longer felt like the girl who didn't understand how the world worked, which should have been a sign of how truly naïve I was.

Joey admitted to me much later that in the beginning, he didn't think we were ever going to work out. He thought he was going to "fuck me and use me for a ride"—the dumb country girl from Springfield. He pretended to be my boyfriend, and I took him wherever he wanted to go. I was desperate to be loved and accepted after having spent my entire life trying to fit in. When I smoked a joint with him, it allowed him to see a way for us to be together. He was more comfortable around me.

When we weren't together, I knew exactly where he was. Because I was the one with a license and he counted on me to take him everywhere, I never had him far from my sight. My old life was exactly that: an old life. I found a new existence—an exciting one—and yes, it involved getting high, but I was still fundamentally the same person inside. And Joey was a good guy. Whenever I thought about the devil and his influence in my life, I pushed the thought away and focused on Joey—what he needed, what he thought, and what we were going to do next.

Before I started smoking weed, when I picked Joey up from his friends' houses after ice skating, he never invited me inside. He made me wait in the car. Or he'd have me drive him somewhere and he'd say, "I'm just running in real quick; I'll be back out." I know now that he was going in there to either get weed or smoke weed. And I'd sit out in the car waiting in some sketchy neighborhood with my doors locked, hoping he'd be fast. After I started smoking with him, I got invited inside.

After that first joint, we got high together all the time. I'm not sure if I ever really knew him when he was sober. He took me to a head shop that sold pipes and bongs. He introduced me to all the paraphernalia that went with smoking pot. We also bought whippets: cartridges filled with nitrous oxide that when you inhaled them gave you a wicked rush to the brain. I accidentally broke one open on my finger and it burned me, and that was the end of that high experience. Getting stoned introduced me to a whole other way to enjoy the world. I stopped living in constant fear of religious retribution, my mother's disapproval, and my general lack of direction in life. At the same time, I latched on to him as a lifeline, since I was falling away from my religion, my family, and everything I had ever known. I wanted a savior, and he needed to be saved himself.

Whatever alcohol we needed Joey bought from stores that never carded him. I liked wine coolers and drinking them made me feel more relaxed. He took me to a place that rented hourly hot tub sessions. It was so much fun to sit in the water and lean back, looking up at the stars through the slats in the ceiling, smoking joints, and drinking. This life was perfect for me, and I truly believed Joey also was perfect for me.

We broke up after an argument a few months later. I packed up my belongings, which had slowly started to accumulate in his room, and moved back to my grandparents' home. The breakup was bad, and I missed him terribly. Grandma Clara tried to help and at first, I was inconsolable. But after a long week, I started getting over him.

Then out of the blue, he called and wanted to hang out. Just like that, I was back at his house. I was desperately afraid of being lonely—afraid I wasn't good enough for him or anyone. I was happy he needed me.

I sometimes wonder what life would have been like for me if I had gone my own way. Maybe I could have eventually found a way to go to college or kept working part time at the grocery store job. I could have returned full-time to the meetings and service and focused on the New System and God again. Joey would have been a brief phase where I dipped my toe into the wild side, an imperceptible blip in my mostly uneventful life up until that point.

We officially got back together and celebrated by having sex, playing video games on his bed, and smoking a joint. Shortly after that, he introduced me to acid.

Nothing Else Matters

My mother had another baby, Gabrielle, making me a big sister again. Curt and Scarlett were in high school preparing to graduate. Everyone else had lives, and I was lost and unsure of who I was and who I was supposed to be. Before Joey, I spent my entire life waiting for the end of this system of things so that God's new order could come, and I would be saved. I was warned that some of God's followers would be lured by Satan and the temptations of the world, leading them to be pulled away from His love. If that was the case, I was definitely on that path.

When Joey came along and accepted me and his friends welcomed me, I felt loved and like I was a part of something bigger. Some of the first people he introduced me to were a couple named Christopher and Maggie. They both had long, stick-straight blond hair. Their hair was so shiny and silky, it made me want to reach out and touch it. We made jokes that from behind we could barely tell them apart.

They lived in an apartment complex near the mall with Christopher's parents and his younger brother. When we visited, his parents were nearly always sitting in the living room, planted in front of a television and barely glancing our way as we walked past. We smoked a lot of weed in Christopher's bedroom, and I was certain they could smell it. I was still cautious about getting high in front of adults. But Christopher reassured me it was fine because he lit incense. We smoked cigarettes, or sometimes cloves, immediately after the joint, which made the air in his tiny bedroom grow even thicker. The room became engulfed in one thick cloud of smoke, blue mingled with white, as it floated toward the ceiling. It was always dark because the curtains were drawn over the window shades. Pink Floyd and a variety of musicians displaying skulls and skeletons burst forth from posters on every wall in the small space. A black light glowed in the corner and eerily lit up some of the posters.

Maggie introduced me to cross-stitching. I loved the focus and attention to detail it required. I bought more patterns, hoops, thread, and needles to make my own tapestries. I lost myself in the intricate designs, especially if I was stoned. We sat on the floor and cross-stitched while Christopher and Joey talked or played video games.

One night, the four of us went to the cemetery. We smoked a joint, lay on one of the largest grave markers, and stared up at the night sky. I listened as they talked about their dreams and what they wanted for the world and their lives. Christopher and Maggie were both servers at a restaurant down the road from where they lived. I still had a job at the local grocery store, but I was working fewer hours. Joey planned on going back to college. Being high made it easier for me to push away any negative feelings I had about my own lack of direction. I was older than all of them, but I thought they had lived such wondrous lives already, not having been raised believing that death was imminent all the time.

The cool stone of the grave pressed against me and chilled my back. Water in the nearby river rustled against the shore, providing background music to their voices. The sweet smell of pot and cigarette smoke lingered in the air. I stared at the stars and buried the thought of God punishing me for my sins. I was certain I wouldn't make it into the New System now. Luckily, when I was stoned, I grew numb to falling away from God and the Truth.

Christopher casually mentioned they could get some acid, and Joey jumped on it. I was apprehensive. In the back of my mind, I heard my mother's voice telling me Satan wanted me to do hard drugs, to lead me even farther away from God's love. But I shoved that thought aside. When I expressed my concerns, the three of them insisted it would be fine and they wouldn't let anything happen to me.

We dropped the acid at a Pink Floyd laser light show held in downtown Alcoa. Joey handed me a tiny square piece of paper no bigger than my fingernail. I placed it on my tongue, waiting for some sort of burst of . . . something. The small, nearly tasteless paper turned into a chewy spit wad before I swallowed it. I questioned what sort of impact something that insignificant could even have on anyone.

I found out after about half an hour. Every one of my five senses was operating in overdrive and every synapse in my brain was firing at triple time. Walls blurred together with the ceiling until I couldn't tell the difference between them. The facial features on people became exaggerated, displaying huge gaping maws with tiny beady eyes before switching back again. When I glanced at Joey, his hairline took on an even sharper devil's peak and his blue eyes darkened to nearly black in the evening light.

The Pink Floyd laser light show was louder and more extreme than anything else I could recall in my life up until that point. The lights, sounds, and even the smells were stronger and sharper. On acid, the world was in a different dimension. I giggled uncontrollably one minute and bawled my eyes out the next. Christopher laughed at me, a harsh, barking sound to my ears, and said I was "tripping balls."

I lost eight hours of my life that night, most of it I couldn't recall the next day, or even now. I enjoyed the otherworldly feeling and the happiness and euphoria of tripping, but when things took a turn for the worse, my anxiety, paranoia, and depression were suffocating, like a tight grip around my throat.

Joey and I dropped acid again at a party in an apartment in Grand Heights. I spent a majority of the night freaking out that the cops were going to show up. There was a large number of people crammed into the small upstairs apartment, and as parties go, the noise level increased. It became my obsessive goal that in order to escape the noise and a possible police visit, we all should leave the premises immediately. For most of my acid trip and a majority of the evening, I wandered around, interrupting conversations and assigning people into groups of twos and threes. Looking at them with a direct, large-pupil stare, I informed them when they should leave and how they should walk down the sidewalk so as to not draw attention to themselves. The next group would have to time it before they left so that they didn't catch up to the group in front of them. After a while, during one of my numerous interruptions, one of the guys asked me, "What do you mean, leave? If we leave, we're more obvious. And where will we go?" Someone called me a buzzkill and told Joey I needed to "chill and quit freaking people out."

That dashed my elaborate plans for escape. I rode the rest of the night out on a couch, alone in the living room alternating between muttering about how loud it was and jumping at loud noises. I longed to hide in the closet when I thought the police were coming.

After that experience, one would think I'd had my fill of dropping acid, but Joey loved it, and I was determined to try and make it work for me. Plus, Joey had no problem doing it without me or leaving me home while he did it. I didn't want to be the uncool girlfriend, and I didn't want to be left behind.

On another night, we decided to drop with Joey's friend, Jay. Jay was a good-looking guy—shorter, with sandy-brown hair and a philosophical way about him. Whenever we were stoned, he got quiet and contemplative, rather than loud and talkative. I think at times I must have gotten on his nerves.

The plan was to wait for Jay to get off work at a local pizzeria, and then the three of us would drop together. Joey and I arrived in the parking lot just before his shift ended so we could pick him up from work. Joey and I planned to drop while we waited, then Jay could drive us back to his house. A few minutes before he was supposed to get out, he informed us someone called in sick, so he had to work late. By the time we found out, I had already started feeling the effects of the acid, and there was no way I could drive.

Joey and I stayed in the car the entire time, tripping on acid for eight hours in the back of the pizzeria parking lot.

Eight hours straight.

Tripping balls in a car.

I went through all the phases: laughing uncontrollably, crying my eyes out, and staring blankly ahead. Sometime around 2:00 a.m., I felt well enough to drive us home—though I was exhausted.

The first experience at the Pink Floyd show was the best, but each subsequent trip after that was more like a prison sentence of my mind. When I was on that drug, I couldn't get off—there's no changing your mind. Perhaps that's what

I liked least about it. The effects stayed with me, regardless of what happened during the trip. I also never knew what to expect. There were times I was fearful that I was somehow closer to God under its influence, and I didn't want him to see me that way.

Later, Joey and his friends went through a phase where they tried to sell fake acid to earn money. I discovered that if I removed the colorful ad inserts from a magazine and stabbed tiny, even holes in them with a needle, I could make them look, taste, and feel like sheets of acid. I even wanted to try to dip them in some sort of kitchen cleaner to give them a more chemical acidic taste, but the guys told me to hold off on that.

Joey's friends praised me for my artistic ability. They dug up magazines from home and brought them to me. Joey was proud. I was somebody important with a skill and a useful talent. After a lifetime of not fitting in, not knowing who I was or who I was meant to be, this felt good. This acceptance alone was a drug for me, and I was no longer an outsider. These people didn't care about my religion or my past; they accepted me.

I did that a few times. I got stoned, lit a cigarette, picked up my needle, and went to work. I spent hours leaning over a magazine ad as I methodically pricked a pin into a sheet in even rows to look like machine perforation. I never went with them to sell the sheets to the customers. I couldn't bear it if someone called me out and said the product was fake after all my hard work. Plus, I didn't want to see that part of the business. They sold to nameless, faceless students and dealers who I never met, and I was fine with that. They also had to make sure the person couldn't find them when they discovered the drug was fake. It could get dicey when people got ripped off for a few hundred dollars and had no recourse to get it back. The fewer people involved in the sale, the better.

One night, a group of us went to the dock on the Grand River to smoke and get high. The Grand River ran through an area behind Joey's friend's house. The dock was in a roadside park with a boat landing. Occasionally, we gathered by the river to get high and hang out.

A commotion started near the water with three girls who were gathered at the bottom of the stairs near the river's edge. A small girl with blonde hair was pressed into the fence by a taller Mexican girl leaning over her, yelling in her face. The taller girl weighed a lot more than the blonde, and she also had a friend who stepped in occasionally to point and yell, giving the taller girl a break.

There was something fearless about the small blonde girl. Her voice was deep and throaty as she yelled back at the taller girl. She displayed an aura of disgust and attitude, blended with spitfire. Despite being backed into the fence, she kept coming back at the girls who were trying to intimidate her.

I'd never been involved in fights. When they happened between girls in school, it always inevitably ended up in hair pulling and scratching. Neither sounded appealing to me. These girls looked to be more of the punching sort, or maybe even the stabbing sort, and my stomach churned. I thought someone should stop it. Joey pushed me aside and went down with another shorter guy to pull the girls apart.

Eventually, with the help of Joey and the shorter guy, the fight broke up. The taller girl left with her friend, both flashing hand gestures to the blonde, but she didn't appear fazed at all. She flipped them off, glanced around and located her cigarettes, which she had apparently lost in the scuffle.

After the two girls left and things calmed down, Joey introduced me to Justin, another one of his good friends, and the shorter guy who helped break up the fight. Justin had dark hair that was shaved close to his head and sported a dark goatee. He had various tattoos lining his arms and legs and there was barely a spot on his skin that wasn't covered in ink. Justin was stocky and loud and got progressively louder the more he drank. Every one of his sentences ended with "man."

His girlfriend, Brandy, was the small blonde girl in the fight. Up close, I realized Brandy was a lot younger than I'd originally thought. Loud and sassy, she had long dirty-blonde hair and dark brown eyes, hooded by thick, unplucked eyebrows. She didn't wear a lot of makeup, which made her appear even younger. I loved her spunk and wished I'd had half of it when I was seventeen years old.

We hit it off right away, and the four of us frequently hung out. I enjoyed my new friends, and having people in my life who accepted me was something I had always been searching for. I eventually gave up ice skating. I let go of that dream, of competing and performing in sparkly costumes. I justified giving skating up by drawing the conclusion that since I'd started at a later age, I wasn't going to be great at it.

Besides, I had found new friends and a new way of life.

Never Tear Us Apart

The more time I spent with Joey and his friends, the less time I spent trying to connect with my mother. She had always been the biggest reason I kept going to the meetings; I never wanted to disappoint her. I knew people in the congregation asked her where I was and why I wasn't attending the meetings or service anymore. She bravely showed up and faced them, giving them some sort of excuse.

I also knew how she felt about Satan throwing things in our way to stop us from serving God. And yet, here I was, her oldest daughter, doing drugs and partying, and hanging out with worldly people who God considered bad associations. The further I grew away from the religion, the more she disapproved of my lifestyle. She grew quiet when I did visit, no longer trying to convince me to come to the meetings. She didn't care to hear about my life or my new friends because in her eyes, I was doomed to die. She considered me lost to Satan and this system of things.

I officially moved out of my grandparents' house and into Joey's bedroom at Joseph and Karen's. Grandma Clara was unhappy when I moved out. She used to wait up for me to come home when it was late at night, acting like she wasn't waiting but immediately falling asleep the minute I came home and went to bed. Unlike my mother, my grandmother was supportive and happy for me. Worried, but still happy. Every time I visited my grandparents, they lit up the minute I walked through the door. Grandma Clara loved to hear about my friends and my adventures. I left out the part about the drugs, but I wondered if she somehow suspected it.

After my first missed period, I bought a pregnancy test at Target before I was supposed to meet Joey at a restaurant nearby for dinner. It was one of the restaurants that rarely carded him, so he liked to drink there. I had half an hour before I was supposed to meet him.

Taking the test in the Target bathroom, I read the instructions over and over while I waited. After I received the positive results, I threw that stick away and bought another one, choosing a different cashier this time. Back to the bathroom I went, heading for the same stall.

The two lines showed up again, dark pink slashes on the white stick.

I was nervous about telling Joey. On the inside, I was happy about this development. I had always known in the back of my mind this could be a possibility. Joey used condoms sparingly, if ever. We weren't careful even though he knew I wasn't on birth control. I was scared about telling him and had no idea what he would say, but I could guess that he wasn't ready for this any more than I was. There was a part of me that knew I loved him and needed him in my life. I wanted a piece of him, no matter what, with me always.

But I was also scared because this was not something the Bible condoned. Having a baby out of wedlock was the height of immorality in God's eyes, thus I was committing a sin against him. I was sealing my fate and moving even farther away from God's love. I also wasn't sure how to tell my mother.

I met Joey at the restaurant and sat down at our table, fidgeting with my purse. He already had a mixed drink in front of him and slid another one over to me. He always had to order for me since I could rarely order a drink and not get carded. I pushed it back and asked for water instead.

"What, you're not going to drink?" he asked, surprised.

"I'm pregnant," I said, waiting for his reaction.

His expression went blank and then he exhaled. "We're not ready for this."

"We can be ready."

"We're too young to have a child right now."

"I'm keeping this baby," I told him with finality.

He was shocked initially, but when we talked it out, we agreed to make it work. When we got home, we told Karen. She was ecstatic to be a grandmother, and she told us she would help in any way she could. Joseph was less confident and more of the mindset that Joey needed a full-time job now more than ever, and we needed to focus on our futures instead of partying all the time.

I knew I had to tell my mother. I also knew what her reaction would be, which was why it took me a while to build up the nerve. When I finally told her, she insisted I return to the meetings and prove I was repentant to the elders so that I wouldn't get disfellowshipped. Being disfellowshipped meant you were excommunicated from talking to anyone in the congregation, including your family members. In their eyes, it was God's way of showing you He loved you by cutting you off so that you could see how much everyone's love meant to you.

When my mother was pregnant with me, she had shown herself to be repentant about her mistake (the mistake being me), and they allowed her to remain in the congregation. She was adamant that I should repent and get the congregation to support me.

Basically, I had two choices: Repent, break up with Joey, and rejoin the congregation, or formally leave the congregation and the people I had known my entire life, including my family.

I knew choosing to stay with Joey could lead to the death of my baby in Armageddon. God wouldn't care about my child if I left the congregation. My unborn baby's life was in my hands. My mother alluded to that in our conversations. If I left the religion, the baby's death would be my fault since I was responsible for the child.

On the other hand, how could I leave Joey? I was reckless and wild with him, but I loved him. Perhaps there was no turning back. My dice had been thrown, my lot in life chosen.

As soon as the pregnancy became public knowledge in our small town, the elders were adamant that they had to meet with me. My mother told me she couldn't hold them off any longer since they constantly asked her where I was and how to find me. They wanted to discover if I was repentant or if I needed to be cut from the flock. I was a single woman and pregnant, which reflected poorly on the elders if they didn't act. They couldn't have others in the small-town congregation witness me flaunting this worldly behavior.

I was tired of running and hiding, so I finally agreed to a meeting with two elders from the congregation, John and James. I had known them both my entire life.

At the meeting, I said right away, "I'm not leaving Joey, and I'm not marrying him. I'm happy about my pregnancy."

"You understand what this means, of course?" John asked, concern etched across his features.

"Yes, I understand."

They wanted to pray, so I held my head down and bravely held back my tears. They informed God that they'd made the decision to disfellowship me, which was no surprise given my lack of repentance. They spoke of an open-door policy, which meant I could return, but no one could speak with me until the elders decided if my intentions were true.

So just like that, all the people I had grown up with for twenty years, all the families I had known, the days out in service knocking on doors, the get-togethers and the meetings were all erased and meant nothing. The congregation was no longer allowed to associate with me, and it would be announced at a future meeting. My family was no longer allowed to talk to me unless it was absolutely necessary. I lost my religion, which was basically everything I had ever known since birth.

I went to my mother immediately after the meeting with the elders.

"Well, it's done," I said.

"What happened?" She leaned toward me with hope in her eyes, cautiously optimistic that perhaps she had been wrong, and I actually had repented and wanted to come back.

"I'm disfellowshipped."

She turned and left me standing in the kitchen. I didn't go after her. I stood still and looked around the house I had grown up in. The water jugs—some empty, some full—were still piled in the corner. The bare floor, with torn linoleum and subfloor exposed beneath, desperately needed sweeping. The dirty dishes piled in the sink, waiting for their turn to use some precious water. Beer cans littered the kitchen table. And little Gabrielle, my baby sister, who was now an active toddler, looked up at me, her chubby cheeks smudgy with food. I picked her up and hugged her close while she squirmed in my arms.

My whole life, all of it, was condensed into this one room and this one moment in time. The world was closing in on me. What had I done? I didn't just lose my mother; my decision also meant I could no longer see my siblings. In good conscience, my mother couldn't let my brother and sisters associate with me either. In her eyes, I was no longer welcome in their home. I had turned my back on God, so she turned her back on me. She considered me an outsider. She took the religion very seriously; if I wasn't repentant, she didn't want the elders to know she was still talking to me. From that day forward, she made it clear her relationship with God was more important than a relationship with me.

Now I was pregnant with no support, emotional or financial, from my family. I had a deep-rooted fear that when I was cut from the flock, I was cut from God's love. I was going to be one of the people who died in Armageddon. I was going to die, and my child's death would be on my conscience. I was going to be a single mother who was just dating the father and was cut off from everything I'd ever known, facing certain death when Armageddon came. I was now considered an apostate.

I pushed those thoughts aside and tried to focus on my future. Despite my fear, I looked forward to Joey and raising our child together. I lost my family but had gained another and didn't regret being pregnant. I was excited to have this baby. Karen and Joseph were supportive. My grandparents were excited, too. I was hopeful that maybe this child could bring Joey and me even closer together.

I was ready for this, or so I thought.

The Tide is High

In the beginning, I think Karen was hopeful this baby would bring Joey around. He had never held a regular job for long; his main excuse was that he didn't have a driver's license. Karen wanted us to be responsible and raise this child together. She and Joseph had been married since they were younger than us, and they had raised a family together. I wanted that for Joey and me and our baby.

Karen and Joseph allowed us to live in one of their rental homes in Alcoa. It was a small two-bedroom house on Oakland Avenue, in a seedier part of town. Despite the location, it didn't dampen my spirits. Joseph had renovated it, and to me it was a perfect first little home for our family. I dreamed about having our baby and both of us working hard to eventually get our own place someday.

After we moved in, I discovered how sketchy the neighborhood was. Our neighbor to the right was a man who fought pit bulls in his basement. The neighbor on the left was addicted to crack and sold it out of his house. Karen didn't know about these people. I didn't, either, until we had lived there a while and Joey clued me in.

Joey enrolled in community college at his mother's insistence. She said he should apply himself like his older brother. Allen attended a university and was doing well. She wanted the same for Joey, and so did I. I drove Joey to college and waited in the car, reading or cross-stitching to pass the time while he was in class.

Sometimes I simply laid back in the seat, with my hand resting on my belly, and dreamed about the future. I wished I could go to school too. I figured if Joey got his career started, then that could set us up for success after the baby arrived. Joey would graduate, get a good job, and then watch our baby while I went to school. I daydreamed about what a career for me might look like. And I dreamed about our baby and how much joy she or he would bring us.

I found out later that most of the time when I'd dropped him off, he hadn't been attending classes at all. He would wave goodbye to me as he walked to campus, then call his friends to pick him up and spend the hours getting high. Later, he would get dropped off and walk back to the car after his class was supposed to be done.

Right away it was clear Joey and I had different ideas about the house on Oakland Avenue. I wanted to make it a home for our baby who was on the way. Joey was thinking more along the lines of a bachelor-pad-let's-have-the-guys-over place. Weed paraphernalia and skeleton statues were laid out on the end tables. Black lights and scary posters lined the walls. Our "home" was more like a teenager's bedroom on a larger scale. Karen gave us pots, pans, and dishes and helped us get beds and dressers. I couldn't wait to decorate the second bedroom as a nursery.

Then Joey informed me he had invited Justin to live with us. Justin needed a place to stay, and Brandy was coming too. I never had a say in the matter. When I confronted him and told him he never discussed it with me, he reminded me that it was his parents' house. Therefore, it was his house and not mine, and I could leave if I wanted. I wasn't happy about it, but I didn't want to leave and had nowhere to go. The plus side was that they could help with the bills.

Karen was furious. She saw the writing on the wall. She, too, wanted this to be a place for her grandchild to be raised, but Joey didn't see the problem and refused to back down.

Justin and Brandy moved into the room that was supposed to be the nursery. After some initial adjustment, it wasn't that bad. It was nice having another girl in the house. Even though Brandy was younger than me, she had street smarts I didn't possess.

They loved playing cards, and since I was the fourth person, they taught me how to play. I learned how to play euchre and how to keep my face from giving my hand away, which was called a poker face. I learned how to read other people and recognize their facial expressions and tics that gave them away. We played into the night and early morning hours—laughing, joking, and telling stories. While they smoked weed and drank, I drank water or juice. There was a small part of me that was sad because everyone was having a great time, and I was stuck being sober. But I focused on my baby and how happy I was about that.

Brandy was jealous of my pregnancy. I knew she and Justin were trying hard to get pregnant. Each month that went by with her not getting pregnant, she grew more upset, crying on our kitchen floor after her period had started again like clockwork. She had so much freedom and life in front of her. I couldn't imagine being pregnant at seventeen. But Brandy was determined, and she knew what she wanted.

Eventually, her period was a few days late. She was excited and rushed out to buy a pregnancy test. I thought for sure she would take it right away as soon as she got home. But as it turned out, they were all planning on dropping acid that weekend. When I asked her if she was going to take the test, she said, "Dude, we've planned this acid trip for a while. I'll just take the test later."

A few days later she took it, and it was positive. Both of us were pregnant at the same time. I was due in late May, and she was due in October. Even though I had my reservations about her youth and apparent immaturity, I was excited to go through my pregnancy with someone else. Things were going great for a while.

Soon my car broke down, which was no surprise since it had a lot of miles. I had no job; therefore, I had no money for another car. Justin and Brandy didn't have a car either. We were forced to take a city bus everywhere. Sometimes Brandy and I went to the store and bought baby items, which made the anticipation for our babies' arrival even more exciting.

I learned that Brandy had lived with her mother growing up, but she ended up moving in with one of her friends in Alcoa. Brandy didn't like living with the girl and her family because the girl's mother was addicted to crack. She said the mother received food stamps every month and bought milk, bread, and some boxes of mac and cheese and then traded the rest for crack. She had a lot of kids, including twins, and everyone was hungry. Brandy said she felt bad for the children and couldn't stand living there any longer.

We didn't have to worry about going hungry at our home since Justin loved to cook and made great meals for us. We took the bus to the store and bought food with our food stamps, stocking up our fridge with all the essentials.

Frank, one of Justin's cousins, was a frequent visitor. He was tall and built like a linebacker. He had brown hair and a permanently stoned gaze. He came over at all hours of the day or night, sometimes with Penny, his on-again-off-again girlfriend. They had a daughter when they were young, named Kathryn, a toddler with big brown eyes and soft brown hair. Sometimes Frank brought her with him. I couldn't wait to see what my own child would look like when he or she was born.

There were anxious nights Penny came to the house late looking for Frank. She sat on our couch, staring out our window and smoking cigarettes, with a worried expression etched on her face. She was hoping Frank would come because she didn't know where he was. Kathryn was in her pajamas, a pacifier in her mouth, crawling around the floor and trying to get into the weed or the bongs on the end tables. Joey told me Frank cheated on Penny, and that was why she always needed to know where he was.

Sometimes Brandy and I walked down the alley at the end of the block to Sulan's Party Store. A quiet Indian man ran it, and he was the only person I ever saw at the cash register. Sulan's had the normal run-of-the-mill staples, including liquor and beer. We loved the big barrel near the counter filled with pickles that were bobbing in their brine and garlic. He accepted food stamps and WIC coupons, so we each carefully chose a pickle and spent our WIC coupons on milk, cheese, and juice. Sulan's was always open, even in the middle of the night, which was great because we always had a craving for pickles.

Things were good for a while. It was becoming a happy little home despite my initial reservations. We had plenty of guests visit us, friends of Justin and Joey. Sometimes they brought their girlfriends along and I met new people.

And then Joey and Justin started disappearing.

Black No. 1 (Little Miss Scare-All)

As good as things seemed to be going, with the four of us living together in the tiny house, sometimes it felt crowded. Having no vehicle and relying on public transportation didn't help. Justin and Joey occasionally left to go for a walk or to get out with their friends. They claimed they had to escape the hormonal women.

Joey grew distant, and his attitude toward me cooled. He was no longer enrolled in classes at the community college. No matter what we did, we never seemed to have enough money. Brandy and Justin weren't moving out anytime soon, and my dream of a little house for our family dissolved. I relied on Karen for a lot of things to prepare for the pregnancy, and she kept her word. She was always there for us when we needed her and was truly helpful to me as my pregnancy progressed. She had taken over as the mother in my life since I had been disfellowshipped.

One night, Justin and Joey had been gone for a particularly long time. It was a cold evening, and they had left earlier on foot. Brandy stared out the window and intermittently walked outside to look down the street for them. I, too, wondered where they had wandered off to for so long.

"What the fuck!" she yelled from the kitchen.

Brandy pointed out the window to the broken-down car next to the house, as she furiously yanked her coat on. The windows in the car were steamed. I could barely make out movement in the vehicle. Joey and Justin were smoking crack. For weeks, they had been visiting the dealer's house next door, buying crack, and smoking it in the abandoned car while telling us they were going for walks or visiting other people.

I was stunned. Joey had been distant, but I thought it was the baby's pending arrival that was stressing him out. I didn't realize it was anything else. Once Karen found out, she kicked everyone out. We had nowhere to go and ended up moving back in with Karen and Joseph. Justin and Brandy had to find a new place. I missed Brandy, but we both knew we couldn't stay in that house any longer. Even though I wasn't thrilled to be living with Joey's parents again, I was somewhat relieved to be away from the bad influences in Alcoa that were pulling Joey away from parenthood.

Joey was furious about the decision. He was close to everything when we lived in Alcoa, including all his friends, and now he was stuck back in Springfield. His behavior became more erratic as the due date loomed. Most of the time, I wasn't even sure if he wanted to be with me anymore. On more than one occasion, he said he felt I had trapped him.

But he showed up to my birthing classes with me. And after a while, I think he even started getting a little excited. He joked with the other soon-to-be parents in the class. We found out we were having a girl, and he helped me pick out names. He even got a job.

Things were looking up for us.

On our last day of the birthing class, we got a call from the doctor and found out that according to our last ultrasound, our baby was breech. If she didn't move, she would have to come out by C-section. I was devastated. Somehow, I had failed, and I wasn't going to have a "natural" childbirth. Joey comforted me; he made jokes and tried to make me laugh. The old Joey was coming back to me, and that made me feel good.

I gave birth to our daughter, Riley, by C-section in June 1995. She was tiny and weighed just over six pounds—a beautiful baby with blondish-red hair, like Karen, and large dark blue eyes, like Joey. She didn't look like me at all. Karen said she already had my stubborn attitude when she refused to latch on for nursing.

I loved her fiercely the moment I laid eyes on her. For once in my life, I had someone outside of myself to love completely.

After three days in the hospital, we went home to Joey's parents' house. We tried to settle in while I healed from the surgery. A new baby only compounded the issues Joey and I'd had up until that point. It was only a matter of time before things between us started getting worse. We got into a fight the night before my baby shower, when Riley was less than a month old. Joey punched me and gave me a black eye, which forced me to wear a ton of eye makeup to cover it up.

Karen helped me with Riley and was a lifesaver during that time, but she strongly supported her son. As things worsened, I felt more and more trapped. I had nowhere to go with a newborn baby and no job.

Allen came back from college for a visit and asked if we wanted to go to an amusement park in a nearby state. I was still breastfeeding, but Joey made it clear he was going with or without me. He had grown so distant, and I still wanted the life I had before Riley came along. It became clear she was going to be my sole responsibility. I resented that he got to get up and go to an amusement park with no concern about me or our daughter.

I ended up going, but it was an overnight trip. I missed Riley so much and felt guilty about leaving her and spent some of the time secretly crying. I also was suffering from intense pain caused by not nursing. When we returned home, my breasts felt like they were going to burst. Karen told me Riley had hardly eaten and had been difficult to soothe. Karen didn't support my breastfeeding from the beginning. She didn't want Riley to become too dependent on nursing because then no one else could watch or feed her. I cried and held Riley close and promised I wouldn't leave her again.

I tried, but I couldn't keep up with caring for a newborn daughter and partying with Joey. He never excluded me, but he made it clear he was doing what he wanted, regardless of whether I was with him or not. If there was a party in Alcoa or a group of his friends were hanging out, he was going. He expected either Karen or me to give him a ride. He liked to be around people and thrived on parties and getting high. I didn't even want to party that much. I wanted our little home and our goals back. But the more I thought about it, the more it became clear those were *my* goals. I constantly felt like Joey wanted to be away from me and our daughter. I kept trying to keep him closer and was thankful he didn't have a license to drive.

Joey eventually ended up cheating on me with a young girl at a party. I was home with Karen, Joseph, and Riley when he'd gone out with his friends. After I found out, I was sick to my stomach. The girl was only fifteen years old, as young as Scarlett. Somehow, this was my fault. I felt as if I had failed—failed to be a good girlfriend. I thought if I would have been with him, he wouldn't have cheated. But if I went with him every time he wanted to be somewhere else, my little girl would miss me. I couldn't be everything to everyone.

It all unraveled after that. Even though Joey apologized profusely and said it would never happen again, I began to see the painful truth. I had thought I could change him. I thought if he could see how much Riley and I meant to him and become the man I knew he could be, we would be fine. But it wasn't turning out that way.

I was extremely hurt when he cheated, but I didn't leave him. I couldn't. My mother wasn't speaking to me, my grandparents were getting older, and there was no room for my daughter and me at either of their homes, anyway. Plus, I was too invested in this relationship to quit now. We had a child together. I had no self-esteem and was deathly afraid of being alone. The devil I knew was much better than the devil I didn't.

So, I chose to stay.

Rock of Ages

The need to be independent from Joey and his family grew stronger. Because I had experience from high school in my typing classes and learning office work, I got a part-time receptionist job at a water softener business in a nearby town. I moved into an apartment on my own.

Even though it was a step toward independence, my fear of being alone won out, and Joey ended up moving in with me. We were on-again-off-again in our relationship, with Riley being the main reason we stayed together. He made me laugh, and we still had good times. Even though we had problems, they were *our* problems, and he was the father of my daughter. I loved him in my own way. Even though we fought constantly, the apartment was in my name, so I felt less trapped. I occasionally still hung out with Brandy, who now had her baby, a little girl named Rayla.

On one of the off-again periods when Joey and I were fighting, I impulsively contacted Jenny Jones to be a guest on her show. A male guest was going to choose a girl out of three finalists to go on a date. They called me and told me that out of the thirteen hundred applicants, mine was one of three they'd chosen. When they interviewed me on the phone, I broke down and admitted Joey and I were sort of in a relationship. They politely declined extending me the invitation to the show.

During one of our on-again moments, Joey informed me that he, Justin, Frank, and some of their other friends were going to a strip club for a bachelor party. I threw a fit. I was convinced he would cheat on me again, simply because he was going to be looking at beautiful women wearing skimpy clothes. I had heard about what those girls were like. In my mind, this was as good as cheating. I had no idea what happened in those places, other than that men went there to get turned on by loose and immoral women. I was positive he was going to meet a beautiful woman and betray me again.

After a long, drawn-out argument, Joey refused to listen to me any longer and left with his friends. I was beyond upset that I couldn't convince him to stay. Even Karen told me it wasn't that big of a deal.

I worked myself into a frenzy and managed to get a couple of the other girlfriends upset too. I convinced them this was a terrible idea and we needed to go drag them out of this club for cheating on us. Penny was there, and she didn't need any further convincing that Frank could be cheating. Brandy didn't care about Justin cheating, but she was down for the excursion and agreed to drive.

When we arrived at Jordan's, the downtown strip club, we got out of the truck unsure of how to proceed. I had been highly motivated on our way there, but when we arrived, I was struck with indecision. The club was located three stories up, with stairs that went to the top. I didn't want to go up there and risk seeing any naked, godless women, so I resorted to yelling in the parking lot at the men hanging out by the entrance. Brandy lounged against the side of the truck;

she didn't want anyone messing with her vehicle. Penny stood by me, huddled in on herself, smoking a cigarette and occasionally yelling with me.

The men ended up being the club's bouncers. They warned us we'd better leave; one of them said he was calling the cops. This frightened the other girls, and they were ready to call it quits. Brandy was mainly concerned about what kind of money Justin was spending in there. Penny grew quiet after the threat of the cops. For all I knew, she may have been frightened she was violating some sort of restraining order against Frank.

I hovered around the truck, crying and screaming. Eventually, Justin and Joey came out to make us leave after the bouncers informed them we were there. I cried frantically and clutched Joey's arm, trying to convince him to come with me. I kept reliving him cheating on me with a fifteen-year-old girl. I couldn't get that out of my mind.

He refused to leave his friends. He told me strip clubs were not what I thought they were, and he convinced me he wasn't after any of the women in there. The girls and I had no choice but to leave.

When things were going well between Joey and me, we decided to move out of the apartment and back in with Karen and Joseph. They watched Riley for us whenever we needed, and now that she was weaned to a bottle, it was much easier. They grew close to her as she started sitting up and paying attention to her surroundings. It was nice to have a built-in babysitter, not only when we were working, but also when we wanted to go out. It wasn't hard to slip back into a lifestyle of drugs, drinking, and partying when we had such willing sitters. Karen adored Riley; in fact, she enjoyed us being there at the house with her because it allowed her to keep an eye on how we were raising her granddaughter.

When we moved, I quit my office job at the water softener company. Joey and I found various restaurant jobs making ends meet for things like diapers, weed, and cigarettes. I found a job at a restaurant called Sammy's Lounge in Alcoa. I started as a hostess, but they eventually moved me up to a daytime waitress.

Joey and I continued our roller coaster relationship. I still resented him for his infidelity, and most of the time during our arguments, Karen stepped in and took Joey's side. She also formed strong opinions about how we should raise Riley—when we should give her milk, when to potty train her, when to feed her, and her bedtime schedule. I stayed high enough to let her have her way most of the time. I was unhappy, and having a child or a man in my life wasn't fixing my happiness. But I had nowhere to go and no ambition to figure it out.

On a whim during one of our on-again times, I got my belly button pierced. Joey came with me to hold my hand. We went to a tattoo studio in East Alcoa. I lay back on the bed and studied the fierce drawings on the walls that would eventually be someone's body art. An image of the devil peered down at me from one of the drawings. I thought of Satan watching me as I desecrated my body, a gift from God. I shoved the thought from my mind as a needle was driven through my belly button.

The piercing hurt like hell, but I liked how it made my stomach look. My body was slowly coming back again after giving birth. I was self-conscious about my C-section scar, but even that was flattening out. I had gained quite a bit of weight during my pregnancy, but because of my youth, good genes, and smoking, my weight had dropped off significantly.

Cocaine

Joey and I started hanging out with Sheena and Calvin. Sheena was a sassy redhead, super friendly, and talkative. She smoked nonstop and would never be caught without weed. She had a young son and daughter, both of whom spent a lot of time with their grandparents. Calvin was her boyfriend and Joey's long-time friend. He was tall with shaggy blond hair and permanent dark circles under his light blue eyes. Sheena was loud and vivacious, and Calvin was quiet and contemplative, which made them the perfect couple.

Sheena lived in a sketchy neighborhood, but she had Section 8 government assistance, so she was able to get help to pay her rent. If there was a deal to be had, Sheena knew how to get it. She had contacts everywhere, mostly because she was smart and friendly. If you weren't her friend, it meant you didn't know her yet. She could talk to anyone, anytime, and find something in common to discuss.

One night, Joey and I paid them a visit. Her apartment reminded me of my own home growing up, messy and cluttered. Sheena wasn't much for cleaning, but she always welcomed people in with open arms and a joint.

A heavy layer of cigarette smoke hovered near the ceiling when we entered. A tray tin of weed sat on the table, with a package of Zig-Zags nearby. After introductions to a couple of other people at the table, something else caught my eye.

A mirror, a razor blade, and a rolled-up dollar bill.

Upon closer inspection, I noticed a tiny mountain of white powder on the mirror. It looked like baking powder.

Cocaine.

I'd never seen cocaine before. Another one of my imaginary boundaries popped up in my mind. Another progression. The pot smoking, the acid tripping. Those were natural to me now. I didn't even think of myself as a "druggie."

But this. This was hardcore. This was crossing boundaries into something else.

Cocaine was the dangerous drug. I'd always reconciled my consumption of drugs in my mind with "at least it's not fill-in-the-blank-with-a-hardcore-drug-like-cocaine." How much farther up the chain did it have to go before *all* drugs were normal and not hardcore?

Joey put his arm around me. "Want to try it?" He glanced at the others. "She's never done this before," he added for their benefit. They stared at me, and I hated how it made me the oddity. Somehow, Joey had dug up a girlfriend who had never seen anything like this.

I shrugged my shoulders. I tried to act cool about it, nonchalant, as though I'd seen it before but had never taken the time or opportunity to try it. But I was curious. I watched as Calvin pulled the mirror toward himself.

"What's it do to you?" I asked. I was determined not to get trapped into an eight-hour trip like acid, thinking of Riley at home with Karen.

"Makes you feel excited, happy, free," Calvin said as he picked up the razor blade.

Everyone at the table leaned in, excitement and anticipation in their eyes like a movie had started rolling. They smoked and continued their conversations, trying to play it off as casual, but everyone's side-eyed gaze went back to that pile on the mirror.

Calvin cut a little line out of the pile, using tiny chopping motions. He rolled the dollar bill into the shape of a straw and leaned over the mirror.

Whiiiip! The line disappeared up his nose, as the dollar traced it like a vacuum cleaner.

He ran his finger over the streak and rubbed it on his gums, then passed the dollar bill and the mirror to Sheena. She chatted happily with me as she did the same thing and cut herself a line, while Calvin carefully watched. It appeared everyone else wanted to watch each other experience it—and also keep an eye on how large a line they were cutting for themselves.

"Cut her a small one to start," Calvin said nervously. His leg jiggled and some ash fell on the floor from his cigarette.

Sheena handed me the dollar bill after she cut me a line. What could it hurt? I wanted to fit in, and these were my friends.

My grandfather used these old-fashioned blades in his razors. He didn't believe in disposables. *Push that thought from your mind.*

I stalled and made sure the dollar bill was rolled up tight. Everyone stopped talking and watched me, their eyes bright and intense. As I leaned over, I saw my own reflection in the mirror, up my nostrils. Sheena gently grabbed my hair and held it back. She was still talking, and the sound of her voice intensified after she did the line.

I sniffed hard and followed the line with the dollar bill.

A chemical taste instantly hit the back of my throat, and a burning sensation spread throughout my nasal cavity. The cocaine smashed into the back of my eyes like a freight truck, and I was instantly wide awake, alert. I was flying inside my own head, and the only thing holding me to the ground was my body.

"Rub your finger over your line, and swipe it across your gums," Joey told me. My mouth tasted like metal, and my gums grew numb.

After we each did a line, we began talking a hundred miles an hour about everything.

We smoked joints, which only heightened the experience. And then about thirty minutes later, we cut up more lines. It didn't last like a hit of acid. When I dropped acid, I was stuck in it for at least eight hours—a good or bad trip. If I smoked weed, its effects lingered, but it gently faded until I rolled another joint. Cocaine wasn't like either of those drugs. It dropped off quickly, like a crash, and it was severely missed when the feeling was gone.

I instantly loved cocaine and loved who I was when I was on it—vibrant and alive. I was on top of the world, and it was amazing. Joey was instantly funnier and more likable. All the bad shit about us faded away with only the good stuff left. But the high didn't last very long, and the only way to get the feeling back again was to do another line.

Our little pile started to diminish, and the intensity in the room increased. The thought of having none left seeped into our collective minds.

We ended up getting more and doing it all night.

That was my introduction to cocaine. I knew it was addictive. I could tell immediately as soon as I was coming down. I wanted another line, and I didn't want to lose that feeling. We finished and hung out for a while longer until it started to fade. Everyone made room for each other on Sheena's couches, smoking and edgy, depending on where they were in the coming down process. Now that we'd done coke, weed was a pale comparison, but it did help take the edge off once the cocaine was gone.

Later I asked Joey about how much it cost. How did we get it if we wanted more?

He knew someone, another friend of his who sold it if we ever wanted some. Buying drugs was always nerve racking for me. Dealers don't like drug traffic at their homes, and I hated meeting people in public. The cops were a constant problem, no matter what drug we were looking for. As for the cocaine, we didn't have to worry. It was expensive, and we didn't have the money to spend on that kind of high, which in a way was a good thing.

I still waitressed during lunch at Sammy's. I smoked pot regularly, but I had steady income, and that was what was important. Joey and I continued partying. I made enough money to make sure we always had a bag of weed.

Joey decided to grow pot plants, and some of our evenings were spent in a cornfield, moving the plants in fear that either the police would confiscate it, or his "friends" would steal it. The plants grew to over nine feet tall. They were impressive—towering, green, and stately in their large, round planters. As they grew taller, the fear intensified that someone would find them and steal them. Any helicopters flying overhead would send us into a frenzy.

When it came time to harvest them, Joey cut them and hung them upside down to dry. Then he cut the buds and trimmed the edges. I helped with that part of it. We had shoeboxes full of weed stacked in his closet. His entire bedroom smelled like a skunk. As scary as the thought of getting caught growing and harvesting weed was, it was nice to not have to buy it.

Joey and I were more comfortable when we had money. We got along better. We sold some of the weed we harvested but kept most of it to smoke and also held back seeds for the next time we planted. We weren't struggling as much with the supplemental income we had from selling the weed.

While working at Sammy's, I met a fellow waitress named Jan. She was petite with light brown hair and a large smile. A couple of years older than me, Jan was friendly enough, but she reminded me of the type of girl that would have made fun of me in high school. She lived with her parents and had her own space in the basement. One day after work, she invited me over so that we could go out to some local bars.

When she said she stayed in her parents' basement, thoughts came to my mind of the dark, dank Michigan basement at my parents' house, filled with spiders and unknown horrors in the shadowy corners. Her basement was nothing like that. Jan's bedroom was completely furnished, done in pale pinks and whites. The doors opened to a spacious patio outside, letting in beautiful daylight. She had her own private bathroom, complete with sparkling clean tiles. Her bathroom counter was filled with name-brand lotions and facial washes.

I thought of growing up in my own home, with a toilet that didn't flush, and a bathtub filled with garbage bags of clothes and broken chairs. She came from a far different world than what I was from. One that was very unfamiliar to me.

"Wanna do a line?" she asked.

I was surprised. I knew she smoked pot, but I didn't realize she was into coke. She seemed too rich to be into drugs like that. Jan's life seemed perfect. I noticed she wasn't surprised that I did coke, though.

"Sure," I said cautiously. I hadn't done a lot of drugs without Joey around. It was weird to not have him here with me while I was doing a drug—kind of like I was cheating on him.

She pulled open a little baggie and broke out a line for each of us on her bathroom counter, casually chatting about work stuff. The lines were easily as big as my pinkie finger. I wasn't even sure it would all go up my nostril.

I glanced around. "Are your parents coming home soon?"

"No," she said, licking her finger and rubbing the coke on her gums. "They're never home."

We each did a line. And then another one. My chest pounded, and I had a ringing in my ears. I had never been higher. She made us a drink, and we both couldn't stop talking each other's ears off, our conversations firing back and forth in rapid discussion.

We left after she finished getting ready (I had no idea how she applied eyeliner after doing those lines). We hung out at a few different bars that night. She was fun, but I could tell her problems were different than mine. She was spoiled in a way that I had never been, and while I enjoyed spending time with her, we only hung out once outside of work.

I wasn't ambitious at that point in my life. I had all but forgotten my dreams of a happy home for myself and my daughter. I didn't think about my goals of going back to school or bettering myself. I existed, and that was the extent of my life: survival.

I enjoyed hanging out with Joey and his friends, who then became my friends. We got high together, and there was no expectation that life should be anything more than what it was. Joey took me to the head shop again, and I bought a small one hitter for cocaine and a joint holder for my purse. I added those items to my collection of drug paraphernalia.

I fit in with Joey, provided we were getting along. I fit in with that lifestyle.

I finally belonged somewhere, and it felt good.

Suicide Blonde

Riley was getting bigger. You couldn't put her in a playpen to amuse her any longer. She was growing up and was now a full-sized toddler—running around, exploring. When she fell and hurt herself, she sought out Karen. When she discovered something cool, she ran to Joseph to show him.

When Karen began to take over some of the parenting roles for us, I let her, but I didn't like it. I felt inadequate as a parent and also felt guilty about the drugs even though I knew Riley didn't understand what they were yet. Joey was relaxed at parenting. When Karen was around to help, things went easier for me. She was always there if we needed a babysitter and she never complained.

On top of that, Joey and I started fighting regularly again—actual physical fights that involved shoving and yelling, and sometimes it happened in front of Riley. She would stand there and cry as we screamed at each other. I never wanted her to grow up and see what I had seen as a child. I knew I had to do something. This wasn't working anymore.

After a full-blown physical fight, I finally made the decision to move out again and take Riley with me. I found an ad in the local newspaper for an apartment and went to check it out. Karen told me I could use her as a reference. I was grateful because I didn't have a good reference for an apartment after breaking a lease before, and I wouldn't have a cosigner.

The interview went well. The apartment was small, but adequate for the two of us. The woman told me she was contacting my reference, and two days later, she called me.

"I'm sorry, but I can't rent to you. I spoke to your reference, and she said you and your boyfriend fight all the time. I'm not even sure why you listed her as a reference?"

I tried to explain that it was Karen's son who was fighting with me and that I was trying to get away from him, but she didn't want any part of that trouble. I was embarrassed, but I thanked her and apologized for wasting her time. Karen had sabotaged my attempts to move out. She wanted me to stay with her because then Riley would stay with her too.

It affirmed that I had to get out of there. I decided to keep looking for a place and not let anyone know.

I quit working at Sammy's Lounge and took a waitress job at Cracker Barrel. It was while working there that I met a hostess named Tamara. Tamara was small with pixie-like features. She had short brown hair, and her eyes squinted when she smiled. She was quiet and nervous, which was fine because I had a tendency to be loud and brash, so we hit it off right away.

Since we both smoked, we took our cigarette breaks together. I told her about living with Joey and his parents and how no matter what I did, Karen always took Joey's side. It was always my fault. I explained how I felt I had to get myself and my daughter out of there. Tamara told me she rented a place from her mother in Amherst, a nearby town. She said I could live with her while I got on my feet. We could split the rent, and it would help her save money as well. I quickly agreed, and after a week of planning, I packed up what little I owned and moved myself and Riley out.

Karen was upset and wanted to know where I was taking Riley. I gave her the address and told her we would still be in touch. I never intended on taking Riley away from her grandparents or her father. Karen was upset, but there wasn't much she could do.

Tamara lived in a small, two-bedroom trailer. It was technically three bedrooms, but the third bedroom was filled with her mother's belongings. Various knickknacks and household items were scattered about that weren't Tamara's style that I figured also belonged to her mother.

I stayed in the bedroom at one far end of the trailer. That, too, was furnished and filled with personal items, as if at any point, someone could show up and be surprised when they discovered me in their space. I didn't own a lot of things, so it didn't bother me.

There was no room for Riley in that bedroom and definitely no room anywhere else in the tiny trailer for a crib. I had no choice but to place her playpen in the hallway in front of the third bedroom squeezed into the doorway, but it didn't fit in the room completely. The first time I rented an apartment, Riley had her own room. I hated this situation, with my daughter sleeping in a playpen in the hallway, but I was desperate for a place to live. I didn't have many choices. When Karen came to pick up Riley the first time, her lips pursed together when she saw the room filled with boxes and unused furniture.

"This isn't an appropriate place for a child to sleep," she informed me. She clearly thought I had lost my mind, moving out of her comfortable, spacious home and dragging my child to sleep in a hallway.

I shrugged my shoulders. The only other option was to move back with her and continue to live with Joey. I couldn't and wouldn't do that. I didn't know what else to do. I was twenty-two years old and doing the best I could with no support from anyone else in my life.

After I moved in, Tamara became my guidance counselor. I enjoyed having someone to share my concerns about my ex, Karen, and money problems with. Tamara always listened intently, sitting in her spot on the couch, smoking cigarettes, sharing her thoughts and providing advice when it was appropriate. It reminded me of when I first graduated high school and lived with roommates. I realized I missed that camaraderie. I could tell she didn't like it when I didn't heed her advice, though.

I continued working at Cracker Barrel and still barely made ends meet. The rent wasn't high, but I was spending a lot of gas driving Riley back to Springfield to have Karen and Joseph babysit. It turned out that daycare was cost-prohibitive and hard to obtain on waitressing hours, so it was often easier to have Karen keep Riley for a couple of days at a time, especially if I was working two days in a row. Karen didn't mind and never argued, and she always made herself available.

One evening, Tamara introduced me to one of her friends. Jenson was tall and muscular, a former football player, with short dark brown hair. His gaze flickered down to watch my mouth move when I talked. He cracked a shy smile when I made him laugh, and something inside me opened a little bit. I hadn't even considered being with anyone since Joey, and it was nice to have his attention. Tamara warned me he was in between relationships. He had been dating his high school sweetheart, and they had recently broken up. Regardless, I could tell he was interested, and when he asked me to hang out, I said yes.

Jenson drove an amazing sports car. He didn't have children, and he made it clear he wasn't interested in putting Riley's car seat in his vehicle, so we only hung out when Riley wasn't there. I allowed Karen to get Riley more often, even when I wasn't working, so that I could spend time with Jenson. A part of me enjoyed that freedom—the feeling of no responsibility and fun. It almost became a relief to me when Karen came to get her. I watched the clock and waited for her to show up, then loaded Riley in the car seat with her overnight bag. I felt guilty that I was so anxious to send her away, but she was excited when her grandmother showed up, clapping her hands and trying to carry her own bag, that I figured it was a good idea for both of us.

During those times, I had the opportunities to grow closer to my daughter and I didn't. I even felt like if I wasn't going to be a good parent, I needed her to be raised by someone who was. Karen offered to adopt her at one point when she was a baby so that she would have "good health insurance," but it was more because she wasn't sure what direction I was going in my life. I wasn't comfortable giving up custody and I refused.

Jenson and I went to a comedy club for one of our first dates. I dressed up in one of my cuter outfits—a plaid schoolgirl skirt with a matching bolero vest and tall boots to go with it. For the first time since having a baby, I felt sexy. Jenson dressed up, too. I sat in his sports car, with my hair and makeup done and my new outfit. It felt good to be "normal" in a relationship. Joey and I never went on dates. It was weird to have fun and not make finding a bag of weed part of the date night focus.

Jenson was upset about the breakup with his ex. He spoke of it often. I wanted to be understanding, a listening ear, but I also wanted to stake a claim to him. I thought that if I could show him how much better I was, then he would see that dating me was the best choice. I figured I could make him see things my way if I got him alone. I pursued this plan even though he didn't like children, he was fussy about his vehicle in a way that annoyed me, and he was nervous about sex.

I got a hotel room for our first time. I hadn't been with anyone since Joey. I rented the room because Tamara made it clear she didn't like our growing relationship. She acted weird about us going out, like she didn't approve of me dating Jenson. Maybe it was some sort of leftover loyalty to his ex, or maybe it was because she had given me guidance and I refused to follow it. As it turned out, she was right in hoping I wouldn't pursue something with him.

After a short period of time, Jenson broke up with me and decided to give it another go with his ex. I was devastated. I thought I really liked him. The reality was that we had very little in common other than me being a listening ear and finding enjoyment in dating someone with a car, a driver's license, and a steady job. But in my mind, our breakup meant I wasn't good enough for him. A cool guy like that didn't want to have anything to do with a struggling single mom and waitress at Cracker Barrel. After we broke up, I bought myself a bottle of tequila and a lemon and did shots on the couch until I passed out watching the Jenny Jones show.

Shortly after that, I got back in touch with Brandy. We started hanging out again, and it was like no time had passed at all. The more we hung out, the less I was home with Tamara. Tamara made it clear after one introduction that she didn't care for Brandy. And Brandy felt the same way about her.

One night, Brandy and I went out, and we agreed she could stay with me since it was so late. When we got back at 2:00 a.m., I whispered to her that we needed to be quiet because Tamara was probably sleeping. The front door creaked open, and we stepped inside the trailer. The orange tip of a lit cigarette was the only light glowing across the dark room.

"Where have you been?" Tamara asked, exhaling the smoke into the dark.

"Out," I answered, still whispering. "Sorry if we woke you."

She didn't answer but silently stared at us as we crept back to my bedroom.

"Dude, was she waiting up for you? That's creepy, man," Brandy whispered.

I laughed it off but agreed it seemed weird. Tamara was very involved in my life. Probably because she was concerned that I couldn't keep up with my end of the bargain for bills and rent (rightfully so).

Stephanie was another friend I met at Cracker Barrel. She, too, was from Amherst and was friends with Tamara. She came over one night to hang out with us and filled us in on Jenson's girlfriend, who had temporarily taken up waitressing at the local strip club in her spare time to raise money for her parents' anniversary cruise. I had seen pictures of his ex before. She wasn't what I considered pretty. In my opinion, she wasn't attractive enough to work in a strip club. I briefly wondered what sort of money a waitress could make there, but then it slipped my mind. I wasn't pretty enough to work at a place like that.

We talked about Cracker Barrel, and I admitted I wasn't making shit for money waitressing. Stephanie said serving at a bar made more money than a restaurant like Cracker Barrel because a bar tab makes better tips. Given my experience at

Sammy's, I had to agree. Waiting tables for average-income families after church on Sundays was a struggle. It was hard to keep up with the bills, and even though Karen helped me with daycare, I was still broke all the time.

I hated not having money. It reminded me of my childhood. My parents could barely make ends meet, and they struggled to find money to keep food on the table and pay regular bills.

I didn't want to end up like that.

Edge of the World

After a few months of waitressing at Cracker Barrel, I realized I didn't like working there either. I hadn't gone to college, and I didn't have any leads on better jobs. No one had told me when I was growing up that I would need to plan for a future. Anytime I considered the future, it had always involved the New System, where I wouldn't need college or a job.

But in this current system, it was clear I needed to pay rent and buy diapers. Waitressing was in no way fulfilling to me as a career, and I was barely scraping by. The more Riley was with her dad and his family, the less time she was with me, and I started to look forward to my alone time without her. I had become focused on surviving, so I honestly didn't know what my goals and dreams were anymore. Furthermore, I didn't see a way out of this existence.

Jennifer was another waitress I had befriended at Cracker Barrel. She was a petite blonde who was friendly to everyone and smiled a lot. She reminded me of a cheerleader with her perky smile and upturned nose. She, too, was a single mom with a young son. Jennifer made good tips because everyone loved her, and some people even requested her when they came in.

One day, Jennifer didn't show up for her shift.

People quit without notice all the time, but everyone was surprised because Jennifer had been there for a while. This wasn't like her. After a few days, it was discovered that she had been murdered by her boyfriend and left in her car behind Kroger's, the local grocery store. Someone noticed the car parked behind the store and found her in the vehicle. Her boyfriend confessed. It was discovered that they argued, and he killed her in a fit of rage. I couldn't help but think of her young son who no longer had a mother.

Rumors circulated soon after her death. It was mentioned that she occasionally stripped at Déjà Vu, a nude club in Alcoa. I was horrified yet fascinated. She was such a normal girl, delivering extra syrup to customers for their pancakes. But there was another side of her—a side that took her clothes off at a gentlemen's club, and I couldn't figure out how to reconcile the two sides. I thought about her death often after that and how little I actually knew about her.

One Friday evening, Stephanie and I carpooled to work. Shortly after our shift started, she received a phone call in the office. Her uncle had passed away, and she had to leave work early. Our manager wasn't happy about it, but she let her go. Stephanie was my ride, and I had no idea how I was going to get home that night after my shift ended. I spoke to our manager, a woman named Lisa, and let her know my predicament.

"Look, I can't worry about how you're going to get home. I have a restaurant to run." She brushed past me to handle some sort of kitchen dispute.

I stood there a moment trying to figure out a solution. The whole reason I carpooled was to save money. I was torn and didn't know what to do. No one was available to give me a ride home after work. Amherst was quite a drive from Cracker Barrel, and I obviously couldn't ask Stephanie to come back and get me.

When I got back to the kitchen, Stephanie was leaning against the counter with tears in her eyes.

"I'm so sorry to do this to you," she said. "I have to leave and pick up my mom. Are you coming with me or staying?"

At that moment, one of the hostesses let me know they sat a family at a table in my section. Stephanie and I discussed my predicament a few moments longer. I still didn't know what to do. The hostess reminded me of my table.

"Don't leave," I pleaded with Stephanie. "Give me one minute to greet the table." In the back of my mind, I already knew what I was going to do.

A large family was seated in my section, two adults and a handful of children. I put on my fake smile and took my pen and paper out of my apron.

"Good evening. I'll be your server. Can I start you off with something to drink?"

The man at the table glared at me. "As long as you took to get here, of course we know what we want to drink. And by now we're ready to order," he fumed. His face was a dark shade of purple, and his eyes bulged out of his head. He spit when he yelled at me.

Granted, this was probably deserved since they'd been seated for a while before I showed up. After his grumbling bitch session, he turned to his wife and sweetly asked her to tell me what she wanted to order.

It's amazing how I can look back with clarity and recognize those pivotal moments in my life—moments plucked from time and expanded upon when they become past memories. This was one such moment for me. Maybe the man could have been nicer. I could have sent Stephanie on her way. I could have broken down and called Karen, Brandy, or anyone and begged them for a ride. I had the option to pay someone at work to drive me across town after my shift, or I could have thrown myself on the mercy of Lisa. Who knows how things would have turned out?

But what I knew right then and there was that I couldn't handle waitressing at Cracker Barrel any longer, and I believed this was a sign. I knew beyond a shadow of a doubt there was no way I was bringing that ugly man or his vapid wife and ill-mannered children anything to drink or eat.

I smiled through clenched teeth and put my pen to paper. I don't even know what they ordered because all I did while they spoke was scribble "blah, blah, blah." My pen dug into the paper, and my fingers turned white with the pressure of my pent-up anger.

"I'll be right back with your drinks." I smiled at everyone around the table. The man waved me away impatiently. I was clearly a servant and didn't need any attention.

Stephanie was anxiously waiting for me with her coat on. "Have you decided what you're going to do?"

I glanced around the bustling kitchen. Servers, sweating and scurrying, flew by us, vehemently pressured into performing quickly for two dollars an hour. The rest of their duties included kissing ass to every customer who came in, regardless of how they were treated.

I removed my apron and set it on the counter. "I'll get my coat," I said with finality.

And we left.

Of course, there were options. I could get any customer service job if I tried hard enough, because I was friendly and outgoing. I had an engaging smile, and most of the time, I could make people laugh and like me. If I couldn't live on my own for lack of employment, I'm sure Joey would have taken me back. I could have moved back to Karen and Joseph's and tried to find another waitressing job or maybe even an office job.

But an idea had grown in the back of my mind. I knew where I wanted to work, and I knew what I wanted to do. I wanted to wait tables at a bar again—and not just any bar. I wanted to work at a strip club in Alcoa. Of course, I knew I couldn't dance with my stretch marks and a C-section scar. I wasn't beautiful; I had acne scars and some remnants of baby fat left. But I was attractive enough to wait tables and hopefully make more than at Cracker Barrel.

I was average height, around five foot four, with long brown hair and blue eyes. There wasn't anything ugly about me. Sometimes, I even felt pretty. Men had hit on me constantly when I worked at Sammy's Lounge. What was the difference? I could handle getting drinks for people, no problem. I thought of Jennifer who apparently made money at Déjà Vu, she was friendly and smiled a lot, like me. Jenson's scrawny girlfriend worked at a club and made good tips, what did she have that I didn't?

I left Cracker Barrel that night nervous and afraid, because, oh my God, what had I done? I had less than a hundred dollars in tips in my pocket to last until I found something else. I had a child to take care of and no job. I didn't even know for sure if the strip club was hiring. I walked out with no notice and no reference.

Stephanie dropped me off and went to pick up her mother. When Tamara got home later, she was surprised to see me on the couch. I explained what happened.

"You *quit*?" She gaped at me. Of course, she was worried about how I would come up with my share of the rent.

I told her not to worry; I had an idea.

Girls, Girls, Girls

On Monday afternoon, after quitting my job at Cracker Barrel on a Friday night, I carefully applied my makeup and got dressed in one of my nicer outfits. I drove to Dreamgirls, the topless club in Alcoa, smoking one cigarette after another. This club was the one where Jenson's girlfriend had worked at for a short time, and I thought it might be the best place to start.

I parked my car and sat for a few minutes to build up the courage to go inside. The single-level building ran the length of the parking lot and a bright pink-and-white sign hung out front. The voice in my head told me I was crazy to think I was good enough to even approach that building and ask for a job. I was a girl raised in poverty, who had some acne scars, small boobs, and no outstanding physical features. I imagined the manager laughing at me when I walked in and the entire crew pointing at me as I returned to my car in shame.

I recalled going to breakfast at Denny's restaurant with one of my roommates after I graduated high school. Megan and Haley, two popular girls from school, sat at a nearby table with glitter on their eyes and fully done makeup. They laughed loudly and seemed to be having a great time with a couple of guys. Someone told me they were strippers at Dreamgirls. I came to Denny's in my sweatpants and a baggy T-shirt at 3:00 a.m. for the breakfast special. Meanwhile they looked beautiful and runway-ready. In my mind, an exotic dancer was just that—exotic, like Megan and Haley. A dancer was ethereal, beautiful, and the epitome of every man's dreams. Isn't that why the slogan for Déjà Vu club was once "One hundred beautiful girls and three ugly ones?" I wondered how they chose the ugly ones. I didn't want to ever find out. Hopefully the same criteria didn't apply to the waitresses.

A red carpet fit for royalty ran beneath the covered walkway and led to the club's entrance. The doorway, made of stained glass, was impossible to see through.

The first thing to hit me was the thumping bass coming from inside. I couldn't tell if it was my anxiety or the loud music that made my chest compress. A lit-up marquee hung on the left side of the entrance featuring a young woman in a thong bikini wearing dark lipstick with seductive eyes. I briefly recalled my Bible studies where the elder referred to harlots sent by Satan. That image could have been used as a modern-day representation. I averted my curious gaze. I had been standing there ogling her. I'd have to get used to seeing women like that if I waitressed here, and I didn't want to be a prude.

A thick, burly man stood behind a podium to the right. He held a clipboard in front of him and glanced up at me. He was probably a bouncer. I asked him for an application and then waited to see if he'd laugh at me. He nodded and told me to wait while he located the manager.

So far, so good. He didn't kick me out or act like I didn't belong. I stood at the podium, swaying a little to the music and trying to act like I didn't have a care in the world.

I saw the bar directly across from me where a bartender walked past and grabbed some liquor off the shelf. Flashing lights bounced on the walls around me in time to the music, but I still couldn't see inside.

Just then, two amazingly tall women teetered by me, giggling and leaning into each other, clutching small glittery purses. They wore short skirts and what looked like bikini tops. They were all legs and very thin. One of them turned toward me, her face fully done with makeup. She didn't smile. She looked away, and they wandered further into the bar and out of my line of vision.

I nearly turned around to leave. *What am I doing here?*

Just then, the bouncer reappeared with a man who introduced himself as Larry.

Larry was a short, stocky man with dark curly hair and a gruff manner. A toothpick hung from the side of his mouth. While the bouncer had barely glanced at me, Larry took me in from head to toe with a sharp, no-nonsense gaze. I had smoked part of a joint for courage before I came in. I instantly wondered if he could smell it.

He nodded toward a door behind the podium that led to an office. His "office" was a small, cramped space with very little room to move. It probably had been a coat check closet in a previous life. A coffee cup with brown stains on the inside and the phrase "I love titties" printed on the outside, sat next to his computer.

I tried not to stare at the pictures of naked women all over his walls and desk, but he caught me looking too intently.

"She's pretty," I said, gesturing toward a topless woman with a postage stamp-sized piece of cloth covering her vagina.

"Yeah," he said, making a grunting noise as he sat in his chair.

After shuffling piles of papers around on his desk, he finally located an application and a pen. It was a standard job application except there was a place for a stage name. I left it blank because I wanted to waitress, and I didn't think waitresses needed stage names.

He busied himself organizing a stack of papers and phone messages at his desk while I completed the form. After a few minutes, he turned back around and took my application. I sat straight up in my chair, figuring this was my interview and it was time to make a good impression.

He briefly glanced at my application, flipped it over, and sat it down in front of him. He switched his soggy toothpick to the other side of his mouth. His chair groaned in protest as he leaned back and placed his hands behind his head.

"You see, I'm not hiring waitresses right now."

My heart sank, and shame washed over me like a rippling tide. Who did I think I was walking in here to get a job? I wasn't good enough. I wasn't pretty enough, even with bad lighting, to waitress there. He must have noticed my acne scars or that my weight wasn't right. I certainly wasn't beautiful compared to the two women I had seen walking by when I first arrived. This, I thought, is how he lets me down easy—how he tells ugly girls they aren't wanted here. I hoped I could at least slink out without anyone seeing. I just wanted to leave.

After a few seconds of silence, he picked up my application and threw it on top of a mound of papers on his desk. That's when I noticed they were all applications. There must have been more than one hundred in the stack. Mine was on top of the huge pile until it slowly slid down to land near the "I love titties" coffee cup.

"See these?" he said, pointing to them. A few more fell off and landed on the floor. He didn't bother to pick them up. "These are all the applications for waitresses I received within the last couple of months. I get applications all the time for waitresses. I don't need anymore."

I was trying not to cry. Rent was due this week. I couldn't imagine Tamara's face when I came back with no job and no prospects. I was going to be homeless with my daughter. I didn't have a plan B. This was my backup plan. I quit my job with no notice. I had one check left, for very few hours, coming next week. I thought of Riley and had no idea how I was going to take care of her.

Somehow, I gathered up my purse and straightened my shoulders. "I understand. Thank you for your time."

He leaned forward in his chair, switching his toothpick to the other side of his mouth. "You know, we can always use another dancer. You wouldn't mind dancing, would you?" He eyed me shrewdly, his gaze pausing at my breasts. "You could make a lot of money."

I almost asked him to repeat himself. He wanted me to dance? Maybe the lighting in here was worse than I thought. I had never taken a dance class in my life. The only choreographed performance I had ever done was ice skating with old ladies as the queen of hearts in a deck of cards. I was neither tall nor graceful. I had stretch marks and a C-section scar. I certainly didn't consider my breasts attractive enough for someone to want to pay money to see.

He took my silent shock as consideration. "It's great money," he reiterated. "You can pick your own hours." His elbow hit the stack of applications and more of them fell on the floor.

"I've never danced before. I haven't had any formal training."

"That doesn't matter. In fact, it probably helps."

I figured I may as well be honest with him. No sense in him finding out the hard way. I blurted out, "I have stretch marks . . . and scars, from a C-section."

He looked confused, like he wasn't sure if I spoke English. "That's got nothing to do with it. Lots of the girls do." He casually tossed his mutilated toothpick in the trash can and leaned back. His chair groaned from the shift in weight.

"You don't have to. It's just a suggestion."

I should have stood up and left there in a huff, told him no way and to only call me if he wanted an excellent waitress. *Harlots and Jezebels*. I glanced at the women in the photographs. My face flushed considering what would happen if my parents found out—my mother. What about my grandmother?

But none of them had to pay my bills. I had no money. I wasn't going to have any money, not anytime soon. I needed diapers. I needed food—and rent. I silently cursed myself for walking out of that job at Cracker Barrel, but I could do nothing about it now. There was no way I could go back.

I still hadn't said much when we stood up and walked out of his office.

"Why don't you come in later this week and audition? If it's not a good fit, then no worries. Come in Thursday night." He escorted me to the entrance and shook my hand again. "See you Thursday."

I hadn't even seen the inside of the club. But there was something inside me that felt excited and exhilarated.

What if. . . ?

You Sexy Thing

After the initial shock, it didn't take long to make a choice. My money was nearly gone. Once I'd made the decision to dance, I knew I needed something to wear. I recalled those girls in their super-tall shoes. How would I ever walk in those? They had to be at least six-inch heels. I caught a brief glimpse of the women, with their beautiful costumes, long nails, and flowing hair. How could I ever transform myself into something like that?

I stopped in at Lover's Lane in Alcoa, two businesses down from Dreamgirls. They marketed themselves as a business that sold things like lingerie and sexy stilettos to bored housewives. Joey told me strippers bought their clothes there, and I didn't ask him how he knew. Their clothes were expensive. My stomach dropped when I noticed the price tags. I needed at least one hundred dollars to get an outfit.

I had no money for clothes and barely had enough for gas and cigarettes. Luckily, Karen had diapers for Riley. Joey knew I had applied; he was the one who gave me a joint for courage. I think he was somewhat impressed, but he didn't have any money either. I hadn't told Karen yet, and I was vague with Tamara at first, letting her know I was going back on Thursday for a "second interview." She was breathing down my neck for rent, nervous that I wouldn't come up with my portion for the bills.

Grandma Clara had a friend named Leonard, an older man in his early sixties. He was tall with a large stomach that protruded over his belt. He was never seen without a baseball cap or a hat to cover his head, and he rarely took it off, especially around me. I think he was uncomfortable about his baldness.

My grandmother lit up when he came over. She enjoyed his company, and it was always, "Leonard this" and "Leonard that." But she never noticed he was creepy toward me whenever I was there during his visits. As soon as I walked in the door, his attention pivoted directly to me. His eyes followed me around the room, and he found ways to strike up conversations the entire time he was supposed to be visiting my grandparents. Sometimes his comments were inappropriate, and he said things that made me uncomfortable, but only when my grandma couldn't hear him.

I figured I had nothing to lose. I drove to Leonard's senior housing apartment in town. His face registered shock when he opened his door. He was busy adjusting his baseball cap on his head. Naturally, he wasn't expecting me.

"Come in. What a surprise!" He backed away, and I stepped into his apartment.

We sat on the couch and made small talk. I could tell he wondered why I was there, and I decided to dive in. If he was offended, then I would chalk it up to a learning experience.

"Leonard, I found a new job."

"Really? Waitressing still? I'll have to come visit."

"No. I'm going to start dancing—" I paused— "at Dreamgirls." To say it out loud was scary, but back then in my innocence, I was a little proud of that title. Of course, I hadn't made it through the audition yet, but I was auditioning in performing arts. I didn't need to be an actress or a model, like my high school report said. I could still be on stage. I could even be exotic.

His eyes took on a lascivious gaze. "Well . . . is that so?"

"Don't tell Grandma," I hastily added. "I haven't told her yet."

"No, of course not." He crossed his heart with his finger against his chest.

"So, I need an outfit. And shoes. I don't have anything to wear. Can I borrow some money to get started? I can pay you back."

He didn't say anything at this point, and I wondered if I had it wrong about him all along. If he said no or didn't have the money, I had no idea what I would do. I didn't even own nice underwear with matching bras.

"Sure, honey. I can lend you some money." He got up from the couch and came back with his wallet. He gave me a one-hundred-dollar bill. "I'm happy to help a struggling young lady in need."

I took the money and relief flooded through me. At least I wasn't wrong about him. My instincts were right.

He sat back down on the couch, this time closer to me. "If you want, maybe you could come and just dance for me. A private show." His gaze lowered to my chest. "You know, to show me the new outfit."

This was something I wasn't prepared to answer. I hadn't thought of that as an option and the thought of dancing for Leonard made me nauseous.

I laughed nervously and carefully folded the money into my wallet. "Yeah, sure. Maybe."

I never went back there, not to dance and not to pay him back. Did it make me feel guilty? A little. But I remembered all the times he made me feel gross with his inappropriate behavior and comments when my grandma was out of range. Then I didn't feel so bad after all.

Next, I went to talk to Brandy at her apartment in Fayetteville. Justin was there with her, but they were in the off-again stage of their relationship. I asked her to come with me to audition.

"Please come with me. I can't go alone."

"Dude, I can't be a stripper." She took a hit off her joint and handed it to me. "In case you haven't noticed, I've got no tits."

"That doesn't matter, Brandy. He didn't say anything about mine. He said it didn't even matter that I never took a dance class before." I didn't know if it mattered or not, but I knew I didn't want to go alone. I'd feel braver if someone were with me. I couldn't imagine auditioning by myself. I didn't even care if she decided to never go back; I needed someone with me the first time.

Justin laughed and took the joint from me after I hit it. "You're both fucking nuts. You don't even know, man. You'd make so much money in there, dude." This bolstered my confidence, since I knew Justin had been in clubs before, given he was one of the guys we had stalked the night of the bachelor party at Jordan's strip club.

I eventually convinced Brandy to come with me. I reminded her about the mad amounts of cash that strippers supposedly made. Money would convince her. She loved money, and she was between jobs too. Justin agreed to watch Rayla. I still hadn't told Karen about my job change, and I was a little nervous. I decided to wait until after the audition.

Brandy and I stopped at Lover's Lane that Thursday night. I had the crisp one-hundred-dollar bill in my purse. I chose a velour, leopard-print crop top that tied in the front with flared, black, sheer sleeves. There was a matching thong and a little black skirt made of the same sheer soft material as the sleeves of the top. I tried it on along with six-inch black heels.

I gasped when I saw myself in the dressing room mirror. The girl peering back at me looked very similar to the girls I had seen in the club. After I'd had Riley, there wasn't much of a reason to wear anything other than sweats or jeans and T-shirts. It was important to me that I fit in with those girls I had seen on my interview. I ended up purchasing both the shoes and the outfit.

Brandy didn't have enough money for shoes and insisted she couldn't walk in tall heels anyway. Unlike me, she didn't care if she fit in with what the other girls were wearing. It was the promise of money that lured her. But like me, she had grave doubts about whether or not she was good enough. She brought little three-inch heels that she may have borrowed from her mom. They looked like shoes I used to wear to the meetings, not even remotely sexy. But I kept that opinion to myself. I was thankful she was with me.

After our purchases, we drove to the club and parked the car. Neither of us got out. My stomach was a ball of nerves.

"Wanna smoke a joint?" Brandy asked. She lit it up, hit it, and then passed it to me.

"Do you think they'll smell it on us?" I asked nervously. I had visions of them turning us away because we smelled like marijuana, but I couldn't imagine going in there sober.

"Dude, who cares? They do so much drugs in this place."

I'm not sure what made her an expert on this, but Brandy had a way of being an expert on any topic, and quite convincingly. We finished the joint and went inside. The same loud thumping music greeted us as soon as we opened the door.

A different guy was at the podium this time. When he saw us, he leaned around the corner and called Larry over.

I introduced Larry to Brandy and told him she wanted to dance too. I wondered if it was awkward to bring someone else along when this was going to be my audition. But Larry didn't act like it was a big deal; he looked her up and down. "You both got something to wear?"

We said yes, and he led us past the bar to an area he called the private party room. It had its own bar at the back and a smaller stage located in the center. Larry led us past the stage to a set of doors that led to the dressing rooms.

A couple of girls were there when we walked in. One was turned away from us, digging in a makeup bag. She wore a bikini top, and her spine poked out from her bony back as she hunched over the makeup counter. The other woman reclined in one of the chairs that lined the long mirror on the wall. One arm rested across her stomach and the other held a lit cigarette. She was topless and watched me with an assessing gaze. She blew out her cigarette smoke and gave me a long stare. I'd never had a stranger in a partial state of undress look at me with such direct eye contact. I smiled nervously and looked away.

I was curious if Larry would apologize for walking in on these women, particularly when one of them was undressed, but it didn't appear to faze him. Then I realized that was because he probably saw them naked on stage anyway, so what was the difference?

This was like a locker room, complete with high school lockers, except in a very confined space. The smell of body spray and cigarette smoke permeated the air. An assortment of perfume, brushes, and hairspray lined the countertop in front of the mirrors. The other girl had located her makeup and was applying eyeliner. I caught her looking at us when I glanced her way.

"Get dressed. Meet me out at the private party room. You can audition there," Larry said as he walked out. "Get on the floor, Misty, Destiny. Can't make money back here."

He left without a backward glance. The one in the chair flipped him off after he left.

Brandy started up a conversation with them. She was not shy and wanted to know about the money and how much could be made. The topless woman was Misty. Destiny was the one applying eyeliner. They were honest about the money.

"You can make money, but you gotta hustle," Destiny said.

"Some girls don't last long, but we've been here a while. It's the best club in Alcoa," Misty added.

Peeling off my clothes to get dressed in front of strangers brought me right back to high school gym class. My hair and makeup were already done. I had put on a lot of foundation to cover my acne scars, but that didn't help my stretch marks and my C-section. I quickly turned away to put on my thong. I wasn't used to wearing one, and it was terribly uncomfortable, but the thong made my legs and butt look better.

I need a drink for this.

Misty lit another cigarette and took a sip from a glass on the counter. Neither of the girls were in a hurry to listen to Larry about getting out there and making money.

"Can we drink here?" I asked, incredulous. Maybe her shift was done.

"Can you drink here?" she snorted. "Yeah, of course."

"I'm only nineteen," Brandy piped up. "Will they card me?"

Destiny glanced at her. "They don't care how old you are as long as you don't get too crazy."

I couldn't wait to get a drink.

Female of the Species

There was a man standing by the stage, smoking a cigarette and talking to Larry, when we came out of the dressing room. The loud music and the flashing lights from the main part of the club filtered into this smaller area. Larry nodded toward the DJ booth and told us to let him know what songs we wanted.

It was decided I should go first. Brandy said it was only right, since I was the one who talked her into coming here. The room was chilly. Lights from the ceiling blazed down onto the stage, and the rest of the private party room was dark. The leopard-print skirt brushed against my bare thighs as I half crawled, half crouched up the stairs to the stage. I was afraid of falling over in my new stilettos. When I stood up, the ground felt like a million miles away.

I tried to move to the music in a sexy way. I chose to dance to "That's the Way Love Goes," by Janet Jackson. That was the last CD I had purchased that even remotely reminded me of sexy music. My only other options were Pink Floyd, Alice in Chains, and Stone Temple Pilots. I hadn't thought the music part through, wasn't nearly high enough for this, and still hadn't had a drink.

In full concentration, I wobbled back and forth, from one pole to the other, my focus solely on not falling onto or off the stage. When I reached a pole, I grabbed it, walked around it and then tried to move my hips a little, emboldened by the fact I had a white-knuckle death grip on the pole itself.

Misty and Destiny came out to watch us, each of them carrying a drink and a small satchel. They sat in the chairs by the stage and shouted instructions and encouragement.

"Smile, girl!" Destiny yelled. "Don't look so scared."

Misty got up on the stage with me and showed me how to hook my leg on the pole and swing around. It was clumsy, and I wobbled. My ankles twisted together in a Bambi-like heap in the six-inch heels, but I did spin a little. She clapped her hands. "Don't worry. The guys aren't really paying attention to anything else. Just remember to smile and make eye contact."

Destiny shouted, "Take off your top."

I glanced toward Larry. The entire time, he wasn't paying attention; he was engaged in a discussion with the customer. I took a deep breath and found a corner in my mind that was somewhere else. Somewhere not really here—on a stage, taking my clothes off in front of strangers. I exhaled and removed the leopard top, letting it fall to the floor. The cold air hit my bare skin, and the girls cheered for me from below. That was it. It was done. The hardest part was over. I giggled nervously and smiled. Larry only glanced briefly at me and then away again. He barely noticed me at all, and I wondered if that was a bad sign.

I made it through the rest of my song and then Brandy got up to do her turn.

She did the same thing. She wobbled across the stage in her three-inch heels, then took off her top, and swung around the pole. We were both stiff and nervous, but it was kind of fun. Destiny and Misty encouraged us.

After Brandy was done, she stepped down and put her top back on. Both of us were giggling.

"Great job. Here's the deal," Larry said, walking up to us. "We take a percentage of what you earn as rent to work here. A table dance costs fifteen dollars, and a VIP couch dance is twenty-five dollars, minimum. You should try to ask for more."

It was anticlimactic to be told we were hired when he hadn't even watched our auditions. I thought our tryouts would have to be considered, but Larry had barely paid attention to us.

Larry led us out to the main club. There was a much larger stage at the side of the room, and smaller stages scattered throughout the floor. He pointed along the back wall. The VIP couch dances consisted of topless women who stood on wooden ottomans while gyrating in front of the men seated on the couches. A bouncer with a clipboard was walking around and kept track of who danced, how often, and when. That way, they knew how much we had to pay for our portion of rent at the end of the shift.

"You should get them to buy you drinks. There's a shot girl that goes around, and it's nice if you can help her out and get them to buy you shots, too."

The shot girl worked the floor, selling shots in what looked like test tubes. Her tray glowed from the bottom, and the light shone up through the shot glasses in bright colors. My favorite was the Slippery Nipple. I eventually discovered I could do a lot with the whipped cream on the top. Raise the bar tab—that was what was important to the club. That and floor rent from us helped the club stay lucrative.

So, we both got our first drinks. Brandy was underage, but like the girls said, it didn't matter.

"You need stage names," Larry told us after the rest of the tour. "Don't pick one that's already taken. Go tell the DJ, Tommy. He'll get you in the lineup."

When we entered the door past the podium, I saw that the DJ booth was immediately to the left. We met the main DJ, Tommy Thompson, on the first night we worked. He was a short Black man who looked permanently stoned. I later came to find out his eyes were bloodshot all the time. He had a smooth voice made for radio and he knew music.

I learned to befriend the DJs, as they could make or break a dancer's career. They announced a girl when she went up on stage, and they had the power to make the audience think she was a goddess—or a dud—thus, the reason we tipped them at the end of the night. Brandy was all about the money and she hated tipping. I took care of Tommy; he was a good guy and I liked him. It was equally important to make friends with the bouncers. Even though we didn't tip them, they could save a dancer's life.

Neither of us brought CDs because we didn't know we had to. Luckily, Tommy had a lot of music to choose from. "You're gonna wanna bring your own music if you like something," he said. He also warned us that girls had their own signature songs and didn't take kindly to someone else using the song if they were working the same shift. Plus, the customers didn't want to hear the same songs over and over again, either.

A small whiteboard was pinned to the wall behind Tommy. It had a lineup of the girls in the rotation working for the night—Tiffany, Alexis, Cherry, Misty, Desiree. Brandy chose the name Brooklyn. I chose the name Jasmine. Tommy added us on the board at the bottom of the lineup. We were officially put on the rotation. Since we were last, we got to watch how it went for a while before we had to go on the main stage.

The DJ called the next girl's name to go up. For the first song in her set, she danced around and did some pole tricks. During the first song, she took everything off except the thong, top, and shoes. The second song, she removed her top and collected tips from the customers who had gathered near the stage. The girls never removed their thongs, which we discovered was against the law in an establishment that served liquor. Girls skirted this rule by wearing the tiniest of thongs and manipulating it on stage, moving it from side to side and around, while still technically wearing it. As soon as the second song ended, the girl collected her money and clothes while the next girl waited on the stairs for her entrance.

After we were added to the lineup, we followed Destiny and Misty out to the floor. They were already close friends and took us under their wings. They led us to a table with three men, and the four of us sat down, pulling up chairs. Destiny told them it was our first time, and the men cheered at that.

The club didn't appear to be full, but it was busy enough. I wondered if I could do that dance again in front of more people, in front of all these strangers. I nervously slammed my first drink, and one of the guys bought me another one.

"Relax, you'll do fine." He winked. I was thankful he bought me a drink.

Beautiful girls, all shapes and sizes, came up one at a time to do their sets. When Tommy called their names, wherever they were in the club, they stopped what they were doing, sauntered over, and climbed the steps to the main stage. The stage had a railing that ran along the back. A front portion of it was built in Plexiglas and was extremely slippery. On either side, there was a catwalk that led to a pole in the corner.

Eventually, Tommy announced me as the next dancer.

"Go get 'em." The guy who had bought my drink reached under my black sheer skirt and squeezed my bare ass. My first reaction was to jerk away, but instead, I smiled and took another sip from my drink. I wasn't fond of him touching my ass, but I knew he would encourage me while on stage, and I needed a cheering section.

I carefully climbed the steps located at the back of the stage. The girl who went before me held her hand out to take mine. She wanted to help me up the steps, as a sort of introduction. I smiled and took her hand, carefully passing by her. All I needed was to trip and take us both down the stairs. She squeezed my fingers gently and leaned in, "Relax. Breathe."

I nodded and tried not to think about the staring eyes out in the audience. The glare of the lights pointed at me, making everything in the vast darkness beyond the stage barely recognizable. I wanted to squint and cover my eyes, but instead, I smiled and adjusted my skirt as the first chords of my song started playing. This time, I chose "D'yer Maker," by Led Zeppelin. Tommy said that song would go over better with the crowd, rather than Janet Jackson.

I couldn't see out into the audience. The lights above me vibrated in time to the music that surrounded me from everywhere at once. A couple of men slowly morphed into focus as they approached the row of tables close to the stage. One of them had a cigarette, and his smoke rose into the air, creating clouds in the lights.

Brandy, Misty, and Destiny cheered me on from our seats. A minute into the song, Misty folded up a dollar bill and approached the stage. She placed it in her mouth and leaned over to me when I danced near her. "Squeeze your boobs together and grab the dollar from my mouth."

Brandy shrieked loudly from our table, "No one is doing that with me! I've got no boobs." Everyone at our table laughed. I laughed too, feeling more relaxed.

Destiny hollered from the audience, "Take the skirt off." She approached the stage with a dollar next.

"It's sheer," I whispered as I took the dollar from her mouth.

"It doesn't matter. You'll make more if you take it off and just have a thong," she said softly in my ear, then winked and went back to sit down.

I danced to center stage and bent over as I removed my skirt. It slid down my legs and landed in a pile on the ground. I carefully stood back up and turned around, adjusting the thong so that it hopefully covered my scar. No one booed me off the stage. No one gasped or pointed.

Then I saw my reflection in a mirror across the room behind the couches. A different woman stared back at me. I truly was taller, thinner. I couldn't see my stretch marks; the bright, flashing lights and alternating darkness covered all that. I looked pretty, and maybe even beautiful. The black lights on the ceiling made anything white glow hot white and my teeth were the brightest they had ever been.

The first song ended, and the second song started. I removed my top and let it fall to the floor. It was easier than I thought it would be. There were more men gathered at the seats around the stage with money in their hands. As soon as I stopped in front of them, they put the money in their mouths, and I clasped my breasts together to grab the dollar bills. One of them had a beard that scratched my chest. It was strange to be so intimately close to someone I'd never met before.

After my set, Brandy did hers. Our table cheered for her, and the men gave me dollars to give to her on stage.

We were officially exotic dancers.

Birthday

We soon discovered why the girls carried little satchels. Paper currency can get unwieldy, especially when it's primarily one-dollar bills, so we needed something to put our money in. It added up fast and was too cumbersome to shove in a cigarette box, which is what we had on us when we first started. The bartender gave each of us a purple Crown Royal liquor bag to carry our money and cigarettes.

At the end of the first night, I paid my floor rent and tipped everyone out. I made more than enough to cover my rent with plenty left over for food and diapers. There was security in knowing I could walk out with cash and have enough to feel stable. It felt good having a job, and I made way more than what I earned waitressing. Plus, I loved this job already and in a way that I had never loved a job up until that point. Shame on the high school counselor for telling me I could only do creative stuff in my spare time. I could dance and make good money.

When I woke up the next day, I handed Tamara my rent money. I knew how concerned she was that I couldn't pay my share. I think she was surprised I had committed to dancing, but she was pleased I could pay my rent and share of the bills.

To save up money, and because I loved my job, I decided to work as many shifts as I could. I committed to five nights a week, including the weekends. This meant Joey or Karen had to keep Riley more often. I got ready for work around 3:00 p.m., then showed up for my shift around 6:00 p.m. and worked until 2:00 a.m. I slept in late every morning and then got up to do it again.

It was a difficult adjustment in the beginning. When Riley was with me, it was hard to stay on schedule. She was a toddler by then and got into everything. Tamara's house wasn't kid friendly. I found it hard to reconcile being an exotic, beautiful dancer and also the mother of a toddler, complete with potty training, sippy cups, and snacks. I pondered how Jennifer had balanced that life with parenting, waitressing, and stripping. My life was easier when it could be divided into compartments.

I loved Riley with all my heart. Yet I was still always relieved when Karen pulled into the driveway to pick her up. The guilty thoughts subsided when I told myself that this was my job. I had to earn money, and there wasn't any other choice. Honestly, there was no part of me that wanted to give up the life of a dancer. I loved the attention and the adoration. I loved who I was with the makeup and the clothes. It was an addiction.

After a short while, Joey and Justin formed strong opinions about Brandy and me dancing. Justin gave Brandy grief about not being around for Rayla, and Joey felt the same way about me "dumping" Riley off on him. They forgot they were the ones who had been encouraging us to try dancing from the beginning.

Brandy and I chose to work the same schedule and take the same nights off. We became club sisters when we worked and used that to our advantage. We encouraged one man to hire both of us together for a dance, or we enticed two men to "swap off" and made double the money than had we been alone. We danced with each other and learned how to touch ourselves and each other in erotic ways to earn more money. While the men were not allowed to touch us, we could touch and tip each other within reason. We giggled and had fun with it, but we knew it was a performance. The key was to make sure the men thought it was real. When asked if we were related, we claimed we were like sisters, which was true.

We also learned right away which customers were there for specific girls. Some girls had regulars, and they generally knew when their regulars would show up. It was bad form to approach someone's regular and try to get a dance. That caused bad blood in the club.

I made friends with one of the bouncers. Tony was a country boy poster child, with a long blond mullet of curly hair that hung down past his shoulders. He had soft brown eyes and long eyelashes. He was trying to grow a beard, but it was coming in patchy with blond tufts of hair sparsely scattered across his cheeks.

Tony was a gentle giant and younger than my twenty-two years, but not by much. There was a youthful innocence to him that was refreshing. He smiled a lot, and I could tell he was attracted to me right away. I was new to dancing, and he was new to bouncing, so we started dating. He made no expectations of my time. He knew I was a stripper. I knew he was a bouncer. He didn't get weird about it, and we remained professional at work.

As for our dating, it was just hanging out together at Tamara's house. I think she liked him because he was a decent guy. I had no delusions that we were going to be together forever. I genuinely just enjoyed hanging out with him and having sex. For the first time, I didn't dream of some picket fence and a family. I was okay with the casual relationship and enjoyed my freedom.

He met Riley once. Tony and I were lying together on the couch, hanging out before we had to work. Tamara was on her favorite spot on the other couch. Riley played on the floor in front of us while we waited for Karen to pick Riley up. If Karen didn't hurry, then I'd have to figure out how to feed her, and that would cut into the time for me to get ready. I hated not having enough time to prepare for work.

Riley approached the couch and shyly showed me her toy, something she had built out of blocks. I snapped and yelled at her to get away from me. Tears formed in her eyes, and she backed away, clutching the toy close to her chest. Even Tamara looked shocked. Tony took the toy from her and told her it was cool while she tried not to cry. Guilt slammed into my chest, and I angrily shoved myself away to the other side of the couch. I wanted to be the person who was free and independent.

Tony and I only lasted a short while. It wasn't a bad split, and we decided to remain good friends. The longer he worked there, the more I saw his innocence disappear. He was still a nice person, but he became harder around the edges, grittier. I wondered how often he thought the same of me.

After a few months, I was no longer a new girl at the club. I started getting regulars who came in specifically to see me. The girls who had been there a while started accepting Brandy and me as official Dreamgirls.

I took that title very seriously. On a workday, I was ready to go when I showed up for my 6:00 p.m. shift. I showered and had to shave my entire body: legs, bikini line, arm pits, and even occasionally my big toes. I washed, blow dried, and curled my long, mid-back-length hair. I applied copious amounts of heavy foundation, designed to cover acne scars. I wore heavy eye makeup to accentuate my eyes and lined my eyes with black liner. I never walked into work "not ready." The minute I stepped into the club, I was a different person. Jasmine was not only beautiful with perfect hair and makeup, but she also didn't talk about money or problems with her ex or bitch about anything. I quickly caught on that my job was about providing a fantasy. Men heard about money problems and child issues at home; they didn't want to pay to hear it at the club. Jasmine became the performer, the exotic dancer, and she was someone entirely different than Holly. Compartmentalizing these two identities made it easier to walk through the club's door every night.

 Brandy, however, showed up with very little makeup and sometimes needed to shave. She said she didn't care; she wasn't going to change her behavior to make a man more comfortable. Brandy hated wasting precious time getting ready at home. Some girls even showed up to the club with their wet hair still in towels. I bought a pink electric shaver once, thinking that would cut some time off getting ready, but it left stubble on my legs, so I ditched it.

 Not every man who showed up at Dreamgirls was a potential customer. Dino and Chuck came to the club nearly every night. Dino was short and round, with dark brown curly hair and glasses. Chuck was pale, tall, and thin, and he had sandy brown hair that swooped forward and covered a receding hairline. They sat in the same place every night and ordered the same beer. If someone was at their table when they arrived, they made a big deal about it but resigned themselves to a new table for the night.

We knew we could never get a dance from them, but Dino and Chuck liked being friends with the dancers. They were like the club mascots. Was a customer being a jerk? Just head over to Dino and Chuck to blow off some steam. They sided with us every time. Paying customers didn't want to hear about money problems, rent, or toddler issues, but Dino and Chuck listened and even offered advice. They were cool to hang out with if there wasn't any money to be made. It was about the realest I could be in the club.

The coke dealers didn't want any dances, either. They strolled in and made themselves at home, but they never needed a dance or wanted to buy any drinks. That wasn't what they were there for. The dealers were local, always had product, and most importantly were let into the club—no questions asked. They were welcomed there, and Larry and the management staff didn't care what they did as long as it wasn't obvious or brought any attention to the club. If the girls were high on drugs, they were more compliant. Drugs made the job of taking off our clothes easier. Not every girl in the club did drugs, but it was a lot easier to do the job if we did.

It didn't take long until someone asked us if we did cocaine. It wasn't a hard stretch of the imagination when we showed up stoned every night after sitting in the parking lot to get high before work. Cocaine was the club drug of choice. It was a level up from smoking weed. I could smoke cigarettes in the club all night long, but there was no good way to smoke pot in there. Cocaine was the logical choice, and it was also the easiest thing in the world to transport.

I'm not sure what other drugs people did outside the club. I'm certain heroin was a thing for some people, but I never saw it. Perhaps ecstasy and meth were also drugs of choice, but I didn't see those in the club either. From what

I gathered; dancers didn't want to do any drug that would affect their appearance.

Brandy and I each bought a small amount of cocaine from the dealer one night. We took our purchases to the bathroom, and each of us chose a stall. I carefully opened my baggie and poured a little bit on the back of the toilet. I cut myself a line with my driver's license and rolled up a dollar bill. I was excited and scared someone was going to walk in.

"Just do it, dude," Brandy said from the other side of the door. She had already done hers and was ready to go.

I quickly snorted it, the rush hitting my brain instantly. I wiped my finger across the residue on the back of the toilet then rubbed it across my gums. None of it should go to waste. My gums were numb and tingly, and my brain was instantly alive. We checked our noses for white powder in the mirror and glanced at each other, our eyes bright and wild. After I realized we could do coke in the club, it opened up a whole new exciting world for me. I'm a loud person anyway, but I got even louder and lost all my inhibitions on cocaine. Cocaine plus Jasmine equaled instant party girl.

Guys came in for birthday parties, living out their fantasies with the Dreamgirls. Their loud and rowdy friends came with them. The DJ called the birthday boy onto the stage, and the Beatles song "Birthday" cued up. A chair was placed center stage, and the birthday boy sat in it, placing his hands beneath his legs, since he couldn't touch the girls. Every Dreamgirl was required to be on the stage. It didn't matter if you were with a paying customer. This pissed off some of the old-timers because they couldn't make money while they were messing around with birthday jokers. No money in that.

At first, it was crazy and fun. We danced around stage and took turns lap dancing for the guy in the chair. It was supposed to be his moment to shine on stage with twenty to thirty women, all milling around for a turn with him. Some of the girls slammed down hard on his lap. It was as if all their repressed rage came flying out and landed on the poor guy. Not all of us were vicious, though. Just dance a little on his lap and rub our tits in his face. It became less fun when more than one birthday boy showed up in a night, since no one was making money dancing for free on a stage.

The other group stage dances were called the Fantasy Dances. It was a sort of cattle call where all the girls had to go on stage for one song. Each DJ had their different songs to use during a Fantasy Dance. A popular song was "Girls, Girls, Girls," by Mötley Crüe. It was the guys' opportunity to check us out and see all the girls in one place. If I was with a paying customer when the Fantasy Dance came on, it was important he knew I'd be right back. The last thing I needed was for him to catch some other girl's eye while he was looking at all the girls on stage.

Of course, if it were a slow night, then Fantasy Dances were the times I could really stand out.

Living Dead Girl

The bouncers were there to protect us, and we trusted them. They took turns walking us to our cars because, inevitably, men loitered in the parking lot and waited for the girls to get off work. I had never met a bouncer who wouldn't put himself between me and trouble.

They were there to provide safety for the girls, but they also carried clipboards to keep track of our income. Every time a new song started, they walked around and made a note next to the dancer's name. They indicated whether it was a table dance or a couch dance. We always charged at least fifteen dollars, but it wasn't unreasonable to ask for a tip on top of that. Sometimes men balked at tipping for a dance. I knew the bouncers only marked what we made minimum for a dance, but they didn't know what we made on top of that.

At first if a customer offered to buy me a drink, I sat with them and talked. Men were always looking for a deal. "How about no dance, but I'll buy you a drink?" In the beginning, I thought that was a good trade-off. But the girls making a lot of money were doing couch dances along the back. I stopped sitting with men who offered only drinks and the guys who only wanted to pay fifteen dollars a dance with no tips.

If a guy took me back to the couches, I tried to get him to stay back there. The money could add up, especially if he stayed with me for multiple songs. That was why a lot of girls didn't like the birthdays or Fantasy Dances. If a guy came to his senses, he could stop spending money or find that his taste was suited to another girl he hadn't seen yet.

As we were informed in the beginning, we paid a percentage to the club out of what we earned. The bouncers kept track of who made what and how many dances we did. Even though we were considered independent contractors, if we weren't working hard, they sometimes came around and suggested we start dancing. They at least wanted the girls to be on the floor and encourage the men to drink.

At the end of the night, the bouncer with the clipboard waited outside the dressing room to get the club's cut of the money. If you bought too much blow (cocaine) or didn't have enough business to make money, they didn't care. They wanted the cut from what you should have earned.

I fell short one night after spending money on cocaine on a slow night. The bouncer said I had to talk to Larry. I was nervous to owe the club money; I didn't want to get fired. Larry folded his arms across his chest.

"I'll let it slide. But next time . . ." he warned.

That was the first time I walked out of the club owing them money. I was relieved I didn't lose my job. When I told Sasha, one of the older dancers, she scoffed, "Don't let them play you like that; that's how they roll."

I didn't know what she meant. I thought that was really cool of them to let me catch up next time. I was grateful they didn't fire me. After all, I had an increase in personal expenses now. I had regular appointments to get my acrylic nails filled. I got treatments and color for my hair. I still had to buy diapers and pay my regular bills. Plus, the cocaine wasn't free. While I was thankful that they let me owe them for next time, I was also determined to pay the balance off the next time I worked.

Later, I realized they weren't cool with the dancers where back rent was concerned. In fact, it allowed them more control over us—when we worked, how hard we worked. It was always something they held over a dancer if she owed back rent. We were in their debt, and we needed to continue to work in order to pay it off. It was a vicious circle—allow dancers access to buy drugs and drinks (even if they were underage) so that they'd make poor choices, then allow them to put their floor rent on a payment plan. This way, they had to continue working.

On average, I made anywhere from $300 to $1000 a night and sometimes more on a good weekend night. For very little work, it was fine for me. On good nights, it was way more. But there were nights where it was also way less, and it was mostly due to drugs. As we made friends with the coke dealer, it became easier and easier to spot him during the night. If it was a busy night, a little cocaine went well with an alcohol buzz. I was already fun after a few drinks; if you added the cocaine, I was downright manic, "party central." If it was a slow night, cocaine was there to make the night go by faster. I could do a couple of lines and find a way to be fun, even during the slow time.

The bouncers were a huge part of the dancer life, but the girls were the ones who made it more bearable. While it was competitive out on the floor vying for men's attention, there was also a natural camaraderie that happened. We supported one another. If a guy was cheap, smelled funny, or gave off a bad vibe, we warned one another to steer clear. If a girl had a cute top and another one liked it, nine times out of ten, she'd let her borrow it right away. The girls I worked with were some of the best friends I've ever made. And I never even knew most of their real names.

We performed together onstage to make more money. If one of the girls was dancing, I could take a dollar and lie across the stage on my back to have her take it from me. We put on a show for the men, which sometimes resulted in a double dance. They did the same for me. We worked together and were competitive, but we knew that putting on a good show meant more money for all of us.

The lines of sexuality blurred for me. If you would have asked the teen me what I thought of this, she would have been shocked at the blatant sexual behavior, and she would've immediately referenced Sodom and Gomorrah. But this new "me," older and wiser, didn't align with the Christian values I'd been raised on. I learned how to separate my sexuality from my identity, which allowed me to perform.

The first time a girl kissed me, or touched my breasts, or ran her long hair over my stomach as she leaned over me on the stage, I was nervous and giddy. But as time went on, it became part of the performance. It was always the show of abandonment and fun. We were the fantasy, and we did our part to make sure we were looking like we were living the dream up there. Did I ever date any of the girls? No. But I learned to pretend like I did, because that seemed to be most men's fantasies.

Here are some of the girls I remember, in no particular order:

Misty—she was so sweet to me on my first day. She remained a good friend to me while I worked there. She always had a smile, was loud like me, and had a boisterous laugh. She wasn't into the drug scene but didn't care that I was. I only worked with her for a few months before she left. I never knew her real name or where she went.

Siarah—she worked the day shift, which was a difficult shift to work. Girls who worked days mostly had regulars who came in to see them. Guys didn't spend a lot of time at the strip club during daylight hours. Siarah was tall and leggy, with long blonde hair. She was sometimes featured on the marquee by the doorway. She never even said two words to me, and I rarely saw her except during a shift change. Girls like Siarah made this their career. Men bought them cars and breast implants.

Iris—she was eighteen years old with long, stick-straight brown hair. She had dark brown eyes and could only be described as wholesome. I was only twenty-two years old, but I was sad that she had landed here at such a young age. She smiled a lot and reminded me of a dark-haired Barbie doll. Men loved her because she was barely eighteen and had a fresh innocence about her.

Angelica—she was in her late twenties or early thirties. Heavyset, with large, natural breasts that hung down, she wore the same black dress and black heels every night for every set and song. She had a large nose and dark brown curly hair. Many of the men I sat with looked at her and wondered how she got in as a "Dreamgirl," but she had her own share of regulars.

Desiree—she was Spanish and exotic-looking, with dark skin and flowing, shiny dark hair. She wasn't thin but had beautiful rounded-out curves. When she wore neon clothes under the black lights, her skin looked nearly black. She appealed to men who had fantasies about women from other cultures.

Kamber—she had to be in her late twenties, which made her an old-timer. She danced to Type O Negative's "Little Miss Scare-All." She was also athletic, hanging from the ceiling's water pipes during her dances. Management grew concerned that her swinging from the pipes would break them, but she flat out refused to stop. I grew accustomed to watching the pipes nervously when she climbed up there, in case of the event that they busted open and water came down on everyone. While she wasn't what would be considered physically attractive in many ways, she had her share of admirers because of her strength in the pole tricks and her I-don't-give-a-fuck attitude. She wore thick black eyeliner with long blonde hair like an '80's rocker. Her main go-to staple were the tall boots that went above her knees.

Those were just a few of the girls I met in my first months of working at Dreamgirls. Some of them began with amateur night, which was a way to encourage new dancers to get a start and let the men see the "new girls." Sometimes, the girls who showed up for amateur night were clearly not amateurs, but rather they were the girls who came from other clubs to check us out. But some showed up to audition and truly had never taken their clothes off before in front of strangers.

I remembered how welcome Misty and Destiny made Brandy and me feel on the first night we danced, so I tried to extend that kindness to the amateurs.

Sober

I quickly learned how to lean in and use my assets. A man who entered the club became someone with a wallet, and I wanted what was in his wallet. I listened to him, I let him talk. It made him feel good when I rubbed his shoulders. I sat on his lap if he asked and pretended like he was everything I had been searching for, which he was—for that night. I behaved as though he were my long-lost friend, like it was amazing that one night had brought us together.

Vulnerability was huge for them, so the savior complex was a real thing. I can't count the number of times men told me I shouldn't be there. They wanted me to get out of that line of work. "You're too good for this" and "why are you doing this job?" At the same time, they handed over their money to me as I sat on their laps or tried to grasp my breast in their mouth when I danced in front of them. They complained about their jobs, wives, and lives in general. I nodded and provided a listening ear. Mastering the skill of listening closely, I sipped a drink while side-eyeing the room for another conquest, in case the current guy didn't pan out or if he ran out of money.

I learned how to tell early on when a guy wasn't into buying the dances. Typically, they didn't overindulge in their drinks, and they were cautious about spending. The men I liked got drunk fast or came into the club that way. They lost their sense of reasoning, especially when it came to their money. Those were my favorite—with their unfocused, glazed-over eyes, the word "yes" on their mouths, and hands in their open wallets.

The club also offered "Funny Money" to customers. A guy could use his credit card and buy little, yellow monopoly-looking money. Credit cards weren't widely used in the clubs and hardly anyone I knew had a debit card. One night, I sat with a lone guy at a table, and he bought me a drink. But I couldn't make money off drinks, so I needed to dance.

I convinced him to get a couch dance. Boom, twenty-five dollars plus a tip.

"You want another one?" I asked, leaning down so my tits swung near his face. He glanced at my breasts and looked in his wallet. I did, too, but it was empty.

"Ah, I'm out of cash."

I stood up and grabbed my bikini top.

He grabbed my arm. "Wait. I have a credit card."

I paused. Something inside me knew this wasn't a good choice. His loneliness was coming off him in waves. He was desperate for conversation, and he'd felt like he had made a connection with me. He didn't want to lose that, and worse yet, he didn't want to see me dancing elsewhere. A sudden wave of sadness washed over me. I saw myself as I really was. My job was to mislead people into thinking I cared and that they had a friend in me, when really, all I cared about was their money. It felt wrong.

But then he grabbed my ass and squeezed hard. "Let me see if I can use my card."

My guilt slid away. "Of course, I'll wait right here." I smiled and sat back down. He took his credit card up to the counter and came back with two drinks and a stack of yellow money, waving it at me with a grin on his face.

I smiled coyly and patted the seat he had vacated. That stack of money was as good as mine. Of course, when I turned it in, I had to pay a percentage out of it for cashing it in, on top of the percentage that he had to pay for taking it out. This was another way the club made its money off the girls who worked there and the lonely customers.

I spent the rest of the night with this guy. He bought me drinks. And I had him back on the couch, one dance after another. I had worked up a sweat from the back-to-back dances. Yellow stacks of Funny Money filled my satchel. I had to convince him to slow down so that I could smoke a cigarette every once in a while.

As the night wore on and the drinks flowed freely, he proceeded to tell me about his grand life and important job, and also how I should live my life. In every way possible, he was trying to make me think he had his life together and mine was complete shit. I laughed at his jokes and rubbed his arm while I smoked my cigarettes (or "cancer sticks," as he called them). Eventually, it became a constant battle to keep his hands off me. I removed one wandering hand from my left breast, and he tried to lean forward to put my other breast in his mouth. I giggled and said, "No, no," while backing away and pushing away his hands.

At the end of the night, all his Funny Money was in my purse. I made more than enough money to pay off my back rent to the club and house rent to Tamara, get my nails refilled, and even put some aside in my savings. I was exhausted but spending most of the night dancing for him had landed me a nice chunk of change.

"Okay, come in and see me again soon," I said sweetly. My mind was already on getting out of my shoes and into sweatpants and sneakers. I gathered my satchel and clothes, ready to leave.

The waitress brought him his final receipt while I gathered my things. It included all of his charges—drinks, Funny Money, everything. It was dark in the club, but that man turned an awful shade of green.

"What *is* this?" he demanded, looking first at me, then at the waitress. He kept staring at the receipt. "What happened? This must be a mistake."

There were no bouncers close by. It was the end of the night, and they were getting other customers to exit the building. Any moment, the lights were going to come on. I hated the bright lights at the end of the night, casting reality all over us like a shower.

He gave the waitress a hard time about his credit card slip. He demanded to speak to a manager. The waitress wasn't having any of his shit. She wanted to leave, too.

I stepped around the table to go, and he leaned toward me. His words were slurred and his gaze unfocused. "Can you tell me what this is about?"

I should have left, but I felt bad for the waitress who had already summoned a bouncer. "It was Funny Money. You paid for it with your credit card."

"I don't want to put *that* on my credit card!" he exclaimed, looking around for backup. "I can't go home with *this* on my credit card. I'll pay for the drinks, but I'm not paying all that extra money."

"You already did," I said, making eye contact with the waitress.

"Well—" he shook his head— "you're just gonna have to give me that money back." He held out his hand. His voice got louder. "I changed my mind."

"I'm not giving it back. I worked for this money." He acted like it was worth nothing for me to have sat there with him all night while he bragged and bitched and tried to manhandle me.

He sneered, "You didn't do shit!"

I turned to go, and he grabbed my arm with a pleading look in his drunken gaze. "Wait, wait, my wife. If she finds out I spent money on *this*," he waved his other arm up and down ("this" meaning me), "she'll *kill* me."

For a millisecond, I pitied him. But there was no part of me that felt bad enough to give him that money back. This money meant diapers, rent. I earned it.

"I'm sorry." I pulled my arm out of his grasp and stepped away.

By then, two bouncers immediately surrounded him; each grabbed him on a side. Men were not allowed to touch the dancers, at all.

He started yelling and screaming. His face contorted into an angry expression so different from the adoring one a few hours earlier.

I rushed back to the dressing room, shaken and nervous, with the promise that he was being escorted out of the building and someone would walk me to my car.

I never saw him again.

But I always remembered his sad, lonely expression when he realized I was indeed not his friend and that he'd paid a lot of money for me to pretend.

Voodoo

This was a dream job. Other than paying to work there and the occasional jerk customer, it was an amazing experience. I was paid to party. I drank while I worked. I came to work high and got high while I was there. I picked out my music and danced to it—choreographed my own performances. I had finally found a way to express my creativity.

I started learning a few pole tricks beyond hooking my leg on the pole and swinging around. I perfected them either on the private stage in the back when it wasn't being used or early in the evening on a not so busy night. I kept the pole tricks to a minimum because there wasn't a need to get too crazy if you had a lineup of men wanting to give you money. The only real mishap on stage was the time I overshot a swing and hit my face on the pole. I saw stars for a moment but easily recovered. Too many White Russians contributed to that clumsy experience.

I figured out some guys would pay me to dance onstage to what they wanted to hear. I learned new songs that way, and it usually generated good tips and money. Not all of them were winners. I danced to plenty of Warren Zevon songs and

"Sweater Song" by Weezer, but if they paid me enough money, I'd give any song a try. If they complained about the "rap music" or lack of music appreciation and taste, I knew they'd most likely be open to watching me dance to their favorite songs. I spent a significant amount of time considering song selection and coordinating outfits. To me, it was an art form.

Brandy was all about the money from the start. She worked the floor as soon as the shift started and kept looking for ways to earn money. She also didn't care about stealing regulars from the other girls. I told her we didn't need to make any enemies.

"If the men want me to dance for them, that's not my fault," she said nonchalantly. She backed off, but she was relentless. If a guy paid her any interest at all, she didn't care if it was someone's regular. She would march over and sit right down on his lap. Occasionally, the previous girl came and took her client back, but sometimes the man liked them both. Brandy had a way of pissing off the other girls, and she didn't care. She wanted money, and she wanted all of it.

Brandy also refused to spend money on more clothes or shoes. She put on the bare minimum of makeup and only washed and brushed her hair. She was a tomboy, and men liked that about her. Some men were attracted to girls who were an A cup and looked prepubescent, so she had her own following at the club. She was loud, abrasive, and pushy, and there were men who loved that too.

After my initial fears about not being good enough to be a Dreamgirl, I considered it an honor that men would pay to see me unclothed. I had changed considerably from the girl in the Jordan's parking lot, screaming at the bouncers about my cheating boyfriend. I realized how foolish that was, because on the other end of it, as a stripper, I did not look at the men in the club as anything but a way to earn money. They mostly bitched about their wives and jobs. And usually after the initial encounter, I knew exactly where the problems had started in their lives. But it was my job to listen and empathize with them, not to point out that happiness was an inside job.

When I wasn't at work, I didn't spend any time on my appearance. This helped me to differentiate Holly vs. Jasmine. I couldn't hide my tan, fake nails, or dyed hair. But Holly wore baggy clothes, tennis shoes, loose shirts, and left her hair dirty in a scrunchy ponytail. Holly didn't like male attention when she wasn't at the club. I thought I was invisible when I dressed like that, and that's how I wanted it. I was back to compartmentalizing my life, like I did when I was younger and trying to fit into the world.

Someone once told me nothing good happens after midnight, and I found this to be true working at Dreamgirls. The club shut down promptly at 2:00 a.m. State ordinances dictated how long alcohol-serving establishments could remain open, and this included topless strip clubs.

Every night, the DJ played some sort of song shortly after last call that indicated the club was closing. Each DJ had his own favorite, but I can say without a doubt "Closing Time" by Semisonic was way overplayed. It took many years for me to lose that anxious feeling when that song started playing. When the last song ended, the lights came up. We were all tired, and we wanted to go home. We grabbed our clothes, gathered our money, and tried to disengage from the customers. Our faces were shiny, and the stretch marks, imperfections, and razor burn that were hidden in the low lights and black lights suddenly glowed brightly. We wrapped up whatever we were doing and hustled to the back, like Cinderella at midnight.

Sometimes, I had a hard time getting away from particularly amorous customers. That's when the reality sets in for them—that it's just a job, and they were just a customer. They spent time with me and wanted to believe it was something more, especially since they bought drinks and dances.

In most cases, my regulars were long gone by then. They didn't need to see me as the night ended. Of course, there were girls who met up with guys after closing. They went to breakfast with their regulars or met up elsewhere. I'm sure they made more money that way. Some of them carried on affairs. I never gave anyone promises of "let's meet up after work," or "let's hang out outside the club." I had no interest in letting any customer see me outside the club. I had plenty of regulars, and I did have a relationship with them, sort of. They came in specifically to see me and asked for me. Sometimes after a couple visits, they tried to wiggle out of dancing. "Don't you just like me?" or "Don't you just want to spend time with me?" I always responded with "Yes, but I also have to make money. This is my job." If they agreed and continued to pay me, then I would stay. If they grew belligerent and responded with "Well you only like me for my money," then I had to go find someone else.

One slow night, there were only around two customers in the club. The majority of us wandered around, chatting with Dino and Chuck or sitting in the dressing room, smoking and sipping on a drink. A few lounged at the bar or at the tables and lazily watched another girl dance her set to a nearly empty room.

Brandy and I were in the dressing room. Monica came in, teetering in her tall heels. She had shoulder-length brown hair and wore it in an '80s feathered style. She was young and had a beautiful smile with perfect white teeth contrasted against her deep, caramel-colored skin. Monica had the largest natural tits I had seen on anyone in the club, even bigger than Angelica's. She flashed a handful of cash made up of hundred-dollar bills. It had to be close to $600.

"Was that from tonight?" Brandy asked, confused.

"Yeah, I'm so lucky my regular showed." She leaned toward the mirror to put lipstick on.

I noticed her earlier. Her regular was there, but she didn't even do two dances. She just sat in his lap and smoked. I'd seen her in the parking lot before; she drove a brand-new car.

Monica finished applying her lipstick. We chatted for a while, and she left.

"She's fucking him," Brandy said, snapping her gum and eyeing the door where Monica had walked out. I had the same thought. Brandy would say something snarky about girls who did too much in the club, but her expression said she wished it were her who had that guy.

I couldn't think about doing that with someone. Not for money. It was a line I had set for myself, like with the drugs.

"Maybe she's not," I said, ever optimistic.

Brandy looked at me and rolled her eyes. "Come on, dude. No one gives you that kind of money to just sit around and talk."

At the end of the night, I peeled my sweaty clothes off and shoved them into my bag. I smelled like stale cigarette smoke and Victoria's Secret body spray. My makeup was smudged and sweaty. It felt so good to put on sweatpants and get into tennis shoes. I tied my hair back in a ponytail and made sure I had my cigarettes and money.

At least once or twice a month, a manager or bouncer barred the way to the exit, when a fight had broken out in the main club area.

The first time we were detained, a man had busted a beer bottle over someone's head. He was arrested. The other guy was taken to the hospital with a gash on his forehead and a blood-doused bar towel draped over his slouched figure. The dancers were trapped in the back until the police were called and were done questioning those involved.

At first, this terrified me, especially if there was yelling or screaming accompanying the fight. I was scared because I knew some customers carried guns and there were obvious inherent dangers involved in a job like mine.

Eventually, I grew numb to it.

We sat down and waited, talking to the other girls who came out. We reflected on what sort of funny shit happened throughout the night and relayed stories to each other and smoked cigarettes. Meanwhile, the police were there asking questions. The bouncers were involved. Sometimes, medical personnel showed up in an ambulance to carry someone away.

We groaned and moaned about being tired and wanting to leave, while someone was escorted out in handcuffs, or worse.

Nothing good happens after midnight.

D'yer Mak'er

The lit-up marquee at the entrance changed images whenever a new feature was coming to town. Features were girls who drew crowds, and they were "famous" in the exotic dance world. Sometimes they were exclusively exotic dancers, and sometimes they were porn stars. Their heavily edited pictures were splashed on the marquee. They were always provocative, sported a boob job, and were dressed in some sort of skimpy outfit with or without a top.

For the two or three days they were there, they were royalty. Some brought in large crowds, and we all benefited from the increased revenue. Weeks prior to their visit, the DJs announced their pending arrival two to three times a night. They were considered guests in our club, and, as such, got a special dressing room all to themselves in the back.

I got excited when someone new showed up on the marquee. I wanted to know what success looked like in that industry. I liked knowing what it looked like to make it big. The thought of getting paid to dance and travel the country fascinated me. But most of them didn't look like their pictures. In fact, for some, it was obvious it had been a while since the picture had been taken. Often, they looked older and extremely tired in person.

They came on stage and performed their sets. Some wandered around and talked with the men afterward. But most just made stage money and then left to go into the back to their private dressing room. The club paid them to come in. They toured the country and did this for a living. Most of the features were coolly distant, so there was no sense in making friends with them, since we'd probably never see them again. This was before social media or cell phones, so there was no real way to keep in contact.

I had been dancing for about seven months at this point, working six nights a week. My nails were done every week to week and a half. My pinky nail had a hole so that I could attach various charms in the tip. My hair was constantly highlighted and maintained. I always had a large stash of cash in my purse, and I paid for nearly everything in ones. I had lost the rest of my baby weight from Riley. My belly had grown leaner from using my muscles for pole tricks. My arms were stronger from holding myself upside down in inversions. I wasn't great at the pole tricks, but I tried to practice and get better. I was unmistakably a stripper.

I dreamed about traveling the country to perform, maybe getting implants and finding out how to get sponsored so I could be like the women on the marquee. But then reality set in, and I knew I could never do that. There was no way I could travel with a young daughter, and I would never leave her behind. Perhaps I had been too young when I had Riley, but how could I have known? Those thoughts racked me with guilt, and I reminded myself she was the best thing that had ever happened to me. Despite my love for my daughter, my life was always about my job at the club, even when I was away from work. I constantly listened to songs on the radio and tried to figure out if I could perform a routine to it. What about another dance outfit to go with the song? Did I need new shoes for that?

One of the features who came in was Heaven Leigh, and she was from the East Coast. Her real name was Jenny, and she was friendly. She talked to Brandy and me about the experience of traveling. She told us she eventually wanted to stop traveling and open her own school to teach people pole dancing. At that time, pole dancing was not a sport. It was something that was done only in dark clubs and by strippers like us and women in Vegas. I couldn't imagine regular women and housewives doing what we did. Jenny seemed to have smart business sense, and she didn't get high or drink when she was there.

On her last night, she was selling a few of her dance costumes. They were laid out on a table, and the girls were looking at what she had for sale.

I found a black tuxedo jacket that came with a vest, hat, and a cane. I'd recently spent the money I had on a gram and had snorted a line, but my regular, Stan, was visiting me that night. I needed to get to Stan before some other girl sat with him; I wanted that costume.

One of the new girls was standing at our table, having a discussion with him, when I approached. When she saw me, she smiled stiffly, said her goodbyes, and melted into the background. I knew how to stand my ground, but I also knew Stan would see no one else but me. Stan, for some reason, had a paternal crush on me.

I greeted him with a kiss on his cheek and in a cocaine-fueled rush explained about the costume and how badly I wanted it.

"Please, please, buy it for me," I pleaded. This was the sort of thing that regulars did for the dancers; it wasn't too much to ask.

"You want a tuxedo jacket? And a cane with a hat?" he asked, laughing a little.

"Please!" I shook his hands in mine. There was an urgency in my voice, because I was both hyped up from coke and wanted the outfit. I didn't want someone else to get it.

He chuckled, shook his head, and reached into his wallet for the money. I squealed, leaned in and kissed his cheek, then ran back to buy it.

I tried it on and immediately fell in love with it. There was even a metal studded garter included for my leg. I did another line in the bathroom before I returned to the table to show Stan. I modeled it and twirled in front of him, holding the little black cane in one hand and the top hat in the other. I gave him a dance and practiced, using the cane and hat as props. He smiled and nodded his approval.

Our biggest point of contention was that Stan didn't think I belonged there. I heard that from guys all the time. He'd tell me I was a nice girl, a "good" girl, and he hated to see me working there. He told me I had a daughter to raise, and I should find a better job. He was my regular, but he was also like a father figure. And he was one of the less creepy guys. I hated when he told me these things, even though it was coming from a good place. It implied that my job sucked. And "too good for this kind of job" girls didn't make good money, and I needed to make money.

Often when he came in, I sat with him, smoked my cigarettes, and cautiously shared my goals and dreams. Being high got me chatty. I was always careful not to get too heavy into issues like money, religion, my daughter, or dealing with Joey. But part of having a regular meant they could become involved in your life at a deeper level. To Stan, that meant he could have opinions about how I lived mine.

During one of Stan's subsequent visits, I grew increasingly agitated as the night wore on and my high wore off. The dealer was late. I was counting the seconds till I could go back and do another line. Stan wanted to talk, and I half listened to him, chain smoking my cigarettes with one eye on the door. When the dealer arrived, I excused myself in the middle of the conversation, jumped up, and ran to the back. When I returned, my eyes were bright, and I was ready to dance.

Stan studied me for a minute, then shook his head and looked down at his drink. He sighed and slowly moved the straw in a circle.

I was so zooted up that I couldn't sit still. After a line, I went from sullen and quiet to loud and reckless, screaming with abandon all over the club. As soon as the buzz wore off, I couldn't wait to go back and do another line.

Stan probably thought he could save me. When I did listen to him, he talked to me about going back to school and how it was never too late for me to reach for my dreams. On one hand, I was cautiously optimistic: what if I could?" But on the other hand, he had no idea how much of a struggle it was for me, just existing, from the very beginning. I still sometimes believed that Armageddon was coming, and I was going to die. What were dreams and goals to someone like me? He wanted to somehow help me get off the path I was on, and he was one of many who became a self-appointed savior. Eventually, Stan went his own way and stopped coming to the club. But the good thing about regulars was that there was always another Stan to come along and try to save me.

Brandy also had her own regulars. She danced to Tool and Aerosmith, and she didn't give two shits what music men wanted to hear. She continued to wear the old lady office shoes, and when she spun around the pole, her ankles were bent so that she could keep the shoes on her feet. But even with her oddly flexed feet and old lady shoes, Brandy made a ton of money. She got up on the stage with her little girl boobs and office shoes, and she snapped her gum. The guys loved it. She talked football and swore non-stop and called everyone "dude." She openly bitched about her money issues and had no qualms about making sure men knew their money bought diapers and paid bills.

"Don't forget to point your toes," I'd tell her. "It's more attractive if it's a straight line from your calves to your toes!"

"Yeah, yeah, yeah. I hate to tell you, Holly, no one's looking at my feet."

Various vendors came to visit the club, too. A woman named Clarice made costumes and sold them to the dancers. Clarice was an older woman with a head full of graying hair. I never knew how she found this niche, selling dance costumes to strippers, but she was good at it. She sewed exotic halter tops and short, leggy skirts. She brought bikini sets and matching garters. If she didn't have something you described, she would work hard to have it the next time she came in. Clarice was firm on her prices, but her quality was good.

Mr. Party was an Alcoa favorite. Visiting the club wearing his black tuxedo, he was a sharply dressed little Black man, with red eyes and a gorgeous Cheshire cat smile. He referred to himself in the third person and always remembered our names. He carried a bucket filled with fake roses. Some of them were fancy and bedazzled with gems and pearls. Some of them were plain red ones. But all of them were sprayed with the most obnoxious-smelling cologne I'd ever smelled. It was overpowering and lingered, and it was enough cologne to choke an elephant. People made jokes that Mr. Party was the real-life Pepé Le Pew. Mr. Party would approach your table and ask your customer if he wanted to buy a flower for the "beautiful lady." Sometimes he was able to make a sale (with a tip, of course).

An artist named Louis came in to draw women on his sketchpad. He was as round as he was tall, with a receding hairline and small glasses that rested on the tip of his nose. Louis brought his pencils and sketchpad and camped out in the back, near our dressing room door. A lot of the dancers knew Louis, and everyone liked him. When I first met him, some of the girls suggested I get my picture done.

He stopped me on my way out to the floor one night and asked if I wanted a portrait. I shrugged. "Sure, how much?"

"Twenty-five dollars," he said, staring at my tits like he was already figuring out how to draw them.

He pointed at the chair across from him, near the backstage. I sat down and hoped it wouldn't take long. One of my regulars was supposed to show up that evening.

He asked me to remove my bikini top and I did, while trying to sit up straighter, hoping my breasts didn't sag.

He studied me for a minute with his hand on his chin. He looked down at his paper and started drawing, occasionally glancing back up at me. When he was done, he initialed the picture and handed it to me. It was a nice profile sketch. The boobs were too pointy and placed way higher than my normal breast height. Maybe he just liked to draw our faces and stare at our boobs while he was drawing.

I thanked him and took the picture back to my locker. Louis was an okay guy and another regular you couldn't expect a dance from. When I compared my picture to pictures of other girls he had drawn, they all looked similar—right down to our facial expressions. Apparently, he thought we all looked the same, with the same boobs. Or he mastered one look and thought we wouldn't notice if we all appeared to be cookie-cutter versions of each other.

I loved to order Mexican food from a place down the street. Sometimes, the girls got together and placed an order to eat before our shift started. After it got busy, I wouldn't have time to eat. I also knew if I decided to buy coke, I wouldn't be hungry after the first line, so I needed sustenance. I planned my food intake around my buzz schedule and when the dealer would be in the club.

The only thing to worry about with Mexican food was gas during the dances. Some of the girls laughed at me, asking why I thought that was a good idea, particularly when I had to spend time in the dressing room with painful stomach cramps. I wish I could say the fantasy eliminated gas, but no, it didn't.

Amateur photographers frequently came in to find models. Many of them proclaimed they needed nude models, which I immediately shot down. I made a friend in the club named Tim who asked for a dance from me. After the dance, he informed me he was a photographer and said he wanted to take my pictures. He said it didn't even have to be topless.

I had set a boundary of not going anywhere outside the club with customers, so I hesitated. But the lure of having my pictures taken was too much. I knew a lot of the girls had photos done, and I wanted some too.

"Where?" I asked him.

"My house."

"As long as I can bring my boyfriend."

"That's fine."

"And it doesn't have to be topless?" I asked cautiously.

"Nope, not unless you want to."

We discussed the details, and he suggested I bring a few different outfits. I asked once again if it had to be topless, and he insisted it didn't and that it could be only what I was comfortable wearing. I told him I wanted copies, and he said that was fine.

I didn't get a bad vibe from Tim. Joey, although technically not my boyfriend, agreed to come with me. I brought my clothes and makeup to a small ranch home in a subdivision in Alcoa. Joey lounged on a couch while Tim and I did various shots throughout his house with sheets draped over his furniture. We also took some photos outside. We shot through a few rolls of film, and he promised he would bring the copies to me in the club after he had them developed.

True to his word, he came in and gave me the copies. He loved the images. He was very pleased with how they'd turned out. But I judged myself with a critical eye. I couldn't stand my thighs—they were too big and flabby on the inside. I had bruises all over my body from dancing on the static pole. I picked a million things apart about myself that weren't good enough. These were the days before Photoshop was popular. There were no apps to fix the things I hated about my body.

When I look at that girl in the pictures now, I see that I'm laughing in some of them. I see the girl that Stan saw—the one he felt was too good for that business. I was young and insecure but still able to find laughter and happiness. In some of the images, I'm gazing at the camera in a way that can only be described as seductive. I had the ability to turn myself into someone who looked like they wanted to have sex. I had picked that skill up quickly.

But Tim had also shot some candid expressions, when I wasn't paying attention. It's in those images that there is an undercurrent of sadness, confusion. It may not have been apparent to anyone else, but the camera caught those moments in a quick click of a button.

I can see it now, even if I couldn't see it then.

No Diggity

Joey and I spent time together on the days I had to go to work so that he could watch Riley. Eventually, we started hanging out again on the days I wasn't working. More and more often, we hung out at Joseph and Karen's. After a few months of living with Tamara, I decided to move out of her trailer and get back together with Joey so that we could live together again. I knew in the back of my mind the potential was there for Joey and me to pick up where we'd left off when it came to fighting. But I found comfort in knowing what to expect, even if what I expected was bad.

Joey and I continued to receive a lot of support from Karen. She didn't approve of my nighttime lifestyle, but she was there for Riley. She and Joseph picked up the slack when Joey and I were gone.

Joey didn't care that I danced, although he threw it in my face when we argued. Once, he came to the club to visit me. It was on a night that one of my regulars, Jack, was there to see me.

Jack was a man in his mid-thirties. He was balding, shy, and wore overly large glasses. Even though he was a quiet man, he spent money on me with dances and bought me drinks. He said maybe ten words the entire night; the rest of the time he listened to me talk and hung onto my every word. This was fine by me, especially if I was high on coke, and my desire to chat superseded my desire to do anything else.

Joey had decided to visit the club, and Brandy was giving him a dance next to our couch. I laughed and told Jack that Joey was my boyfriend.

"My boyfriend is getting a dance from my best friend." I laughed.

Joey swung his arm around to high-five Jack. "What's up, dude? How's it going?"

Jack, however, didn't think this was funny. He was shocked. More than once, I caught him glancing at Joey and then back at me.

This was my first big mistake with a regular. To me, this was a job. Somehow, I figured men had to know we had lives outside this club, especially the regulars.

Unfortunately, I learned the hard way. Jack didn't come back to see me after that. Maybe seeing me choose someone like Joey crushed his dream that I was a perfect, attainable girl. Joey high-fiving him and calling him "dude" probably hadn't helped matters.

Working four nights a week should have been more than enough to live on now that I had moved in with Joey. But I still worked as many nights as I could, nearly six nights a week. I figured Riley was in good hands with Karen, and I slowly grew apart from my daughter. She spent time with me when I was home, but it wasn't quality time. I spent a long time getting ready for work, doing my hair and makeup, and washing and preparing my clothes. It was important that I looked perfect. I found myself wanting to be at the club, even more so now than ever before. Joey didn't complain, because why would he? He watched Riley, and I kept him in beer, weed, and occasionally coke.

I had gone from lean to almost gaunt. I could go days without eating a solid meal. I lived on White Russians, cigarettes, and cocaine. The long hours and bad lifestyle started to take a toll on me, physically and emotionally. But youth was on my side, and I hid the bags under my eyes with makeup and wore loose clothing.

There were some girls who looked like they never ate. A girl on the day shift named Samantha was bone-thin. I never once saw her eat at the club. Her legs were all sharp angles and as thin as my arms, with bones jutting out of her pale skin. She was sweet and ethereal, with large, round, doe-like eyes. When she danced, she floated. Brandy said a slight breeze could carry her away on stage. Her waifish body accentuated her height. Guys loved that about her.

Samantha's hair was long and blonde. The bottom layer appeared unbrushed though, and I often wondered if it was a weave. She ran a large paddle brush over the top layer, but she never pushed the brush to the bottom to get all the snarls out. When I was growing up, I had long hair. My mother didn't brush it for me; I was supposed to do that myself. She must not have run a quality check on my brushing techniques, because my step-grandmother, an impatient and brusque Hungarian lady named Gramma Rose, discovered a knot the size of a tennis ball at the base of my neck, beneath the top layer. Gramma Rose was angry at my mother and spent hours brushing it out. I cried in pain and begged her to cut it out, but she refused. Samantha had that bottom layer of hair on her head.

I expanded my closet with more shoes and clothes for work. I enjoyed locating unique items to wear. Sometimes I bought them from Clarice, or even other dancers. I frequented Déjà Vu's Love Boutique every chance I could and bought new, taller shoes and more clothes. I had to be careful about what

I wore on the bottom because I was still painfully shy about my C-section scar. There was nothing worse than dancing for a man up close on the couch and having him notice my scar and casually ask mid-dance, "So you have a kid?"

It excited me to be able to buy new costumes and then choose coordinating music and shoes to go with them. For me, it was my chance to be the performer I always wanted to be. I had wanted to join dance class or theater in school. I had wanted to be in gymnastics. Now was my chance to do all those things. Plus, I was investing in myself with the outfits, shoes, and music I purchased. Despite all the girls mostly getting along, it was still a cutthroat business. As soon as I walked out onto the floor, I was competing with twenty to thirty other beautiful girls.

Alina was one of the most exquisite women to grace the Dreamgirls's stage. Her real name was Alice. She was stunning in a Greta Garbo or Coco Chanel sort of way. She was tall without heels, at least five foot nine or ten, with dark brown hair that framed nearly perfect features. Her brown eyes were large and set far apart, with dark, long lashes. I always thought Victoria's Secrets models were hidden in plain sight and she was proof.

One of her signature songs was Blackstreet's "No Diggity." No one else was allowed to dance to it if she was working, or if she was even in the building. And no one really wanted to try; she did it perfectly. She barely made eye contact with men while she danced her first set. She stared at herself in the mirrors behind the couches on the other side of the room, as if she were dancing for herself, by herself. While men clamored around at the bottom of the stage trying to get her attention, she ignored them and gazed across the smoky room. By the time her second song started, she had slowly removed her top and acted as though she finally happened to notice them there, then gracefully stepped offstage to collect the money. If she didn't get to all the men by the end of her second song, she didn't care. She'd make the next girl wait while she swooped down and picked up the money from the stage as the men threw more at her.

I loved watching her. She was a class-A snob. She acted like she was better than everyone else, and I was completely convinced she was better than me. She made a lot of money and drew a large crowd. She knew she was beautiful. I wanted to be like her, aloof and calm—there for the money. Once, she asked if I wanted to buy one of her outfits and I did, if anything, just to be more like her. But I was nothing like her. I was boisterous and laughed too long and too loud. I was an open book, while she was a library of secrets. I made it my mission to make her my friend. While we were never close, she did become friendlier toward me.

Brandy didn't like her one bit. "She's a fucking cunt, dude." Brandy didn't like anyone who was a rival for a man's attention. Alina didn't like Brandy much either. She called her my "little friend," even when Brandy was standing right next to me.

One night, a group of us headed to a coworker's house after work. He lived in a trailer on the south side of Alcoa. Alina went too. She was even prettier with regular clothes on. Even without the stilettos and the glitter, she commanded attention. Her sister, Melanie, also a dancer, met us there. All of us hung out in a tiny, crammed trailer. There were maybe ten dancers, the bartender, and a couple of bouncers. We sat around drinking mixed drinks and smoking cigarettes, talking about work and the future. It had been so long since I had a long-term goal or dream. My life had become the club and living day to day. The thought of owning a home with Joey and raising our young daughter was a faraway thought.

The belief in the New System and Armageddon was also a distant memory that I instantly pushed away, made easier by staying high.

Someone broke out a joint and passed it around. Even though it was late and I knew the party would end eventually, it felt good to listen to soft music in the background and people talking. The tiny trailer filled with smoke, and someone eventually cracked a window. Very rarely did I do anything with individuals from the club, so this allowed me to see them as real people. In these less-guarded moments, they were almost like my friends. We stayed up talking until the sun rose in the sky. I had to get home because I had to work that day, but I hated for it to end.

A rumor started at the club that Alina was pregnant. I had always been a little jealous of her with her perfect body. My stretch marks were a horrible curse to me. I would have been nearly perfect if it weren't for those marks on my stomach and the acne blemishes on my face. No matter what I did, it wasn't good enough. I didn't compare. So, when I heard Alina was pregnant, an evil part of me hoped she would also get stretch marks. Maybe she would have to have a C-section too.

I was sitting on a man's lap, trying to get a dance from him as Alina strolled by. She had a way of walking with her head held high, disdain bordering on disgust for those around her. My customer watched her as she passed and made a comment about how beautiful she was.

"Yeah, she looks great for being pregnant," I said.

This was a buzzkill for any guy looking to fantasize about a girl in a club. His face fell.

"Really? Hmm." And we went back to our discussion.

Later, Alina approached me in the locker room.

"Your little friend went and told everyone I'm pregnant!"

I was horrified, mainly because it was me. But I didn't want her to find out. I acted surprised but didn't correct her.

"Tell her to keep her mouth shut, or I'll shut it for her," she threatened, leaning into me.

Soon enough, she did start to show. So, she really was pregnant; it wasn't a rumor. When she could no longer hide it, they made her a waitress. She still wore a skimpy outfit, but it accommodated her growing belly. I found it hard to believe they had maternity versions of the skimpy clothes waitresses and shot girls wore. I'm not sure how many tips you could expect to make as a pregnant waitress in Dreamgirls, particularly when you used to be one of the main acts. But I got the feeling she didn't have a lot of choices. The loss of money had to be hurting her, and it became clear she needed this job.

I was relieved because she'd been my competition. Before she got pregnant, when I arrived at work and saw the lineup of girls, I always had more confidence if she wasn't working. She went from being the best-looking woman in the club, to someone who started rounding out and gaining weight. Her face broke out in acne. Some of the girls she used to be mean to let her know in no uncertain terms that she had fallen from her pedestal; they didn't push shots or drinks if they sat in her section.

One night, she motioned for me to follow her to the dressing room. She waddled to the back with me in tow. She was getting larger every day; the skimpy outfit for waitresses was getting too tight. She pulled a bag from her locker, the corner locker closest to the entrance. I made a mental note that when she left, I was taking her locker. It was the best one in the dressing room.

The bag contained several sandwich baggies with the telltale white powder in the corners—twisted and tied off like little plastic snowflakes.

"Do you want a bump?" she asked quietly, glancing over my shoulder.

I couldn't remember a time when I answered no to that question.

"Sure," I said, acting casual. I hadn't planned on buying any that night, but there was no time like always. I reached into my satchel for the cash.

She pulled one of the baggies from the pile and handed it to me. Her stomach was in the way when she bent to shove the bag back in her locker.

"You're not—" I paused, searching for inoffensive words—"doing that, I hope?"

She looked at me and rolled her eyes. "No, of course not." She snapped, glancing around. "I just need the money. And don't tell your little friend, the snitch."

Shortly after that, she had her baby, and I didn't see her for a while. She came in once when I was working. She had a little boy, a half-Mexican baby named Joe. Having a baby had rounded her out. While she was still tall, she was no longer sharp lines and angles. Her face was softer, and her eyes were kinder. She'd taken on a gentle quality. When she talked about Joe, she had love and adoration in her eyes.

The next and last time I ever saw her dance was probably close to a year later. She had lost all her baby weight. Her face had cleared up, and she had no stretch marks that I could see. She was back to dancing and had a new tattoo, a butterfly on her butt cheek. She was still beautiful, but somehow having a child changed her. She seemed older, more mature.

That was the last time I saw her as an exotic dancer.

But for the time being, I had the best locker in the dressing room.

Closer

I tried to limit my cocaine use to when I was working. I considered it a perk of my job. But soon, I wasn't limiting my drug use to the club. It was so easy, since the dealer was nearly always there and ready to serve. Joey knew I did it at work and kept an eye on how high I was or how much money I spent. He was jealous of my job and got upset if I came home after work and didn't have any drugs for him. He constantly reminded me he was stuck at home "watching the kid" while I was out getting high and drunk. So many evenings, even as the night drew down to a close, I sought out the dealer and bought some to bring home. That way Joey and I could do some together the next day before I went to work.

One morning, my nose started running. I put my hand up to stop it, and when I pulled it away, it was bloody. At that point, I had been doing coke for a few days straight—at night, at work, and then at home in the mornings. My nose had always stung, but it had never bled before. My first concern was that the blood would block the cocaine from going up my nose.

Joey was getting skinnier. I was, too. But I didn't believe that to be a problem. I wanted to be lean and thin. That meant more of a model-like stature, so I wasn't upset about weight loss at all. At five foot four, I weighed roughly 103 pounds, soaking wet. Joey was six foot two and didn't weigh much more than me. We were both addicted.

One time, Joey suggested rolling a line of cocaine into a marijuana joint to smoke. I liked the high it gave me—a wild buzz that lifted me up and also calmed me down. Someone told me that smoking rock cocaine was basically crack. That same twinge coursed through me, like when I first did cocaine. This was a new level, another one of my boundaries being crossed. But it was a glorious level to cross, and I enjoyed them mixed together.

The nosebleeds were getting worse. Karen had concerns, but she did the best she could by taking care of Riley when Joey and I couldn't. She took Riley while Joey and I did what we wanted. I worked as much as possible to have money for drugs.

Of course, if you had asked me if I had a problem, I would have said no. I didn't believe it to be a problem because I felt I could stop at any time. I drank five or six mixed drinks a night, enough to feel extremely buzzed. On top of that, I either smoked weed or snorted cocaine every day. In my mind, I could stop at any time. I just didn't want to.

It started off as a good night. I was wearing my pink sparkle bikini top with a matching thong. I had a tiny matching skirt that went with it along with my black platform shoes. It wasn't a busy night, but I was having fun.

Two guys came in named Steve and Chad. I sat on Chad's lap. Right away, I knew they weren't going to be great at paying for dances. It was a slow night though, and the dealer wasn't here. I figured at least they were worth getting drinks from. Anna and Amber sat with us.

They bought us a drink, and I ordered a Long Island iced tea. If this ended up being the only drink I got from them, I wanted something strong.

After my Long Island, they bought Flaming Nazis, shots that consist of Goldschläger and Jägermeister. The shot glass is lit on fire. Most bars used to ban lighting drinks on fire, but not Dreamgirls.

"I want to do one!" I said, clapping my hands.

They glanced at each other and ordered one for me too. Anna and Amber opted out, casually sipping their first drinks.

My Long Island was nearly finished, and I was already buzzed. I tried to remember the last time I ate anything, considering that maybe I should order something later or raid the fridge when I got home. But the club was slow. What else did I have to do?

I stared at the burning blue flame as it licked the edge of the glass. My job was to be fun, a good time—a break from reality for these guys. I was nervous about my long hair, and I could see this ending badly. As buzzed as I already was, I still knew that my hair and makeup were quite flammable.

"Will it burn me?" I asked.

"No, not at all," Steve said. "But blow it out first." They laughed.

I blew it out. The warm rim of the shot glass touched my lips, and I took the shot.

The tiny chunks of gold in the bottom of the shot glass swirled toward me as I swallowed. The liquid burned my throat all the way down to my stomach.

I can't recall much of the night after that.

Somehow, I got up, and the floor swam in front of me. I knew I had to make it to the bathroom. It took all my effort to walk in heels as I lunged toward the restroom.

"Where ya going?" Chad asked. He laughed with his friend and tried to grab my hand. "Hey, you wanted it."

When I was in elementary school, nerdy, poor, and an outcast, a popular kid brought some candy onto our bus. He held a few pieces loosely in his hand, looking around for his friends. I jumped into the seat next to him and asked him for a piece. He smiled at me shyly.

"Are you sure you want a piece?" he asked.

I nodded my head, hoping the other kids on the bus saw the popular kid giving me candy. He was including me, letting me join his cool circle.

"Are you sure?" he asked again, still smiling.

I laughed and held out my hand. He dropped a piece of candy into it. It was in a normal wrapper, twisted on each end, and looked no different than my Grandma Clara's candy in her candy jar. He glanced at his friend and back at me.

I shucked the wrapper off and tossed the candy in my mouth, savoring not only the tangy candy but the fact that out of everyone he could have shared it with, he shared it with me. And as I sat there allowing the candy to melt in my mouth, I thought maybe, just maybe, I was sort of cool too.

Suddenly the tangy candy melted away, and something horribly bitter replaced it. And not only was it bitter, but it melted and stuck to my teeth. My mouth watered, my eyes teared up, and I had nowhere to spit it out since I was at the back of the bus. The kid laughed and pointed at me, elbowing his friend so they could both laugh. Shame washed over me as I realized it was trick candy and not real candy at all. It was filled with something awful but coated in something sweet.

That shot reminded me of the candy. I had no clue as to its alcohol content, but my already malnourished body was no longer having any part of this. I collapsed in the public bathroom on the floor. Anna and Amber came to check on me right away, but they couldn't wake me up. I wavered between consciousness and unconsciousness for hours on end.

In moments of wakefulness, I was able to hear almost everything, but I couldn't move. The music thumped in the club, and it got louder every time the door opened. I knew exactly who was on stage by the music that was playing. I could visualize everything, but my body didn't work.

I wasn't alone, because the girls working that night took turns coming to check on me. Amber, Anna, Toni, Jamie. In ones or twos, they showed up. Most of the time, they were coming to use the restroom and then took the time to check on me afterward. Luckily, women didn't visit clubs often, so dancers were the only ones who used the public bathroom.

At one point, someone gently lifted my head and tried to make me drink water. It dribbled down my cheek and landed on the tiled floor next to me. She put my head down and my face landed on the spilled water, a cold spot on my burning hot skin.

"Does she need to go to the hospital?" someone asked.

"No, she'll be fine. Let her sleep it off. We'll keep checking on her."

"Shouldn't we move her?"

"No, we don't want anyone to see her."

They didn't want management to find me. I found out later they'd told Larry that I wasn't feeling well. Although I'd been missing for hours, management hadn't come in to check on me. They didn't care as long as the customers didn't see me.

During one bout of consciousness, I discovered popcorn stuck to the corner of my mouth and a small bowl of it placed in front of me. Someone had also placed a cup of now-cold coffee next to my satchel of money and cigarettes.

I struggled to sit up. My head was swimming, and my stomach was in turmoil, so I lay back down.

I stayed there, dreaming on and off about who I was. What this life was. This wasn't glamorous at all. This wasn't what I thought it was supposed to be.

The girls kept checking on me. Eventually, it was 2:00 a.m. Anna and Amber came to me one last time.

Anna pulled me to a standing position. "Girl, you can't stay here. You have to get up."

They walked me back to the dressing room, where the rest of the girls were boasting about their earnings. It had gotten busier, after all. They felt bad for me, but it was my own fault. With me down for the entire shift, it meant more money for them.

"You okay now?" Heather handed me a cup of scalding coffee. It was dark black and thick from being on the burner all night. I took a small sip.

"Yeah, I'm good."

After I got dressed, I packed my bag and made sure I had my cigarettes and money. I only made eighty dollars that night. When I checked out, they put my rent on arrears.

"Sorry you didn't feel well tonight." The bouncer smirked. "Maybe you could work Sundays, too, to make a dent in this and pay it down."

I nodded and drove myself home. I had no idea what happened to the guys who had given me the shot. I never saw them again.

Jungle Love

I still thought about having a "real" job again someday. It was never far from my mind that this wouldn't last forever. I was nearing my mid-twenties, which was getting old for club age. I knew some of the girls approaching thirty had to work harder and do more to get and keep customers.

Sasha was one of them. She was in her early thirties and had been dancing for close to ten years. She knew the bar inside and out. She was short, even with platforms, and bone thin. She smoked a lot of cigarettes and had a raspy voice. Her eyes were set close together and she appeared to squint most of the time. Her lips were two thin slashes across her mouth, accentuated by dark lipstick. She was not what you would consider conventionally attractive, but she knew how to work the stage. Her gimmick was her flexibility. She laid on her back on the stage, put her feet behind her ears, and pretended to lick herself to anyone who was directly in her line of vision between her legs. She did contortions, and some men liked that. One day, she showed me her driver's license, and I stifled a gasp at the image. She looked nothing like her persona at the club. In real life, she wore thick, coke-bottle glasses and had feathered hair.

Near the holidays, Victoria's Secret ran an ad in the newspaper for retail clerks. I thought this was a perfect opportunity and a good fit for me. I could work there and get a discount for clothes in the club. It was a win-win. I had some retail experience from working at a clothing store after I graduated high school and lived in Alcoa with my friends. I could work their hours and still go to the club and make extra money.

I was proud of the fact that I was a performer. To me, I was a performer above all else. I never considered that a lot of people thought it was demeaning. I transformed myself into one of those beautiful women in the club. I knew how to seduce men, and I could get them to give me money. How much better at sales could I get?

I completed an application and turned it in. The woman was pleasant, asked me a couple of questions, and told me they would contact me.

A few days later, they called and asked me to come in for an interview. I bought a new professional outfit and showed up early at the store.

Another dancer from the club showed up in the waiting area. Relief flooded through me. They were hiring for more than one position. Perhaps we could work here together and at the club.

The other applicant's stage name was Honey. She was one of the girls who didn't say much to anyone when she was there. She was dating one of the bouncers, Jake. He started working there first, so he had convinced her to audition, and she started shortly after that.

Honey wore a wig while she danced, which fascinated me. She was the only girl I ever knew who did that, other than Samantha with her weird combed-over hair. Honey came in wearing a golden blonde wig, and when she took it off at the end of the night, her natural hair was dark brown. That wouldn't end well if it wasn't attached securely. It also seemed like a lot of extra work. I didn't need that added to my long ritual of getting ready for a shift.

I thought it was cool she could change her looks like that. She told me she wore a wig so that no one recognized her. She was the first stripper I knew who didn't seem proud of this line of work. I didn't hide it from people. In my mind, it was a creative job. I made a lot of money to party. What was shameful about that?

When she saw me in Victoria's Secret, her face paled.

"Don't tell anyone about the club," she whispered to me in the waiting area.

It annoyed me a bit. Who did she think she was? She was going to come in here and get this job for the same reason as me. What difference did it make if we told these women what we did?

They were doing group interviews, and we went back together. I discovered her real name was Jessica. We went through the usual mundane questions: Where have you worked? What is your experience? What do you want to do with your future?

"I'm in law school," Honey answered, her voice clear.

Law school? I looked at her in shock. I had no idea. I thought the phrase "stripping your way through college" was a joke. There weren't any girls in the club who went to school as far as I knew. But then again, I had never asked.

"And you?" the woman turned to me.

I wasn't going to lie. I was proud of the job I'd landed at the club. I applied to be a waitress, and they wanted me as a dancer. Men desired me. Men wanted me. They paid me a lot of money.

"I'm an exotic dancer," I said proudly, sitting up tall. "At Dreamgirls," I added for clarity.

The woman was silent, and I took that to mean she needed me to further discuss my interest in the position. "I need clothes for work. Obviously, this would be a good fit—I'd be spending my entire check on clothes."

I'm not sure what I expected the woman to do once I told her. Perhaps get gushy and lean into me to ask questions. Most people are morbidly curious about what happens in clubs, and they ask lots of questions.

But she grimaced, her expression turned stricken and awkward. She glanced down at the application as though maybe she had missed something the first time around.

Honey looked down at her lap. I floundered, feeling suddenly uncomfortable. This woman wasn't interested in my exotic dancing life. She wasn't curious. In fact, she looked at me as though she thought I was going to tuck the store's panties into my purse on the way out or take my clothes off and stand on the display tables.

I was confused. This woman worked at a store that encouraged women to dress in a sexy manner, but when women actually *behaved* in a sexy manner as a job, that somehow made it wrong.

"Okay, well, thank you for coming in. Both of you. We'll be in touch."

We shook hands, and there was a marked coolness in her attitude toward me.

Needless to say, I didn't get the position. I learned that perhaps I was the only one who thought being a Dreamgirls dancer was a coveted job.

I wasn't dumb. I mean, I wasn't so proud of it that I shared details of my work openly with my family. I obviously knew there was *some* shame attached to it. Grandma Clara wasn't happy when I told her. I don't remember what she said specifically, but it was something along the lines of "do you really have to do that?"

My mother was extremely disappointed. After I was disfellowshipped, she barely spoke to me. And she never talked about my career choice. Later on, when I paid her a visit, she told me she had to go to court. My biological father had never paid regular child support for me, so by my twenties, he owed thousands of dollars. When he went before the judge to fight against the judgment, in a last-ditch effort to avoid paying, he pointed to my mother and told the judge I was a stripper, and it was her fault for the way she'd raised me. When my mother told me that story, she sounded like she wanted me to reassure her that my career choice wasn't her fault. That she did nothing wrong to contribute to how I had turned out, working as a stripper.

I'm not sure why it had to be someone's fault that I had become a stripper. Somewhere in that conversation, shame again had attached itself to the position. My mother was ashamed of me.

I never found out if Honey got the job. Her boyfriend was a bouncer for a while, but she gave up dancing after a month or so.

Some people weren't cut out for this line of work.

Fool in the Rain

Larry had friends who hung out at the club. Some of them waltzed in as though they owned the place—chatting it up with the bouncers and bartenders. They were more men who refused to pay for dances. Memphis was one of Larry's good friends who showed up a couple nights a week.

Memphis was an older, balding Black man, quiet and unblinking. When he walked, his feet slid along the floor in a swagger. Brandy called it a pimp walk. At first, I thought he was hard of hearing and trying to listen intently when I spoke, but then I realized he was merely an intense person. Many of the girls who'd been there a while ignored him and chose to stay away. All Brandy and I knew was that he was one of Larry's friends, and he was someone to talk to when nights were slow.

He was the type of guy who rested his hands on your backside, casually caressing, lower and lower. I had grown accustomed to men who felt they could touch me. Regular customers got kicked out if they got too handsy, but bouncers, DJs, and even management felt they could put their arms around you, touch your butt, etc., without any repercussions.

I learned how to feign interest in someone, even if everything in me screamed that the guy was a complete sleazeball. And there was definitely something off about Memphis. He behaved like he was better than everyone in the club. He swaggered in and leaned on the bar, snapping his fingers at the bartender, expecting him to know his drink preference. He listened to me during our conversations but then tried to talk down to me. There was a subtle, pretentious attitude and underscore of "I'm better than you" running beneath it all.

Once, when I was in junior high, I was out in service, and it was my turn to go to the door. A man answered after a few knocks, bright and early on a Saturday morning. He invited us in to "talk about the Bible." He sat across from me at the table with his legs sprawled open in front of him. He didn't pay any attention to the woman with me or the Watchtower pamphlet I tried to show him. Instead, his heavy-lidded, hungover eyes wandered over my body the entire time I was talking about God's promise for the world. I was extremely uncomfortable, but the woman with me was excited. She said I should put him on my list of callbacks, because he had expressed so much interest. Even at that young age, I could discern what types of interest men held for me.

Memphis reminded me of that man.

It was a bad night at the club with very few customers. I needed money, and it wasn't busy at all. If I didn't start paying down my floor rent, they'd get shitty with me. They knew drug use occurred in the club. And while they didn't actively condone it, they took notice if girls spent their money on drugs and didn't pay rent. They started nosing around and paying closer attention to how much a girl was dancing.

Memphis listened to me bitch, commiserating about how slow the night was going. He rested his hand on my lower back.

"Come to the office with me," he said.

"I don't think so," I said, moving away, laughing lightly. "I need to be ready in case a customer shows up." I knew going into the office with him wasn't a good idea. I'd heard he tried to get other girls to go back there.

I glanced around, looking for Brandy, but she was with a customer. At least she found someone who wanted a dance.

"Come on. Let's just go talk. I can't hear out here." He nodded his head toward Larry's office, gently pulling me away from the bar. He then nodded to Larry, who glanced at me, nodded back, and then turned away to talk with the bartender.

Larry knew what was happening. I didn't want to be difficult, and Memphis was one of Larry's friends.

I walked with him to the office. It was like someone had taken over my body, and I was floating above myself. I found myself in the office, with the same piles of papers and waitress applications that went back years. By then, I knew most of them had been convinced to dance, just like me.

I leaned against the desk, and the hard metal edge cut into the back of my legs. I fidgeted and tried to make conversation. Memphis stared at me with his black eyes. He didn't say much and simply leaned against the opposite desk with his arms crossed in front of him, listening.

As I nervously chatted, he casually removed his dick from his pants. He gently stroked it, never breaking eye contact with me. "I can help you if you need money."

I refused to look at it. I didn't know whether to laugh or be offended. A part of me wanted to giggle at the ridiculousness of this situation. But a large part of me was uncomfortable and feeling sick.

I knew I didn't want to be in this office anymore. I knew what he wanted: sex or a blow job. I wasn't even high enough for this shit.

This was another one of those boundary moments. I thought of all the things that I had to deal with in this club from men. All the criticism, opinions, making sure I looked a certain part so that I could be a man's fantasy. The "I'm-better-than-you" boys, the "save-me-from-my-wife" guys, the "you're-too-good-for-this" men. And dealing with the nights like this when I could barely make floor rent, let alone have enough money to bring home. I knew if I crossed this line, there was no going back. Then I really would be what the Victoria's Secret manager thought of me. I couldn't cross that line.

"I'm not doing that," I said, my voice firm.

He fondled his semi-flaccid dick for a few seconds more and then put it back when it appeared I wasn't going to back down. I stood frozen in place against the side of the desk. I grew concerned that if he didn't like my response I was trapped in this office. I wasn't sure if I could get around him.

"Hey, relax, it's okay. I'm not going to hurt you." His deep voice was almost calming. The distant rumble of bass from the club cut through the office walls. His black eyes bored into my soul. "Let me help you."

He came closer and set his hand on my shoulder. He slowly leaned down and pulled my thong aside, then placed his head between my legs and tried going down on me. While he struggled to part my legs, I clenched tightly, and the desk corner cut deeper into my skin. My mind screamed "No! No!" in time to my racing heartbeat.

After only a few seconds, I said, "This isn't comfortable." I backed away farther on the desk. There was nothing remotely pleasant about this experience at all.

He stood back up. His expression was stiff with disapproval.

"I'm sorry," I apologized. "I'm so sorry. I just can't."

This was my fault. I had been bitching about making no money, and he was trying to help. Plus, he was friends with Larry. Would he tell him?

He stayed silent while he buttoned his pants. I wanted out of this room, and I wanted away from him.

"Don't worry about it." His smile was forced and didn't reach his eyes.

After he zipped his pants, he pulled out a money clip with stacks of hundreds. He never shared what he did for a living. I heard he had some sort of important job. I wondered why he never spent any of that money on us for dances.

He pulled a fifty from the stack. "Here." He handed me the money.

We didn't do anything. Cash for sexual acts equaled prostitution. Was that what this was? I didn't know, but I took the money. This, I guess, officially made me a prostitute. After that, we left the office.

Memphis nodded to Larry. He left me to go to the bar without saying another word, and I went to the dressing room to clear my head.

A couple of the other girls left as I walked in. I changed my clothes, lit a cigarette, and reapplied my lipstick. My hands shook, and my face was pale. I took a sip of someone's drink left on the makeup counter to settle my stomach. I looked at myself in the mirror and for a moment, I saw myself as I truly was. A frightened young woman, far too thin, with gaunt, haunted eyes, and too much eyeliner. A former super Christian girl, who let a stranger go down on her, if only for a few seconds, for money. I thought of my daughter at home, being watched by my boyfriend, who was waiting for me to make enough money to come back and bring him some cocaine.

What have I become?

I'd been in the dressing room for a good half hour. I needed to find Brandy. She always knew the right thing to say. At the very least, I had to warn her about Memphis.

But I couldn't find her anywhere. She wasn't dancing at the tables or couches. She wasn't in the dressing room, because I had just left there.

Then I saw her coming out of Larry's office with Memphis. He was smiling and she was laughing.

I pulled her aside after she left him at the bar.

"Where were you?" I asked.

"You look like shit, dude. What happened?" she asked, avoiding my question.

I told her about the office and how he wanted to have sex with me, but I couldn't because he was gross and creepy.

"Yeah, dude. He just tried that shit with me too. What a dick." She looked away and shrugged it off.

It was another bust of a night. I made enough to pay off some of my back rent, but not much to take home. Nights like that made me wonder how women always talked about making so much money stripping. Tuesday nights were not the most happening times for clubs.

We counted our money at the end of the shift. Brandy had a stack of money. A couple of hundred-dollar bills flashed in her wad of cash. We had been together all night. I knew how often she danced. That was way more money than what she could account for in the number of dances she did, even with tips.

"Where'd you get that?" I stared at her wad of cash.

"Tips. The guy in the red shirt." She shoved it into her purse.

I remembered her walking out of the office with Memphis, both of them smiling and laughing. He had his hand on her back and had leaned into her. I had a hunch she did more than just talk to him in the office, like she'd claimed. I didn't say anything, mostly because I wasn't sure if I wanted to know.

As a relatively new convert to the "worldly" life from a former strict religious existence, I couldn't do it. I couldn't meet a stranger at the club and then leave and have sex somewhere. Not only from a moral standpoint, but also because of the danger in it. I couldn't trust most of these men as far as I could throw them. Looking back, I realize there were women far less privileged than I who had fewer choices and no options, and they were forced to do that to make ends meet.

I'll admit when I am wrong. I'll admit I drank too much, did a horrible amount of drugs, and had some bad parenting skills during that period of my life. But one boundary I couldn't cross was sex for money.

Crash Into Me

Whenever I hung out at home, I dressed down with sweatpants, a ponytail, and glasses. It helped me compartmentalize my life—my mom life and my club life. When I did opt to go out, which wasn't often, I wanted to dress up. I wore leather pants, halter tops, glitter on my face and eyelids. If I was dressed to go out, I looked like I did at the club. There was no in-between.

Brandy and I occasionally went barhopping. We could leave with five dollars in our pockets, get completely smashed before the night was done, and end up with the same five dollars in our purse at the end of the night. While men appreciated our presence in the bars, most women didn't find our company so welcoming. Once at a bar party on Halloween, I got called the "Halloween hooker" by a group of local catty women because I was wearing a crop top and tight leather pants.

Brandy's preferred place to hang out was her small hometown of Fayetteville. She still wasn't old enough to drink, but she knew everyone there which mostly eliminated the problem of underage drinking.

We often hung out with Brandy's Aunt Sharon. Sharon was wild and older, but she was fun and acted our age. She had short brown hair that swung around in wild curls on her head. She was tall and extremely thin, with a smoker's laugh and the beginning of crow's feet around her eyes. We sometimes went to her apartment to get ready and smoked a couple of joints before we headed out for a night on the town.

One night, Brandy took me to a biker bar in Fayetteville. Her Aunt Sharon recommended it. The bar was on the seedier end of town, and I had never been there before. The parking lot backed up to some sort of salvage yard, with a chain link fence surrounding the perimeter. The bar itself was small and dilapidated with tiny windows and a slanting wet roof that would soon need major repairs.

We picked our way across the parking lot in our heels and swooped into the entrance, anxious to get out of the misty rain before it ruined our hair. The interior was muted and dingy; cigarette smoke gathered in the ceiling lights. The floor was dirty in some spots from the mud tracked in by the patrons. The tables that did fit in the tiny room were scratched, and the chairs didn't match.

Judging by the expressions of the customers, we were the only ones who had ever walked in there looking like we did. The entire crowd, which was a small group of people, turned to stare at us when we entered. I wore my six-inch stilettos with low-rise bootcut jeans and a halter top, my flat stomach bared with my belly piercing on display. When I glanced around, a shiver of warning and fear rippled through me. Every one of these men looked rough. I exhaled, flashed a smile, and convinced myself this was a public place. No one would do something to hurt us in a public place.

It was too late to turn back, anyway. Brandy was fearless; she wasn't leaving if this was where she wanted to be. We both boldly stepped inside and navigated between the tables, careful not to slip on the mud. Brandy squeezed up to the bar and elbowed her way between two burly, bearded men who wore leather jackets with matching insignias on the back. I hung back but surveyed the room and pretended I was Alina, somewhat inquisitive, but also bored.

While we waited for our drinks, prepared by an apprehensive bartender side-eyeing us, Brandy asked the guys how they were doing.

As exotic dancers, we'd developed a specific set of skills. We knew how to negotiate conversations and put men at ease. That was our number one job. We lit cigarettes and talked to them for a while. The men eventually warmed up to us and bought us drinks, and we returned the favor. Then Brandy and I got high in the parking lot, came back in, and drank some more.

A jukebox was playing background music from the corner of the bar. There wasn't a dance floor, per se, or if there was, it wasn't being used. But that didn't matter to me. I was buzzed and wanted to dance. That was when I was most comfortable.

I put some change in the jukebox and chose Dave Matthews Band, "Crash Into Me." I loved the song but never danced to it at the club. It's very sensual, and that song touched my soul when I danced to it.

The music took over as I slid onto a central area on the floor between the tables. Soon, Brandy joined me, and we danced together, putting on a free show for the guys at the bar.

They enjoyed it.

We enjoyed it.

These men ended up being kind, funny, and no danger to us at all. But we were fearless in ways that makes me hold my breath today. I was lucky in so many ways. I see them on the news all the time—the girls who aren't so lucky. It could have ended so badly. We left the bar that night, boozy and laughing and getting stoned again before heading home, and I count my lucky stars for the guiding angels who watched over me.

Some nights, I stayed out so late because I knew Joey had Riley. There were a few times I was high at four in the morning, and then my daughter was up at seven, fully rested and ready to start her day, while mine was just ending. And there was no one to watch her but me and Joey. Those were the bad days—the days I wasn't present for my daughter, or if I was, I wasn't the best mom I could be.

On the days when we were stoned, tired, or both, we propped Riley in front of the television with her toys and let her watch Barney. Barney was our babysitter, and Riley loved him. She watched an episode, demanded we rewind the VCR tape, and then watched it over again, dancing to the music. I bought tickets to the Barney Circus and took Joey and Riley. We sat close to the front and Riley was ecstatic. It made me glad to see what the money I earned could do for her. I wanted her to have experiences like that. I enjoyed giving her nice things because I didn't have that growing up.

Spending money on her made me feel better about not being present as much as I should have been. Joey and I went all out for Riley's birthdays. We took her to Chuck E. Cheese, a gigantic indoor playhouse for small kids. They served pizza, and their mascot was a giant rat, which ought to tell you something. The entire place smelled like pizza sauce and piss, but Riley loved it there. Everyone was invited. Joey's friends Frank and Penny brought their daughter, Kathryn. Brandy and Justin brought Rayla. Sheena had her two children, Brody and Carmen. The adults drank, ate pizza, and got stoned in the parking lot. We bought Riley presents and made her day as special as we could. It seemed to make up for the fact that I wasn't there as much as I should have been, even on the days when I wasn't working. And given that I never celebrated holidays or birthdays growing up, I wanted to make sure my daughter didn't miss out.

Once, Sheena took her kids to the Barnum & Bailey Circus, and she invited us along. I was hesitant to go with her. My mother hated the circus, and some of that had rubbed off on me. She'd felt bad for the animals that were subject to abuse by the trainers. I, too, felt bad about the animals being forced to perform for the people in the audience, whether they wanted to or not. They performed, but they always seemed so sad, there for show and entertainment, and for those who paid the price of admission.

Bette Davis Eyes

Cocaine became like weed for me. The problem with getting high is that you eventually need more to get and stay high. As soon as I woke up, it wasn't enough to just smoke a joint. I woke up and snorted a line. It was taking more and more to keep me high. I still had nosebleeds, so I attempted to occasionally take a few days off in between so as to not completely wreck my nasal cavity. It was a waste of coke if I bled it out, although I could always rub the blood on my gums and still get some tingly numbness from it.

Joey's relatives held a family reunion one weekend up north in the summer, and Joey and I decided to attend. I rarely ever vacationed, so this would be a nice getaway. I worked a week straight to put aside enough money for beer, liquor, weed, and cocaine.

I bought an 8-ball of cocaine, so we'd have it for our trip. Since I wasn't sure if I'd see the dealer before we left, I bought it ahead of time and told Joey not to do any of it. I locked it in a safe; this way, he couldn't get to it while I was at work. When I got home later that night, I discovered he'd spent my entire work shift picking the lock. We got into a fight over it.

He was mad at me for locking it up, while I went and got high at work whenever I wanted. He didn't think it was fair that he didn't have some at home when he knew damn well that I was doing it at work. It ended up that we didn't have as much as we thought for our vacation.

Karen and Joseph took Riley with them, and we were meeting them there. Karen typically kept Riley because she wanted to show her off. But she made it very clear that when Joey and I got there, we were to take over Riley's care, since she didn't want her all weekend. She needed a vacation too.

Joey and I agreed, but when we arrived, we headed out to hang with his cousins at the dock by the lake. Joey's cousins were a wild bunch, in and out of jail and prison.

"You got coke?" his cousin Clint asked.

Unfortunately, Joey and I had done the rest of the 8-ball in the car ride on the way up. Even though Joey had broken into it, there was still a lot left. We just didn't stop doing it all the way there. We tried to save it, but we knew that was too hard to do. We were out of it and coming down. The more cocaine I did, the more I needed it. It was never enough.

It was late that night after everyone else went to bed and we got a hold of Jerron, one of Joey's friends in Alcoa who was a dealer. Jerron didn't like a lot of traffic at his house, but he was in the wrong business if that was how he felt about it. He lived in a house in a subdivision with his girlfriend and a child. He didn't want coke fiends coming to his house, so he met most people offsite, but Joey was his friend. And that night we decided we needed to have it.

"You're leaving now?" Karen asked, incredulous. She woke up when we were leaving. She already said she didn't want to watch Riley the entire weekend. Riley was already in bed, so there was no way we were going to be able to wake up with her in the morning. Karen knew. They all knew what we were doing. They had to. No one would drive back down to Alcoa for just any reason.

We drove three hours back to Alcoa to pick some up from Jerron at ten at night. And then we drove back to Kalkaska. A six-hour drive for cocaine. We stayed zooted up the entire night and did it all with Joey's cousins before morning came.

I don't recall what happened with Riley, if we watched her or if Karen did. The remainder of the weekend was filled with fun activities at the beach and barbecues and general festivities. But Joey and I were coming down from the high and knew it was beyond unreasonable to drive back down to Alcoa for more. So, we stuck with weed and drinking to stave off the cravings.

I knew in the back of my mind that I wasn't happy. This was supposed to be a vacation, a fun time with my daughter and boyfriend. It was strained and awful. As I came down, I snapped at anyone who talked to me. I couldn't wait to get back to Alcoa and back to the club, my second home, where I could have as much cocaine as I wanted.

After the vacation was over and we returned home, in a moment of clarity, I realized I didn't like the feeling of addiction. I didn't like who I was or who I had become. But I was so far into it that I had no idea how to get out. I wasn't doing a good job at parenting Riley, and I mentally beat myself up about it. And the more I beat myself up about my bad parenting skills, the more I craved the drugs that freed me from thinking about my guilt. I thought if I kept away from Riley, then at least she wouldn't be scarred by my behavior. The time she spent with Karen would hopefully undo some of my horrible parenting.

Eventually, our dealer Jerron started doing coke, and it became more of a problem for him. That was a huge mistake if the dealer allowed himself to get addicted to his product.

Joey told me Jerron had gotten high and had become agitated when he couldn't get his son unstuck from the car seat. He'd yanked on him so hard that he broke his legs.

I was horrified when I heard this. At what level did that come in? Again, I had these boundaries that I didn't want to cross. I already had nosebleeds. I convinced myself I could quit anytime I wanted; it was just that I didn't want to quit. I guess if we knew when we were getting close to crossing boundaries, or if someone said "hey, there's a boundary fast approaching," it may have been different.

After we returned and despite my "what the fuck am I doing" epiphany, my addiction didn't slow down. I continued to buy coke either from Jerron or at the club. I always knew where to get it. I always knew how to get it. And perhaps, most importantly, I had the money for it. I bought an 8-ball at a time, and all my "friends" and Joey's friends hung out and got high whenever we could.

The scariest thing for someone addicted to cocaine isn't the idea of getting caught (although that's up there on the list); it's if your dealer or his lead gets busted. That's the worst. Those are hard times because there's no recourse.

And you need your fix when you come down.

Kashmir

Brandy and I needed to make more money. We barely made enough to cover our floor rent and our accumulated back rent after we bought cocaine and weed. We didn't blame our lack of income on the fact we were burning through the money on drugs; we figured we weren't getting good customers anymore. We didn't work into the equation that our entire evenings were spent trying to get coke, do coke, or come off coke, and that was probably noticeable to the men who were there paying for a "fantasy." Most Dreamgirls' clientele didn't want to deal with our fidgety, nail-biting anxiety while we waited for the dealer to show up.

Management continued to allow us to put our floor rent on arrears, and then they encouraged us to work more nights to "catch up." Sasha rolled her eyes at us one evening when a group of us were sitting around, bitching about our back rent.

"You know they do that so you have to work more nights to catch up. You owe them when you allow them to charge your rent." She tapped ash from her cigarette with her forefinger into the ashtray, knowingly shaking her head at us. "This ain't Vegas; we don't have a union here." She laughed her dry, throaty laugh and left us to meet her regular at the door.

I hadn't thought of a union, and the more I thought about it, the more I realized we needed to stand together, all of us girls, and fight how much we were paying in floor rent. I told them we needed to form a union; the club couldn't charge what they charged without us there, and they needed us for that club to run. My rant was loud and cocaine-fueled. Just as I started coming down, the coke dealer arrived, and I gave up the cause.

Not only was I not making enough money, but I grew bored at Dreamgirls. Eventually, men recognized us as regular dancers at the club, and we were no longer considered "new." There was nothing about us they hadn't seen before. Newer girls showed up, shiny, sparkly, and nervous, like Brandy and me the first time we arrived. Men liked new. They liked different. After a while, if they frequented the club enough, they already knew all about you, and after enough conversations, they grew tired of your life. They could stay home if they wanted to hear the same old stories. Unless they were your regulars, they didn't need to stay attached. And sometimes regulars split after you didn't agree to meet them after work or take the relationship to the next level. We decided a change of atmosphere might do us some good.

Brandy and I decided to check out Jordan's, the other topless club in Alcoa. Ironically, this was the same club we had visited when our boyfriends were inside having a bachelor party, a little more than a year prior. A lot of girls who came to Dreamgirls arrived from there. We discovered that girls regularly moved around clubs to switch things up.

Despite still owing floor rent to Dreamgirls, we took a leave and went to visit Jordan's. The manager at Jordan's Showgirls was Gerald Kline. He was an imposing man of Italian descent with thick dark hair and sinister eyes. Something about him was oily, like a used car salesman. He was tall and had a stocky build. He could have replaced a bouncer, maybe even two. He didn't appear to be a man people argued with.

"You girls came from where?" he asked.

"Dreamgirls." Brandy piped up in an effort to be heard over the music.

He gave us a cursory glance, then pointed to the stairs at the back. "Go downstairs and talk to Clara. Let her know you're auditioning tonight. I'll be down in a minute."

Brandy and I made our way to the back of the bar to a set of wide stairs. They were spaced apart at an odd height that made them treacherous, so I grabbed the hand railing. How did girls navigate down these steps in heels?

I was a little nervous because it was a new location. But it wasn't like the first time. We took our bags to the "dressing room," which was really a corner in the basement beneath the club. We had to walk through an area with tables and chairs stacked up, apparently for group events. And just beyond stood a smaller room which served as the dressing room with mirrors lining the side wall.

Gerald came in a few minutes later. His presence was overpowering in the small dressing room. He reached out and smacked the ass of one of the girls who was down there. She giggled and swatted him back. He introduced us to Clara, a woman standing in the corner. She was older and dressed in jeans and a T-shirt. She had wavy brown hair and green eyes. She had been talking to two girls when we walked in the room. There were baskets on the counter beside her containing items like hand lotion, body spray, and tampons.

Gerald told us we needed to tip Clara at the end of the night because she watched our stuff and if we needed something, she had it. She was called a "house mom." This was new. We didn't have a house mom at Dreamgirls. I could see where Clara may have been a dancer herself before age took over.

"Fucking got to tip everyone. I'm sure as fuck not tipping her too," Brandy bitched under her breath. She hated tipping. Even when the DJs worked their asses off to make her feel fabulous on stage. "I'm the one taking my fucking clothes off. Why the fuck I gotta pay them?"

I wasn't keen on tipping more people either; I was there to make money. But I knew if I tipped Clara well enough, she would watch my stuff, and there didn't appear to be many lockers available in this dressing room.

We quickly got changed and went upstairs to audition. By now, I had quite a few outfits to choose from since I'd started. I put on my white, sparkly two-piece bikini set I had purchased at Lover's Lane. I paired it with a pair of strappy white stilettos.

We met the DJ, chose our songs, and were put into the regular rotation. The other girls gave us a once-over as they made their way around the room. They were neither friendly nor unfriendly, just indifferent.

Jordan's was different from Dreamgirls in the layout. The stage was located in the center of the room, and the tables surrounded it. There were poles on either end of the circular stage and mirrors on the opposite sides. I watched the other girls dance to see how to navigate the new stage setup. Dreamgirls had miniature glass stages you could stand on during the Fantasy Dances if you didn't want to go on the main stage. There were no miniature stages here.

The one thing that stood out right away was the shower in the corner. I asked a friendlier looking waitress what that was, and she said it was for a shower dance. The customers had the option of a shower dance, an opportunity for a guy to pay for the girl, or two, to get in there and get wet.

I immediately knew I wasn't participating in any shower dances. I couldn't imagine getting my hair wet and allowing my makeup to run in front of customers. It was hard enough getting ready as it was, a shower mid-shift was a dicey prospect.

Brandy and I approached a table near the stage and sat with a group of guys. We were new there, but not new to the gig. We both needed drinks for courage. We told them it was our first night at Jordan's.

I sipped my drink and glanced around the room while I sat on a guy's lap with my arm draped around his neck. I laughed at his funny stories and paid attention when I needed to. I was kind of nervous and excited. I hadn't been excited about performing in a while. It already felt good to be in a new atmosphere. I practically vibrated with excitement, and I was ready to get on stage. Even though I had done this so many times before, this was a new place. A new chance to shine. The other women were watching us, waiting to see what sort of competition we could be. I was ready to show them. My stomach was a bundle of nerves, and I couldn't wait to dance.

I had to choose a stage name. I decided to go with Alexis at this club. It was a new start; Jasmine was the old me. The new me felt like an Alexis. When the DJ called my name, he announced that I was new to Jordan's, and I climbed up the steps onto the stage. The men and the women in the audience stopped to watch the "new" girl. I made eye contact with the men and held it for a few seconds. I swung my long hair around and let it fall and sway down my back. I was confident and alive and on fire. Seduction was the key, and I had learned my craft well. Quite a few men came to the stage. I made good money on my second song. I was a natural performer.

After the auditions, we ceased to be Dreamgirls. We were officially Jordan's Showgirls.

We were immediately informed about floor rent, which was similar to Dreamgirls. The pricing was similar, too. There were table dances available around the stage. It was often crowded at the tables, and chances were the guys at the next table enjoyed the show as much as the paying customer because of the close proximity. I could see how this would make it easier to push for a more private dance, or couch dance.

Stairs near the entrance led up to the second level, where dancers could take their customers for private VIP dances. The couches lined the wall in a back corner. Another bar was located upstairs for private parties, but that was mostly kept dark and unused. There was also a public bathroom. And of course, there were bouncers with clipboards counting the dances and for security, too.

The stairs leading to the second level were as bad as the stairs going down to the dressing room. They were scary and took some getting used to. We didn't have stairs at Dreamgirls; it was all one level. The first few nights at Jordan's, it took a lot of courage and focus to navigate those stairs after a few drinks, but I managed.

The money was better right away. We were new to this club and used that line on men for a while. Men who frequented the club hadn't seen us before and wanted to get to know us. The DJs were pleasant, and the wait staff was friendly. The girls were cautious at first but eventually warmed to us. We didn't have back floor rent to pay; we were at zero as far as owing money. We started making more money, more often.

Larry tried to warn us that Jordan's was different: seedier than Dreamgirls and not as nice. He proudly told us Dreamgirls was the best topless club in Alcoa with the higher class of girls. But from what we could tell, Jordan's wasn't that much different. The building wasn't as nice, but that didn't matter to me in the end. I figured Larry didn't want to lose us, so that's why he tried to warn us off from Jordan's.

There were many more requests for private parties at this club. Men had no reservations, asking right away if you were interested in doing an outside party. In fact, some of them specifically came in with no interest in getting a dance or spending time there other than to find girls to work their own private parties. They offered lots of cash to come party with them offsite during the day or evening and not in the safety of a club. The requests ranged from a private bachelor party to a company golf event, and anything and everything in between.

I knew plenty of girls who did that. From the number of petitions I had received, I believed they got a lot of acceptance from this club for those types of requests. I knew most of the girls who did that were successful and made good money. But I also heard horror stories. No thanks. I stood my ground and refused to do anything outside the club. I turned them down, and as far as I knew, Brandy did too. But we got asked about them at least once a week.

Deuces Are Wild

It didn't take long to learn what was seedier about Jordan's.

One night, I was making my way down the stairs to change when I heard music coming from the basement near our dressing rooms. I wobbled a little on my shoes as I peered down the stairs. Was Clara playing loud music down there?

The bouncer guarding the stairs laughed and told me to be careful. There was always a bouncer somewhere near the stairs to ensure men didn't follow the women down to the dressing rooms.

"Are there people down there?" I asked, grabbing the handrail.

"Private party."

The entire downstairs area had been transformed, set up with the tables and chairs that had been unused up until that point. A shots waitress wandered around with her tray, and a bartender served drinks in the corner. There were even a few dancers giving dances to the men.

They were crowded in—smoking, drinking, and laughing. Most of the men wore business suits, and some had drinks in one hand while watching the girls dance in front of them.

I navigated through the crowd to get to the dressing room. One guy called out to me as I walked by, but I pretended not to hear him. This was the first time I'd ever seen actual customers this close to the dressing rooms. No men were ever allowed near them at Dreamgirls except the bouncers and Larry or the DJs, but not customers. This made me nervous, like they were too close to the sanctuary where you went to regroup and recharge.

Clara was there, smoking a cigarette in the corner and reading a magazine. She nodded to me when I walked in. How she could read with that music playing was beyond me. The dressing room was less of a safe haven from the customers when they were right outside the door. I quickly got dressed in another outfit and ran back upstairs.

As the night progressed, the party downstairs grew louder. The discussions were punctuated by raucous laughter or cheering. Smoke filled the room, and the entire area was shrouded in a light blue haze. The music downstairs competed with the music upstairs. I kept my visits to the dressing room minimal, except for quick outfit changes.

On one of my visits, I passed by Sadie, a dancer with short, blonde, spiky hair, who leaned against a pole in the center of the room. Her hand was inside her thong, and her finger slid in and out of her vagina. Her back was pressed against a pole, and she bit her lip, lifting her face toward the ceiling. Two men sat in front of her with their faces mere inches from her hand. One was slipping a twenty in her partially removed thong, while the other one caressed the inside of her leg.

Shocked, I pushed past the group and stumbled to the dressing room. We were never allowed to move our thongs like that or allow men to touch us at Dreamgirls. Sure, girls would pull their thongs down, but they never removed the bottom part on stage or in front of anyone. There were no bouncers in the basement to ensure this wasn't happening. Sadie was pleasuring herself in front of the men, and I'm not sure how far it went after I ran to the dressing room.

I saw why some of the girls who came from Dreamgirls found Jordan's not to their taste. It definitely had a grittier feel than Dreamgirls. I kept to myself when parties were held down there. I never offered to work one of them. Gerald once asked me if I wanted to work a private event, and I politely refused, claiming I had something else going on.

Aside from that, Brandy and I felt like we had made a good move. The money at Jordan's was great. The girls eventually accepted us, and we found a few regulars at the new place. This was a fresh start. A clean slate.

I had been there a little more than a month when I ran into Megan from high school. The last time I saw her was at Denny's restaurant, which felt like a million years ago. Megan was one of the popular cheerleaders in high school, but she was always nice to me.

Her stage name was Trinity. I was shocked when I saw her climb the stairs up onto the stage. Her wavy brown hair had been dyed blonde, and the roots were growing in. She wore a pair of small leather shorts, the edges turned down to create open flaps exposing her thong.

I waited until she finished her set, when I approached her at the stage. "Hey, Trinity."

She smiled her one-hundred-watt smile, the same smile from high school, but her eyes did not flicker recognition.

"It's me, Holly," I whispered, leaning in.

A split second passed and then she gasped, her eyes widening in surprise. "Hey, girl." She leaned in to give me a hug. "I didn't recognize you. How long have you worked here?"

We caught up for a few minutes, and I noticed a man in a suit standing off to the side, waiting for a dance with her.

"It's good to see you again," she smiled and took my hand in hers before walking away to the man.

It was hard to look at her and imagine her as the popular cheerleader in high school and reconcile her being here with me at Jordan's. To me, this validated that I was just as good as she was. I could have been popular and pretty in high school, too, had I not been poor. If I hadn't been restricted to having no friends outside my religion.

I loved dancing all over again. I had confidence in my ability to make money. I knew how to do my makeup, how to walk, how to sway my hips, and how to lower my eyes to look sexy. When I entered the room, I scoped out who appeared to have the most money. I made my mark and acted coy, glancing at the guy through hooded eyes until he made eye contact. Nine times out of ten, he approached me after my stage set and asked for a dance. It took me over a year, but I had perfected the art of seduction.

Brandy was doing okay but got very restless when she wasn't making what she considered enough money. She was cutthroat when it came to her customers. She was pushy and had no problem sharing her money problems with her clientele. This was a turnoff to some men, but for the older ones who wanted to be her daddy, it worked.

And then there were some who were plain sickos. She had no boundaries with men and their weird fetishes. She told me once that a guy paid her a lot of money to grind her knees into his nut sack. No dancing, just leaning on her knees into his balls. She said he was crying out in pain, and when she asked if she should stop, he insisted no.

When I screwed my face up in disgust, she laughed and said, "If I don't do it, someone else will."

For the most part, I didn't attract those types of guys. If I did, I didn't stay with them any longer than necessary. Creepy was another boundary for me. When men asked me if I enjoyed being choked or if they could pay me to urinate or defecate on them, I deflected until I found a way to escape, usually after a drink or a dance.

I enjoyed talking to businessmen. I could spot a successful man right away, not just by his suit and tie, but by his demeanor. I became really good at reading men and learning how to interact with them. I could swear like a truck driver, or I could behave like a coy flower, if only for a short period of time. I read often and absorbed what I read. I tried to keep up with the news, national and local. I formed opinions either way so that I could discuss current events. I was cautious about voicing what I thought until I heard their opinions. Whatever they needed me to be, I became.

I liked the businessmen because that wasn't a world I was accustomed to. I grew up in poverty. Businessmen were frowned upon by my parents, who often referred to them as yuppies. It made me feel a sense of power and control over them when they came into the club. Cell phones weren't a regular thing back then, so when a man in a business suit came in and was taking calls on his phone, I knew he was the one I wanted.

One night, a man in a suit and tie tipped me on stage, slipping a twenty into my thong and asking me to come see him after I got done with my set. Robert was a tall man, with brown hair and the hint of a receding hairline. He reminded me of someone who may have been a football player in his younger days. He was in his mid-to-late forties and was still what I would consider handsome.

Robert paid me to talk with him and said I didn't have to constantly dance. Some men were like that. They knew I had to make money, but they didn't demand dance after dance or try to weasel me into staying with them for free. He didn't want me to leave, so he paid me to sit on his lap and listen. He talked about his job and failed marriages. He traveled a lot for work; he was some sort of consultant. After my next set, I sat back down with him. He removed my shoes and rubbed my feet. I listened to him talk while I smoked my cigarettes and sipped my drink. I added comments every now and then and asked questions as appropriate. I was curious what it was like to work in a business environment, to wear a suit and consult with people on cell phones and have conference calls. That world seemed so far away from me.

Every once in a while, he paused in his story, nodded his head to the beginning refrains of music, then suggested that I dance because he liked the song. But then it was back to getting another drink or lighting my cigarette.

"So, Alexis, do you like seafood?" he asked as I danced in front of him.

"I love seafood," I gushed. I hadn't had a lot of seafood other than fried shrimp at a late-night truck stop, but I loved that, and I was quite certain I would like all seafood.

"Oh yeah? What's your favorite seafood restaurant?"

I racked my brain for a nice seafood restaurant in the area. "Red Lobster," I said, proud I had come up with the name so quickly.

He threw his head back and laughed. "Red Lobster is not real seafood. That's like fast food seafood." He shook his head. "I can't believe that's the nicest place you've ever been to. I could take you to a *real* seafood restaurant on the east coast." He paused. "You should fly out to Maine with me; I have a place there. I could show you what real seafood is."

What upset me the most was that he'd put down my response. He denigrated me and my opinion. I was embarrassed and ashamed that I didn't know any better about Red Lobster. To me, it was fancy. They had a lot of commercials, and their food looked delicious. I hadn't known nice restaurants growing up, and they hadn't been a priority in my life thus far.

As embarrassed as I was, the thought crossed my mind. What if I did go with him? This guy wanted to fly me to the east coast, just for seafood. I knew what it meant. It wouldn't be free. He would want sex from me, even if he said he didn't expect it. In broad daylight and real life, I knew what this offer meant.

Would it be so horrible to have sex with someone twice my age? Was it really that different than dancing in here with my top off? Other girls did it all the time. Hell, other girls were driving new cars and doing it. What would it be like to have someone give me money and take me places and buy me nice things? I wouldn't have to worry about bills. And if Robert wasn't enough, what if I added one more to the mix? Who was to say I couldn't have two men who provided for me when they came into town?

Riley. My daughter. This wasn't the mother I wanted to be. Taking trips with these men would only make it worse. It would take me even farther away from my daughter. I wouldn't fault other women for doing it, but it was another boundary I didn't want to cross.

I told him no. I made up some excuse, but I made it clear I wasn't going anywhere. He was fine with it, and our night went on.

But he left a scar long after that night ended. The dirt-poor girl from my past raised her head into this current world, the one who didn't know which restaurants weren't good enough. I was the "fast food Red Lobster" version of strippers. And as much fun as I had seducing men and acting like I belonged in their world, deep down I knew I didn't belong, and now this man knew too. My poverty stung with a vicious bite and reminded me I wasn't adequate and would never be good enough. My stepfather once told me our family was the fly on a wedding cake when we went out in public. No matter how many shiny clothes I wore or how tall my shoes were, I was still the unwashed poor girl beneath the glossy veneer. I fought hard to keep that attitude hidden, and it was so much easier when I was high or drunk.

I was making enough money where I could take a couple of days off during the week, but I kept working six nights a week. My desire to be desired and accepted superseded all other things in my life.

The Dope Show

It didn't take long to find the coke dealer at Jordan's. At first, I was determined cocaine and drinking would only be part of my job. Jasmine, at Dreamgirls, couldn't control her cocaine use, but Alexis at Jordan's wasn't going to have that problem. I didn't want to bring it home anymore. I had gotten the nosebleeds under control and decided that drinking and snorting cocaine were part of what made the job easier; therefore, it was only going to happen at work.

This lasted a short while. It was difficult to leave the club at 2:00 a.m. coming down from a cocaine high, knowing I wouldn't have any more until the next time I worked. I either had to show up to work again or buy a little bit for home. I was already working six nights a week, so I started spending a little more money at the end of the night to bring some home. Plus, Joey was tolerable about watching Riley if he knew I was bringing something back for him.

We still lived with his parents. I made enough to live on my own, but with the constant drug use for both of us, it would have been tight at times. Living with Joseph and Karen allowed us more money for drugs and free access to childcare.

My beautiful daughter was growing into a little girl. She wasn't going to be a toddler for much longer. There were painful moments when I realized what I'd missed out on in her life. She had full conversations and opinions. Her stick-straight blonde hair with reddish tints was growing longer. She looked absolutely nothing like me, with my dark brown hair. My idea of spending time with her before work meant I sat on the couch with her while she watched Barney. I thought being in the same room meant we were spending time together. I got stoned and watched the clock until I could get ready for work. Occasionally, she brought me a book, and I read to her. I enjoyed reading, and she liked books, too.

I always felt like I was failing as a parent, but I didn't know how to fix it. I wanted her to be able to have someone to go to, because I thought I was mostly too fucked-up to parent her. She didn't deserve a bad mother like me. These "I'm not good enough" thoughts made it so much worse. The more critical and inwardly ashamed I was of myself, and my parenting only drove me farther away from my daughter. But I was dealing with addiction. I was addicted to the money, the adoration of guys who thought I was a goddess. Addicted to the drugs. Addicted to the job.

One day, I was backing out of the driveway. I had my work bag in the car, my mind already at the club. Riley stood sobbing at the window, her tiny blonde head peering from behind the glass with her finger in her mouth. She cried when I left and held her arms up to me. We'd had a good afternoon. I read to her, and we ate lunch together. She didn't want me to go. I hugged her, said "Mama has to go to work," and walked away. As soon as I was in my car, relief flooded through me. I was escaping.

I had a job to do, and it was one that meant more to me than being her mother. I wish I could have shaken myself awake and said, "Be there for her!" Or better yet, I wish I could have found a desperately needed support system that showed me I could have done so much more with my life. I needed to be there for my daughter, but at that point, I needed to be there for myself first, and I didn't even know how to do that. Even though I thought I was making my own choices at this job, I wasn't. I did not feel empowered, because if I were truly empowered, I would have had the options to make other choices in life. I would have had options that allowed me to also be a better parent.

It didn't take long to make new friends at this club with the other girls. They asked us about Dreamgirls and what the money was like. We asked them where else they had been. Sometimes, the girls were there for a long time—lifers—sometimes they were there for a month, maybe less, then gone.

Our friendships with these girls were competitive on the surface but also ran deep in many ways. I made out with so many women I didn't know. I laid back on stage, and a girl leaned over me and licked my stomach. I moaned and arched my back like it was enjoyable (maybe it was), yet the entire time, I wasn't thinking about anything but getting a dance from someone who was shoving money in our thongs.

Sometimes a man wanted two girls at once. It didn't matter if you liked the other girl or not. For at least one song, we were besties and girlfriends. We were adept at hiding any sort of differences if it meant losing money. But most of the time, there weren't a lot of differences between us. I grew close with some of the women. In some of our chattier, drug-fueled discussions, I learned about their lives, their goals, how they became sidelined from the dreams they originally had in life.

And then one day, they were gone. They'd moved on to a new club, and you never said goodbye. And worse, you never even knew their real names. Or if you did, you didn't know their last names. They were simply gone.

"Where did she go?" I asked after not seeing someone for a while.

"She must have gone to another club," was the inevitable answer. It was never "she got sick of this shit and quit."

Jordan's also let us start an account and charge our floor rent. Inevitably, I ended up owing rent there too. One night, I caught a glimpse of the clipboard and saw all the girls who had balances. It was pretty much everyone. Jordan's was a bit stricter about owing back rent. They insinuated that you couldn't quit working there if you owed them money. I never had a problem leaving a club and coming back, no matter how much I owed. They always let me come back. I was a hard worker, and I didn't start fights. And perhaps, most importantly, I knew how to draw a crowd.

Brandy and I heard about The Landing Strip, near Romulus. It was the cream of the crop for exotic dancers everywhere. One of the girls at Jordan's mentioned you had to have a license to dance there, though. She also said it was definitely an audition. Most "auditions" meant you automatically got a job. This place was particular about who they accepted. Brandy wanted to check it out and suggested we go on one of our nights off.

Immediately, my insecurities took over. I knew I was pretty enough and good enough to dance in Alcoa, but what about a place like Detroit? They required you to obtain a license with the city to dance. I guess it was sort of a permit-type thing. Did they drug test for it? And most importantly, would I even pass an audition?

Regardless, Joey, Brandy, and I took off one night to check it out.

Joey liked to think he was cool hanging out with two strippers. It was the easy life for him to spend time with us, because he knew we always had an abundance of drugs. While we lived together and raised Riley together, I knew that our relationship wasn't going anywhere for the two of us. I had lost my starstruck love and adoration for him. I cared about him, but I knew he wasn't the one I wanted to spend my life with. As they say, "He wasn't Mr. Right, but he was Mr. Right Now."

We arrived in Detroit and pulled into the parking lot. It was a large nondescript brick building from the outside. The large words "The Landing Strip" glowed on the front sign facing the road.

The inside of the club itself was amazing. The entire stage was lit up like a runway, where the women walked the catwalk. Everything was so bright. To me, everyone looked super rich. I immediately felt out of my element, the Red Lobster of strippers.

The women here were of a different caliber. They looked taller on that stage, looming over us with the bright lights shining on them like halos. Their makeup, skin, and hair were flawless. And most obviously, at least to me, none of them had stretch marks or a C-section scar. They all seemed to have implants.

Brandy had no sense of anything not good enough about her, or me.

"We can do it, dude," she said, her eyes lighting up as one of the guys neared the stage and threw a fifty down for the girl performing.

I wished I had half her confidence. She still never spent extra money on shoes and clothes, she didn't shave unless she felt like it, and she waltzed into this ritzy-ass club like she owned it. And because she was so different from all these girls, she probably could make a killing here. For me, it was a constant inner battle. I was average in my own mind, and I had to fight for attention.

It would be hard to start over in a new club. And these lights were so bright. Everyone would see my stretch marks. I didn't see anyone here who had them the way I did. As the evening wore on, I grew more miserable and less excited about the experience. Perhaps I'd only be good enough for the Alcoa market. As powerful as I thought I was when I put on my makeup and clothes, there wasn't anything I could do about these lights. Men would see me for the sham I was—a poor girl who grew up without running water, not good enough to deserve fifties on the stage. I was disheartened.

We didn't audition. We stayed for a short while to observe and then left. The car ride was quiet until Joey and I started arguing. We fought the entire way back. I was upset about not being up to par for that club, and I wanted to go home.

Brandy took my side as Joey antagonized me, which further enraged him. I was so angry, and I wanted him out of the car. I made fun of his stuttering, which he did when he got agitated. I knew it upset him, but I was hating myself right then. I wanted him to hate himself as much as I hated me. I egged him on as we were taking the freeway back to Alcoa. It was pitch-black as we raced down the freeway, my foot pressed on the gas pedal matching my revved-up mood. Brandy grew quiet in the back seat, smoking a cigarette.

Joey was lighting his cigarette with the car lighter; he pulled it out and it was red-hot. He suddenly reached over and pressed the burning spiral into my cheek.

I screamed. My face was on fire. I was livid. There was a wild thought in my head to take the car off the road, just run into the guardrail and kill us all. That would teach him. But Brandy was able to separate us and calm me down.

I had planned on working the rest of the week, thus the reason I took that night off. But the escalated argument between Joey and me made it so I couldn't work for a couple of days while my face healed.

Mouth (The Stingray Mix)

Karen insisted we enroll Riley in a special education class. I didn't think anything was wrong with her. She was a quiet child, observant and watchful. But she was a happy kid, and she seemed to be learning fine. But because I wasn't active enough in her life, Karen kept demanding that I couldn't see the problems.

At Karen's insistence, and after she pulled some strings, we took her to her first day of preschool with special education children.

When Joey and I dropped her off for the first time, both of us stopped dead in our tracks as soon as we entered the classroom.

The children in the room had serious medical issues. Some of them had missing limbs, and most couldn't verbally communicate. Riley jumped for joy and ran to the toys to play with the other children. The other parents glanced at each other and then stared at us like we were crazy.

Shame washed over me. Why was our healthy, beautiful daughter in this room? We introduced ourselves to the teacher, and I stumbled around answering questions about

Riley and her abilities. She had no disabilities as far as I was concerned, but I had a hard time answering some of the questions. I wasn't around her enough and started second-guessing myself.

When we walked out of the room, I let Joey have it. This was his meddling mother who thought our kid needed to be with children who clearly had far more serious issues than ours. Our daughter being in that class also meant some other child didn't get a place in the room. He was as upset as I was.

The teacher had tried to hide her shock after she saw the burn scar on my face, but I'd caught her expression. At the end of class, she reported Riley's progress to us and walked us to our car.

"Is everything okay?" she asked gently.

I told her everything. How I was driving and Joey burned me in the face. Joey got explosively defensive. I thought we were going to fight again right there.

The teacher told us we needed to work this out one way or the other, because our daughter didn't need to see this. Riley was playing near the car while we screamed in the parking lot at each other. How many times did she have to block out our fighting? Maybe our behavior did mean she fell into the category of needing special assistance, but this wasn't good for Riley. I grew up seeing my parents fight like this. What damage was I causing my little girl?

I wish I could have said that was the last straw, but instead, I withdrew deeper into the life I lived at night. I only truly felt at home in the chaos that was the club life. The drugs, the alcohol, the men, the loud music. It was my life. Even my beautiful daughter couldn't save me from myself.

Brandy and I never ended up applying to the club in Detroit. Driving that distance in Michigan winter weather would have been horrible. I was secretly relieved. But we still wanted to check out other clubs.

On another night off, we drove to Battle Creek. We didn't take Joey with us this time. We loaded up our car with our clothes, got high, and took off. Battle Creek was a lot smaller than Detroit and not as far away. The good thing about driving home at three in the morning is there's hardly any traffic. But that's also the worst thing about driving home at that time. If you're even slightly buzzed or high, a cop could pull you over in an instant.

Once, after leaving the club in Alcoa, I was pulled over while driving on the back roads. I was likely sobered up by then, but I always had joints in the car. I had most likely smoked one when I was on the way home. The officer pulled me over, told me I had a headlight out, and let me go. The entire time, my heart was pounding in my chest. I had an unhealthy paranoia of cops.

We showed up at the strip club in Battle Creek. We followed written instructions and a map to get there. We eventually located a small, single-level building set in a factory district. It was a tiny one-room building set up similar to the biker bar in Fayetteville. It seemed seedy as all hell from the outside. I was hoping it looked better on the inside. There weren't many cars in the parking lot, which was another bad sign.

The inside consisted of a large room with a hardwood floor. There were chairs and tables set around in a circle. When we walked in, we immediately searched for a stage but there wasn't one. There was a pole in the center of the floor, but there was no separation between the customers at the tables and the dancer.

We walked in the doorway, allowed our eyes to adjust, and stood for a moment, trying to decide if we should even stay. Maybe this was no longer a strip club? A waitress behind the bar saw us and glanced at the bartender. They exchanged some words.

"Let's just sit down and figure it out," I suggested. The bar was nearly empty, but a few people glanced our way. We sat at the table nearest to us.

The waitress approached. "You need to be escorted in the club."

We had never heard this before and looked at each other. Brandy piped up, "We just want to check this out. Can we get a drink?"

The waitress gave us a dirty look and then sighed as though we were dumb. "Women need to have a man escort them into this club."

Brandy and I looked at each other, puzzled.

"Why?" Brandy demanded. "Can't we audition?"

The waitress immediately brightened up. "Oh, you want to dance?" She then explained that the hiring manager wasn't there, but he was on his way back and we could wait.

There were a handful of times when a man brought his wife or girlfriend into the club to get a dance. Some men had that fantasy and brought them, in the hopes that maybe their girlfriend would enjoy it. Or their girlfriends were curious. Whatever. I'd danced for plenty of wives in front of their husbands. To be honest, I don't remember any women coming in alone. Apparently, this was a small enough town where that sort of behavior wasn't accepted.

There were only a few customers present, and they were seated at the bar. It wasn't early; this place should've been busier by this time of the night. We took this as a sign that we wouldn't be making much money. I hadn't even seen any dancers yet, just the lonely floor-level pole in the middle of the room.

We each smoked a cigarette and sipped our drinks. Brandy caught my eye and we both nodded. This was another wasted trip for us and another night we weren't working. As we stood up to leave, the waitress rushed over and held out her hand to stop us.

"He's coming right back," she insisted.

We thanked her and told her we weren't interested. She kept insisting we stay and talk to the manager, who was due back any moment. The men at the bar swiveled around to watch us. We still had yet to see any dancers working. Brandy was determined. If there was no money to be had, we weren't staying.

We left there feeling defeated and agreed that we should probably stick to the local clubs for a while longer.

Fred Bear

Jordan's is located in downtown Alcoa in a business district by the river. It's near other bars, some restaurants, and a ballpark. We made the best money when the event center across the street was booked. The Alcoa Center hosted different types of events nearly every weekend. The club knew this and took advantage of it, setting up signs on the sidewalk that welcomed the patrons of the event center to our bar after, or even during, their event. One of the first things I did when I walked in the door for work was ask the DJ if there were any events. He usually had a scoop on the schedule across the street.

One of the most lucrative events was the annual hunting and fishing expo held at the Alcoa Center prior to the commencement of hunting season. Men from all over showed up with their friends. What better way to spend the evening after an exciting day male bonding with your buddies than at a strip club?

It was the first night of the hunting expo. Jordan's was packed, standing room only, and had a line at the door. We were making more money than we could handle. I danced for one guy, and another asked me to find him next, mid-dance. I had to put my cigarettes downstairs because my purse couldn't hold my smokes and all the cash. When I opened my satchel to shove money in, more money fell out.

A lot of the girls, myself included, danced to what we knew. If I heard a cool song on the radio, I was already choreographing it in my head and figuring out which outfit would work best. If a girl strictly liked and danced to rap music, then in a room full of country boys, she had to work extra hard to overcome their aversion to the music. The same with country music in a room full of men who enjoyed hip-hop. A good dancer learned how to read the room and adjust.

Jack was the DJ on the first night of the expo. He was a tall guy, clean shaven, with dark brown hair—a family man with a wife and kids. He loved his job and was always friendly. Brandy and I both liked him as a DJ. She rarely even bitched when she had to tip him out.

My turn on stage was coming up. I had been working so hard that I didn't have time to tell Jack what songs I wanted for my set. I fought through the crowd and stood at the bottom of the stairs leading up to his booth.

"Whaddya wanna play tonight, beautiful?" he asked, winking at me.

I glanced at the crowd. There wasn't a square inch of room that didn't have someone wearing camouflage. "Play for me whatever you think this crowd wants to hear, and I'll split what I make on stage with you."

"Are you serious?"

I laughed. "Sure, why not? Give it your best shot."

I gave him a high five and he turned around to flip through his music.

The DJ knows he gets tipped out at the end of the night. As I mentioned before, if you're a good tipper, he'll make you feel like a goddess on stage and will encourage the crowd to tip you. But when he knows he's making *half* of what I earn on stage for a set, then he goes *all out*.

My first song of the set he played was Ted Nugent's "Fred Bear." I wasn't sure I would be able to dance to Ted Nugent. I wasn't exactly a fan. But if hunters in the audience thought "Fred Bear" was the jam and it was paired with my tits, it was heaven for them, which meant money for me.

The noise was deafening as soon as the opening chords of the song started playing, and I ascended the steps to the stage.

I didn't have to worry about choreographing movements to the song. I had a wad of money strewn across the stage before Nugent even started singing. By mid-song, I had to wade through it to get to the guys who had money in their mouths and were standing there like fish waiting for bait. I kept removing the money from my thong and throwing it behind me on the stage, to make room for more money. I'd get a ten-dollar bill from one guy's mouth, while another pulled the string on my thong to shove money in there. I had it everywhere. Money was literally sticking to me.

The second song was "Stranglehold," also by Ted Nugent. Both songs were extremely long, and Jack let me stay up there the entire time. When the song ended, they gave me some time to grab the rest of my money off the stage and pick it out of my thong. It took a few minutes into the next girl's song because I was wading through the cash. The fame trickled down from the stage and followed me. Men immediately asked me for dances as soon as I stepped down. I went to Jack's booth and gave him half of what I made. We both made a killing that night.

There was one other night that was crazy like that, but it had been at Dreamgirls. The exact date was June 28th, 1997. It was the night of the Mike Tyson fight, the one where he bit off Evander Holyfield's ear. That evening started off wrong for me. I just didn't feel like dancing. I pouted and smoked in the dressing room. Sitting back there, belligerent, with my arms crossed, I refused to dance. A couple of times, Larry came back and tried to get me to go out. The place was packed with hundreds of men. I could hear the music, so I knew a couple of rotations had gone through.

The guys were seeing the girls over and over again, not that they cared. The girls were making a killing. They'd come back to get changed or smoke a cigarette, but they made it quick because they didn't want to miss out on making money. With me staying in the back pouting all night, it meant more money for them.

Brandy eventually came back and tried to talk me into working. "Dude, it's busy and you need to make money. Let's go."

She was right; I needed the money. There was no good reason for my behavior other than sometimes I'd get stubborn. But eventually, I put on a cute outfit and got put in the rotation.

When the DJ finally called me up, no one had seen me yet. It was late in the evening. The only people who did that were the features. And here I came, a fresh face, to all sorts of yelling and screaming.

To me it was acceptance. Validation. It was wildly addictive to have everyone chant my name, even if it wasn't my real name. It was for me. They were yelling for me.

Moments like those were when I didn't know what the worse addiction was—the crowds going wild for me, or the drugs.

The Beautiful People

One day, Brandy called to ask if she could stop by Joey's house. I was there with Joey and Riley. I grew concerned when I discovered she had been crying. When she arrived, we sent Riley and Rayla to play outside.

She said she stopped at her mom's apartment and passed a guy in the hallway. He greeted her, and she didn't think anything of it. Her mom later told her that man was her biological father.

All along, Brandy thought the man who raised her was her father, but she found out that day he wasn't and that her brother and sisters weren't her full siblings. She was in shock. I understood her anger and hurt. I had a biological father I hadn't met either.

We smoked a joint, and she calmed down, hurt and pissed at her mother for lying to her all those years. I asked her if she was going to meet her father, and she said she didn't know. She was in too much pain to think about it.

I knew my stepfather wasn't my "real" father. I had asked my mom about my biological father. Growing up, I had my dream that he owned a home with white picket fences and horses. I longed for a home that had warm running water and a place to shower. A roof that didn't leak on my bed when it rained. In her more forthcoming times, my mother eventually admitted that he was a bad person. I found out later he served time in prison for drug charges. He clearly wasn't any good. There were no white picket fences and certainly no horses. I understood the pain Brandy was going through.

I had my own shocking family situation around my birthday in 1998. My beloved Grandma Clara had passed away, with my step-grandfather following afterward. After I fell deep into the club lifestyle, I'd hardly visited them at all. It was easier to say life had gotten very busy, but I know it was because I wasn't proud of who I had become. I didn't want my grandmother to see me high. Maybe it was because I couldn't refrain from being high long enough to visit her. I didn't know how to still be her granddaughter and the person I was when I wasn't with her.

Grandma Clara had defended me when my mother cut me off. She never would have judged me, and she loved me. She was perhaps the only person I had ever known who loved me unconditionally. But before her final days, I hadn't been to see her in months.

My mother called me when Grandma Clara got too sick to stay home anymore. She said she was asking for me, and I'd better go see her at the hospital. The way she said it told me grandma wasn't returning home. I'd never had anyone I was close to get sick or pass away. I was at the height of my dance life and working nearly every night. The thought briefly crossed my mind that I was too busy to go, that somehow not showing up would push off the inevitable, but my mother insisted.

Joey said he'd come with me, for which I am forever grateful. Joey and I had a lot of problems, but when push came to shove, I could always count on him to be there for me. We brought Riley, and Joey laid her in the hospital bed next to Grandma Clara. Riley was scared, clutching back at

Joey to pick her up from the bed. She didn't recognize the woman lying there.

Grandma Clara was frantically clutching for something on the nightstand. She hated not having her "falsies" in, as she called them. She'd sooner be caught naked than without her teeth in public. I could tell that was what she was reaching for, but I couldn't find them on her table. They must have been removed by the staff, who maybe thought that someone on their deathbed didn't need to worry about teeth any longer.

I hated seeing Grandma Clara in that sterile, pale-yellow room that was somehow supposed to represent a sunshine color. Someone had plucked my once-vivid and buoyant grandmother from her flower garden at home and stuck her here instead, where she clearly had wilted. The bed looked uncomfortable, and the bars on the side trapping my grandmother in reminded me of a horizontal jail cell. Someone, possibly a patient, screamed in agony from the hallway. A man with a vacant zombie stare wearing a hospital gown not fully closed in the back stumbled down the hall outside her room. The staff brushed past him as though he weren't even there.

My grandmother grabbed my arm. "Get me out of here," she said, desperation in her rheumy eyes.

I couldn't hold back the tears. I tried to be positive, but I didn't know what to say. I hated being there, too, in that hospital. But there was no way she could return home. My grandfather needed full-time care. Right up until the end, my grandma had smoked unfiltered cigarettes, and now her blood wasn't flowing to her legs anymore.

"I can't, Grandma. You have to stay here." I clasped her papery, thin hand in both of mine. We talked for a while; our conversations punctuated by the screams in the hallway. Her face crumpled when I said goodbye. I cried and hugged her. I told her I would come back and see her. But I didn't make it back. I never went back.

My only true supporter and the only person who had loved me most in this life passed away on March 28, 1998—eight days after my twenty-fourth birthday. I wasn't there for her in her last moments on this earth.

My mother had someone from my former congregation officiate her services. But my grandmother had never accepted my mother's religion. Still, my mother insisted that "had she been given more time," she would have converted. I never believed this. Grandma Clara saw the religion for what it truly was.

Other members of the congregation showed up at the funeral to support my mother. They couldn't speak with me since I'd been disfellowshipped, but it didn't stop them from standing around and whispering about my fall from grace, particularly since some of them knew I was a stripper. I tried not to let it bother me while I focused on mourning the loss of my grandmother, but I resented them for showing up to such a private occasion and casting judgment on me.

At the funeral, when they buried my grandmother, they wheeled Grandpa Warren up to the graveside. He was losing his mind to dementia. No one was sure if he knew what was happening or if he was even aware that his wife had died. He wasn't a demonstrative person, anyway. But a few weeks later, he was reading the paper and had an apparent moment of clarity. He saw the obituary for my grandmother in the newspaper and started to cry at the kitchen table and we realized he knew at that point. He passed away a few years after she did. They were the only truly loving and accepting family I had ever known.

My grandmother's best friend, Janet, had passed away too. She was from England and had also loved me dearly.

She'd bought Riley a baby present and told me I should come visit so she could meet her, but I never went to get it. She had never met Riley. I was too wrapped up in my own life to care about anyone but myself.

Whatever the reasons, I always felt horrible that I couldn't make it right in the end with the people I loved the most in life. I was hiding from myself. I had my own pain I was dealing with, which made it hard for me to be there for anyone else.

Pour Some Sugar on Me

I found myself in the same situation at Jordan's as I did at Dreamgirls. It was getting old and stale. People recognized me. They knew my face and knew what I would, and wouldn't, do for money. My songs and clothes were all the same. I was restless, and I wanted to be the new girl again. I once again felt myself losing the spark I had when I took the stage.

Brandy and I had traveled to a few clubs out of the tri-county area to no avail; unfortunately, the only two topless clubs in Alcoa were Dreamgirls and Jordan's. We thought about heading up north to check out some clubs, but apparently, the topless clubs made you wear pasties to cover your nipples. That didn't sound appealing, and we were unsure if we would even make any money, so it didn't seem worth the trip.

I even went back to Dreamgirls for a while to see if anything had changed, but it hadn't. Tony was no longer a bouncer; he had been promoted to manager. He'd lost his fun innocence and his smile no longer reached his eyes which had taken on a steely edge, complete with dark circles. He made it clear that despite our previous relationship, it had no bearing on my past-due floor rent and the money was still due. A huge portion of what I earned went right back to the club at the end of the night.

There was one more club in Alcoa to try.

It was Déjà Vu, the "Vu." There were concerns about that club for me, namely that it was a fully nude club. I had to remove *all* my clothes, including my thong, basically everything but the stilettos. I occasionally met some Vu girls; they stopped into the topless clubs when they wanted a change of pace. Given my poor body self-image, I never had considered it. There was something extremely vulnerable about taking off my thong, even though it consisted of very little material to begin with. Because of my C-section scar, I was hesitant about taking it down to that level. Some of my costumes already had a narrow thong, but I wasn't sure what it would look like if I were completely naked. And what did the Vu girls do when they were on their periods? There wasn't a good way to tuck in your tampon string and hide it behind a thong when there wasn't one.

Another strike against the Vu was that I couldn't drink while working. I wasn't even sure what it looked like to dance completely sober. I don't remember one time dancing where I wasn't under the influence of something—drugs or alcohol or both—while on the job. I needed that to feel comfortable enough to remove my clothes. One of the first things I did when I entered a club was order a drink before I finished getting ready in the dressing room. According to state law, alcohol wasn't allowed in fully nude clubs. What sort of experience would it be without alcohol?

Despite my concerns, Brandy and I decided to audition at Déjà Vu.

The Vu was located in a large building that reminded me of an auditorium. It was full of neon lights—very bright and very pink. It was a similar setup to other clubs, with table and couch dances. The stage was located at one side of the large room and set higher up off the ground.

The manager led us back to the dressing room to get changed. We still had to audition, but it was a formality. By now, anyone could look at us and tell we were regulars in the circuit, with our fake tans, too-thin bodies, loads of clothes and makeup, which we lugged along behind us. We basically had jobs because we'd showed up.

After changing our clothes, we gave the DJ our songs.

We got stoned in the parking lot beforehand and slammed some liquor that Brandy had brought with her. She wanted to bring it in, but that made me nervous. I didn't know how strict they were with the no alcohol policy, but I figured finding out on an audition wasn't the way to go.

The girls never spread their legs with their snatches facing the crowd, which was a relief. They danced basically the same way, only nude. When I asked one of the girls who worked there what they did on their periods, she didn't act like it was a big deal. Just tuck the string up or cut it off; it rarely slid out. The term "rarely" was not reassuring.

I auditioned first. The stage was so high up, it made me dizzy. I took a deep breath and did my set the way I always did. I took my top off in the first song and then removed the skirt. By the second song, I performed a strip tease, pretending to remove my thong, little by little. Little did everyone know this wasn't meant to be a tease. I literally had to build up the nerve to remove it. I had very little pubic hair from my normal removal process down there, just a thin strip up the center called a landing strip. All other hair was removed, but I was more concerned about the scar. I bent over to remove the thong, and the first thing I did when I stood up was look in the mirror to make sure my C-section scar wasn't noticeable.

It was a relief to discover the lights glowed in such a way that those types of things weren't extremely visible. My C-section scar wasn't that bad, and neither were the stretch marks that clawed their way up my concave stomach. They glowed white only because I spent so much time in a tanning bed, but I noticed other girls also had the same scars.

I finished my set and gathered my tips and clothes. Brandy performed next.

After that first night, we concluded that working there wasn't a good idea and opted to stick with the topless clubs. For one thing, the girls weren't as friendly. And because we couldn't drink, it was harder to deal with dancing. We understood from some of the girls they still did drink despite the rules, but it was harder to hide. And it was also hard to get a man to part with his money if he's just drinking pop all night; alcohol opens wallets more often. It was a combination of all those things, but Brandy and I never went back to that club.

A visiting dancer told us about another club in the area called The Barrington located in Fargo. The girl told us it was a dive, and all I'd ever heard about Fargo was that it was dangerous. We had been dancing for over two years at this point, and Brandy was as anxious as I was to find a new place to perform.

We decided to check out The Barrington. It proved to be difficult to find; downtown Fargo was a city made up of multiple one-way streets. It probably didn't help that we were high when we searched for it. We eventually arrived, and a large bouncer greeted us at the door.

We were introduced to the manager and were allowed to audition.

The Barrington was located in a historic building. The tall ceilings were made of pressed tin stained from the cigarette smoke that lingered and rose to the top. The stage looked higher than any I had worked before. All the chairs below were pushed toward the stage, so a person had to crane their neck to look up. It was dark and dingy, with an ominous atmosphere. The crowd seemed big enough, though, so we decided to give it a try.

Even after two years, it still unnerved me being a "new" dancer. The women threw glaring daggers your way until you got to know them. When you're new, it's always a careful dance to make friends with people.

But these women didn't throw daggers. They barely glanced at us, and if they did bother, it was with blank stares. Nothing in their eyes betrayed any emotion. It was odd. A girl next to us gave a lap dance with her eyes half-shut the entire time, like she was somewhere else.

We were shown down another steep set of stairs to a dressing room. Because the building was old, the handrail was set lower and the steps were spaced close together, similar to Jordan's. I'm certain it wasn't up to code. We made our way downstairs to a small dressing area.

What distinctly stood out to me was the sign in the doorway pinned up with a careless tack. "Please wear makeup. Please shower before you come to work. You have to care about what you look like to make money."

I immediately looked at Brandy, whose expression matched mine.

"What the fuck? Gross, dude," she whispered, glancing around.

We were introduced to a couple of girls in the dressing room, and it became clear what the sign meant. These girls were bad off and strung out on heavy drugs. Most of them were so drugged that when they shook our hands, they could barely speak. They didn't even bother with makeup anymore. They were just going through the motions. I couldn't even imagine showing up to work with no makeup, or worse, not showering. I'd been strung out on drugs, and I knew a lot of girls that had serious drug problems, but this took the cake.

Despite all this, we ended up staying there after our audition. We were a hit on the stage and with the men, mostly because despite being high, we were still coherent. We showered, we wore makeup, and we cared about how we looked.

I was quite certain this was a place where human trafficking could get its start. Those girls were so confused most of the time that they were pliable enough to do whatever anyone asked. The vibe I got from that club was the darkest I'd ever encountered in my dancing experience up until that point.

Brandy loved it. She made a killing. She glommed on to the seedier parts of working the clubs. But I didn't enjoy working there. It was dark and dank, and everything about it represented what was bad about exotic dancing.

Stranglehold

I needed to find my own place to live. Joey and I were no longer pretending to get along. I still cared about him, and he cared about me, but we didn't see eye to eye any longer.

I also knew I had to find sustainable employment. I wasn't getting any younger. There were plenty of fresh eighteen-year-olds coming in to replace me. In my mid-twenties, I was getting to be an old-timer in the exotic dance world. Occasionally, the thought crossed my mind that maybe exotic dancing wasn't as fun as I thought it was. There was the constant back rent that forever had to be paid. The freedom of "self-employment" made it seem like we had choices as exotic dancers, but in reality, an overarching patriarchy was in place to keep women where the club wanted us to be—portraying men's fantasies with few options.

I knew for certain I didn't want to return to waitressing. I had some office experience from the water softener company, and office work was something I could do. I found a full-time office job as a receptionist with a local real estate company. I bought business suits and wore my hair modestly pulled back. I started waking up early and I drank coffee. I transformed myself into a professional and worked regular office hours during the week, eight to five. But I still stripped on the weekends to make ends meet. I couldn't give it up.

Shortly after that, I found an apartment in Grand Heights. Riley and I moved in, and we loved it. It was our own place. I enrolled Riley in daycare. I bought groceries and cooked meals. Somehow, having a professional job made me see myself differently. I had bills to pay on my own and responsibilities. Every night after I put Riley to bed, I laid out my work clothes for the next day and packed a lunch to eat in my little lunch box cooler.

It was hard at first. But Riley and I developed our own little rituals. I picked her up from daycare after work, cooked dinner, and after we ate, she took a bath. We read books together. She enjoyed the *Junie B. Jones* series. My mother had read all the Laura Ingalls Wilder books to me growing up and had bought a set for Riley, so I also read those to her. We grew closer and formed our own little family.

The state went after Joey for child support because I had no health insurance when I gave birth to Riley. They wanted to collect from the father for the birth and charge him child support. As soon as I moved out, that opened the door for the state to collect. This was the last straw for Joey and Karen. Despite the fact I had a real day job, they knew I still stripped. They knew how much money I could make, and they didn't feel it was fair that Joey had to pay the money back for the birth by himself.

So, they took me to court for joint custody. They told the mediator I was a stripper and an unfit parent. I was scared. What if they took Riley from me? Even with joint custody, that would be disruptive now that she and I had developed a good pattern living together. It wasn't even that Joey was a better parent; he was trying to avoid child support. Now that I had a professional job, I wanted to prove I could do it.

The mediator took a look at my history—no felonies or trouble with the law. I had a full-time job, and I covered Riley and myself with health insurance. To the mediator, I was a productive member of society, regardless of my exotic dancing on the weekends.

Joey lost his case. I didn't want bad blood between us, so I voluntarily lowered the amount of child support he had to pay to the least amount required by law.

I continued to dance on the weekends and worked the office job during the week. It wasn't easy, but I managed. I had come to depend on the money. I still smoked weed, and I still drank, but I had slowed way down on the cocaine—not that I wouldn't do it if it were offered to me, but it didn't fit me in my new role as a professional working woman.

Occasionally, when I walked onto the stage, I wondered what would happen if someone found out where I worked. What if a coworker saw me in the club? Or worse, what if a customer recognized me? It worried me, but not enough to stop.

Brandy knew someone who owned a limo company. We still saw each other occasionally, but when I slowed down dancing, she did too. One night after work, she drove by my apartment when Riley was with Joey and picked me up with a limo. Other than dancing, I hadn't been out in ages since I had started my day job. It felt amazing to ride in the limo with the top open and the wind blowing through my hair.

We went to her friend's house in Fayetteville, and she introduced me to Carl—a man in his late sixties who knew my biological father. I could tell right away he had a crush on Brandy, and she wasn't doing anything to stop his advances. I discovered he was the hookup for cocaine in Fayetteville, and he supplied her with it when she wanted it. In my opinion, he was a dirty old man, and it shocked me that she cared so little for herself by hanging out with him. It was one thing to hang out with men like that in a club for work, but it was something different to do it in our free time.

One night, I discovered they were shooting a small budget film in East Alcoa. I was invited to show up to be an extra. But of course, I didn't want to go alone. I called Brandy, and we got ready at my house in Grand Heights.

When we arrived at the East Alcoa bar, they were setting up a track on the floor so that a camera could pan across. I spoke with the guy in charge and received instructions on where we were going to stand when the filming started.

There was nothing else to do, so we started drinking while we waited. Brandy still wasn't twenty-one, and somehow, they hadn't carded her, probably because we were there as extras. When she started drinking that night, she didn't stop. She grew wild and crazy and ended up in the bathroom, puking her brains out from Jack and Coke.

I knew I had to get her out of there. She was drunk as hell and underage. I made my apologies to the guy running the show and we left. I decided to leave my vehicle in East Alcoa and take her truck back to my place. Unfortunately, she didn't remember where she'd parked. I eventually found her truck, and we drove back to my apartment in Grand Heights.

I was upset because I really wanted to be in the movie. This was something I could put on a resume for modeling and acting, another dream that I still wanted to pursue. I tried not to be mad at Brandy. She kept mumbling her apologies in a drunken haze.

When we arrived back at my house, Joey was there. He stomped toward me, his eyes angry and flashing.

"Where have you been?" he demanded, pissed off.

He wasn't angry that I came back to my house late. He was mad because he wasn't included.

"It doesn't matter. Get out of my way." I pushed past him into my house.

He stormed in after me.

It eventually turned into a full-blown fight. Brandy lay on my couch and tried to recover. Joey wouldn't leave. He hated being left out, and he still resented me for the child support he owed. There was probably a small part of him that missed hanging out with me too.

"Get out of my house!" I yelled. He refused to leave, and I was worried the landlord would get called. The cops would come if we didn't stop fighting.

He stepped toward me, towering above me, and shoved me backward.

Something inside me snapped. I was angry because I didn't get to be in a movie, and I didn't feel like listening to him bitch at me about my life. All my anger came rushing out, and I punched him in his face.

Hard.

Blood poured from his nose. He was angrier now that I had punched him, and he became even louder.

And that's when the cops showed up.

Save Yourself

Someone once told me people bleed heavier from their heads. Sometimes it looks a lot worse than what it is, because if we bleed from our heads and we're still conscious, it's probably not as bad as it seems.

Joey was bleeding, a lot. We continued screaming at each other as Joey bled all over my floor. Brandy was laid out on my couch with her eyes closed, and her hand thrown over her face.

I opened the door, intent on shoving Joey out so he would stop bleeding on my floor, when two cops appeared on the porch.

"What seems to be the problem?" one of them asked, taking the door from my grasp and holding it open.

"Nothing," I said, stepping onto the porch. I knew if I didn't invite them in, they couldn't push past me without good reason. Like vampires, they had to be invited.

And then my good reason came stumbling out on the porch. Joey stood there with his face covered in blood.

"It's none of your business!" he snapped at them. His eyes looked wild as blood continued to stream from his nose and down his shirt. One of the officers glanced down at my floor, covered in blood, and Brandy reclined on my couch.

We were both detained while they figured out what was going on.

I glanced back as they handcuffed me. Brandy was sitting up now and smoking a cigarette with a calm and clear expression on her face. She had the amazing aptitude of sobering up when she needed to, especially around cops.

Once I was handcuffed, Joey really started yelling.

"Let her go! Let her go! Just take me!"

He flailed around as they tried to handcuff him. He didn't want to go to jail. They pepper sprayed him because he wouldn't calm down. Blood and spray mingled together and ran down his face. He started screaming at them to let me go; his focus had switched to anger at them for taking me to jail.

Brandy jumped in at that point and yelled at Joey to shut up. I kept telling her to stop making a scene (she was underage, so I didn't want to get in trouble for her drinking), but she only shut up when the officer warned her against getting involved.

When Joey wouldn't cooperate, one of them went into my house and grabbed a pillowcase from my bed. They wrestled it over his head to subdue him, and he started screaming that he couldn't breathe.

I yelled to Brandy from the back seat of the cop's car, "My keys are on my counter! Lock my house." And then I added, "It's going to be fine."

She appeared stricken, dazed, and still drunk, but she nodded her head and stumbled back to my house.

Joey and I were taken to jail in separate cars.

At this point, I was tired, and it was late. But at least I wasn't drunk anymore.

When we arrived at the police station, they drove up to the garage and pulled the car inside. Someone opened my door and I stepped out.

This was my first experience with jail, and I immediately slipped into stripper mode. I smiled broadly and asked them their names. It was mostly women I dealt with in the jail, but I was polite and asked them questions when they took me back to get fingerprints. I asked about the ink and if it would stain. They informed me it would disappear and explained how the process worked.

When you're nice to them, they're nice back. I was pleasant and laughing. I even said it was exciting. A couple of them looked at me as though I had lost my damn mind. But I didn't care. To me it was a new experience, like in the movies.

The only time I refused something was when they wanted me to take all my clothes off and put on their jumpsuit and they wanted me to wear their underwear.

"Um, no thanks," I said. I was fine with the jumpsuit, but the underwear was a hard no for me.

"It's the policy."

"I'm not wearing underwear that have been on someone else. I'll just wear my own."

They were preparing to push it as nonnegotiable when I shrugged my shoulder and said, "Or I won't wear any, then."

I'd worked at enough clubs. I knew what sort of critters could be in that underwear, especially if they weren't washed well. They finally agreed to let me wear my own underwear and handed me a one-piece jumpsuit.

I removed my shirt in the room, ready to unfasten my bra. Most people look for ways to hide when they're getting changed, but by then, I was used to getting undressed in front of people. One of the women officers asked me to stop. She nodded toward a window with other inmates peeking through.

"You're causing a bit of a commotion. Can you step behind the wall to get changed?" She pointed to where I should go.

I laughed, apologized, and stepped behind the wall. I finished getting dressed and placed my clothes in a bag they provided for me.

I gave them the bag, signed a piece of paper, and was led to another room. More people in jumpsuits were cleaning and sweeping the area. I later discovered they were trustees who were able to be out of a cell to help out around the jail because of good behavior. A few glanced at me out of the corner of their eyes, but for the most part, they ignored me.

I was put in a one-room cell. A cement slab bed as tall as a regular bed and covered with a thin mattress ran along the right side of the room. A sink and a toilet, both uncomfortably near each other, were located in the corner. Someone handed me a pillow and a thin blanket.

After a short period of time, I told them I was bored and cold. Someone eventually brought me another blanket, a toothbrush, toothpaste, and a book to read (Call of the Wild by Jack London). I liked to believe this was because I was so friendly upon my arrival.

I didn't have a horrible go of it. I read the entire book in one night and had a fitful night of sleep.

In the morning, another trustee delivered food in trays that were stacked on each other in a cart. She handed me my breakfast of cereal, toast, some coffee, and juice. I didn't enjoy the cold toast, and I mentioned it to one of them.

"This ain't a hotel, honey," she said. It was a new shift of workers, and they weren't in the mood to deal with me despite my positive attitude.

After I signed more paperwork and gathered my belongings, I was released. Another shock came when I discovered they weren't going to give me a ride back to my house.

"How am I supposed to get home, then?"

The lady looked at me like I was crazy. "That's not our problem," she snapped.

"I have to walk?"

She shrugged and pointed to a pay phone.

I left the jail and headed down the street. The jail was located in a subdivision, so I trudged past families in front of their middle-class homes, doing middle-class, outdoor things. I was hungover and dressed in last night's bar clothes—not a good combination for me.

Brandy picked me up after I called her. She herself was hungover and not very chatty. She didn't have the same opinion that going to jail was "fun." And after having to walk part of the way, I no longer had the opinion that it was fun, either.

I didn't contact Joey to find out when he'd been released. I'm sure Karen came to get him. The police station never returned the pillowcase that was placed over his head. I'd spent good money on a sheet set, and after what had happened, I was now missing a pillowcase. And I never even got to be in the movie.

Last Resort

Cassie was one of my coworkers at the real estate company. She used to date one of Joey's friends, so I knew her from before. Cassie was sweet, with shoulder-length brown hair and brown eyes. She had no children, but she liked to drink, and we occasionally hung out after work.

We decided to take a girls' weekend trip to Canada. Brandy didn't have anything going on and knew Cassie, too, so she decided to come along. Since I had started working eight to five, I found I had less time to do fun things. My weekdays consisted of waking up, getting Riley ready, taking her to daycare, and then going to work. I got out of work, picked her up, and we usually spent the weeknights at home together. It was a level of normalcy that I enjoyed. However, this trip was a girl's trip, which I hadn't done before. I was looking forward to it and couldn't wait for the work week to end so we could leave.

Joey paid child support to me when he felt like it, and he wasn't happy about doing it. The visitation handoffs of Riley went smoother when Karen was there, or else, she picked Riley up without him. When he found out that I was taking the weekend to go on a trip with my friends, he arrived at my apartment, furious. His three-hundred-dollar tax return had recently been intercepted and instead went to me for his back child support payments.

"Why are you spending my child support money to go whore around on a vacation?" he asked. "That's not what child support is for."

We argued in my apartment parking lot for half an hour. I couldn't make him understand that I paid my bills. I provided for Riley. I covered her with health insurance. I had money regardless of his child support, and I would have gone on this trip one way or the other. That pissed him off even more. It was not what he wanted to hear. I refused to engage him any further. I left him outside and went into my apartment.

The money was helpful in paying off some of my bills. I splurged and bought a couple of new outfits to wear and borrowed some of my sister, Scarlett's clothes. Scarlett was eventually disfellowshipped from the congregation, and we had grown closer. One of the outfits was a blue-checkered skirt and a light blue top that tied at the front. I wore a pair of conservative flat, white sandals.

Brandy, Cassie, and I left for Canada. We passed through customs and located our hotel. After we checked in, we dropped our stuff off in the room and left to see the sights.

That evening, we ended up at Danny's, a male strip club. It was a large building set up like an auditorium, with a long line to get in. When we got inside, it was packed with screaming females. It smelled of body sweat, men's cologne, and cigarette smoke. Cassie knew that Brandy and I were exotic dancers. She never wanted to try it herself, but she was definitely up to checking out the male club.

I fully expected it to be similar to a female strip club, but it wasn't anything like it. The men danced to choreographed routines on stage. When they weren't on stage, they carried step stools, hoisted over their shoulders, to dance for women at the tables. If you wanted a dance, they came over and perched on the stand in front of you. The height of the step stool put their swinging dicks right at face level. The male appendage really isn't that attractive, anyway, but especially not when it's dipping in front of you like a fishing bobber.

Women of all shapes and sizes were perched by the stage. It appeared that some of them were fresh out of work and still dressed in office attire. There were various bachelorette parties, marked by drunken women wearing sashes and crowns. And some of them, like us, were out for a good time. Crowds gathered at the edge of the stage and held money in their mouths. They placed the two-dollar, two-toned currency between their teeth, hoping the men would come get the money from them.

Cassie paid for a dance from a blond, beefy-looking guy named Cash. Afterward, he sat with us, and we told him Brandy and I were strippers in the United States. He relaxed after that. He told us most of the men who worked there were gay, but they made good money—too much to quit. He also shared that he had to shave his entire body nearly every day before he came to work, even his back. This made him a little less attractive to me. I vowed to never again overshare with my customers, even if they seemed like they didn't mind.

Signs posted all over the club claimed Danny's wasn't responsible for any sexually transmitted diseases. That, and the atmosphere itself with its cattle throng of women gathered by the stage, made it seem raunchier than any female strip club I'd been to. Perhaps my clubs were this way, too, but I was now seeing it through a different lens.

The next morning, we woke up and went to breakfast. We were hungover and tired, but it had been a memorable night. We decided to hit a mall and a casino on the way home.

I wore the garden-scene shirt my sister had lent me, with no bra underneath, along with a pair of jeans and some flat sandals. When we strolled into the casino, two guys in the security booth yelled down to us in French.

One of them approached me and gave me a bucket. I took it from him, unsure of protocol. When I peered inside, I gasped. It was nearly filled to the top with Canadian coins.

"Is this for me?" I glanced first at the guy in the booth, then at Cassie and Brandy.

The guy in the booth winked at me and nodded. I never found out why he gave me a bucket full of coins. He wouldn't come down from the booth, just smiled and waved. Brandy, Cassie, and I went to a few machines and dropped in some coins. I've never been much of a gambler. In the end, I turned the coins in for cash. The bucket didn't amount to a lot, but I thought I got lucky that day.

I had a wonderful time with good friends. For once, I had taken a trip that didn't involve obsessing over drugs and how to get them.

Oops! . . . I Did It Again

I eventually outgrew The Barrington. The atmosphere was too dark. I never grew close to the girls at that club, and the neighborhood was terrifying when we left at 2:30 a.m. Plus, there was always a constant fear of running into someone who knew me from the professional world. Nothing would have been more humiliating than having a potential customer or coworker walk in and see me dancing. Unfortunately, it said worse things about me being the entertainment on the stage than it did the person frequenting the club.

Every payday after I paid my bills I had very little left to last two weeks until my next check. The lure of fast cash on the weekends called to me, especially when it was Joey's weekend with Riley. I heard about another club, the Pink Goddess Club, located in Baker. It was an even longer drive, but that was a good thing. The chances that I would run into any coworkers or clients were slim.

I told Brandy, and she wanted to go with me to check it out.

We drove to Baker one evening and arrived at a parking lot for a motel. We kept checking the directions—positive we had made a mistake, but it said we were in the right place.

Eventually we found the entrance. The Pink Goddess Club was part of the motel. A conference center turned into a strip club, complete with drop ceilings and hard chairs around tables. The carpeting was patterned like a hotel, with wild circular designs in dark brown colors. Even the stage was an afterthought added to one length of the room. It was like someone had been given thirty minutes and very few materials to turn a conference center into a strip club, and this was the result.

The manager's name was Mic. He was an older, wiry guy with a receding hairline. He wore thick, coke-bottle glasses, snorted when he laughed, and had a habit of nodding his head in agreement with everything a person said, regardless of whether he agreed or not.

Introductions were made. He said, "It's club policy to take topless photos of all the dancers before they start."

"What do you mean, 'club policy?'" I asked. Alarms went off in my head.

He nodded. "Yeah, it's just part of the rules, and something the owners want to have on file—you know, to keep track of everyone." More head nodding. He scrunched his nose when he needed to peer down through his glasses at me.

I glanced at Brandy, and she rolled her eyes, which said it all. *What the hell?*

Most of Alcoa had seen my tits by then anyway, so what did it matter? We nodded, filled out the applications, and followed Mic to the back room. He pulled out an old Polaroid camera and fiddled with the settings.

I stood against a blank wall in the small office. There was a cleared space that I assumed was used as a background.

"Go ahead and put your arms above your head," he nodded toward me. He was creeping me out with his bobbing head.

But I raised my arms up. My small breasts raised up, too, and the chilly office air made my nipples stand erect. Every club I worked at had never been considered warm. "We need your high beams on," was always the excuse for keeping the temps frigid year-round in a club.

"Give me a sexy smile," he said, leaning into his camera. His voice was nasally, like his nose had been broken in the past. I tried to smile provocatively. But something about him screamed "not right."

Brandy went next, same pose, more head nodding.

We went through an audition, and we were hired. I chose the name Noelle at this club. I liked the sound of it, and it was perfect since we were near the holidays. The girls there were nice to us, but we had the upper hand as far as having the most experience. The dressing room was downstairs in another conference area that had been converted to a wide-open space. I told Mic straightaway that I had a day job, and I only planned on working the weekends.

"Well, I'm really looking to only hire full-time girls. I need girls during the week." He put his hand on his chin, which miraculously stopped the head-bobbing for a moment.

I glanced around at the girls he had so far. Most of them didn't own stilettos or even outfits appropriate for performance. "It's the weekends or nothing," I said firmly. I knew my worth at this point. I could bring money into this club.

When he saw it was nonnegotiable, he backed down, and I told him I'd be back the following weekend. So, we officially became exotic dancers at the Pink Goddess Club.

Even though we were the best performers there, the men were not forthcoming with money for dances or drinks. Baker was considered farm country. Very conservative. Lots of tradesmen, farmers, and men who didn't want to spend too much money on women in a club attached to a motel. But I made decent money overall.

Meanwhile, I still enjoyed working at the real estate office. I had good ideas and came up with suggestions on how to make the front desk run smoothly. The president of the company liked me, and he valued my opinions. His entire family worked there, including his wife and sons.

One of his sons was named Brandon, who was only a few years older than me. He was tall, with short, wavy dark hair. He wore business suits and carried a briefcase. He didn't work at the main office like me; he worked in a nearby town, Amherst, where I had lived with Tamara. But sometimes he came to my office for meetings. He was friendly, funny, and had a devious, joking manner about him. When older agents walked by, he would pick on them under his breath and make me laugh. When I saw him walk through the front door, my stomach fluttered, and I found myself checking my makeup and hair.

He took the time to stop and talk to me at the desk every time he visited. He was recently divorced and had custody of his young son. We talked about the problems involved with being single parents. I spoke about making ends meet (I didn't mention dancing) and paying daycare costs. I discovered his parents helped him a lot. They had also paid for his attorney to get custody of his son. My problems were significantly different from his.

But still, I wondered if someone like me could be with someone like Brandon, a professional who wore a business suit and had a real job and wasn't into drugs—a guy who grew up in a nice home with all the luxuries.

Sometimes, I subbed for the receptionist in the Amherst office. I didn't mind because Brandon worked out of that office, and I could be around him more often. Once, when

I came back from lunch, I discovered someone had placed a rose on my keyboard. I picked it up and looked around. Brandon was standing at the copy machine, looking over the cubicle wall and grinning from ear to ear.

He asked me on a date, and I said yes. I couldn't believe it; never in my wildest dreams would I have thought that someone like Brandon would want to be with someone like me. We ended up seeing each other, and it was whirlwind-fast. I adored everything about him. I was infatuated, and I wanted him to like me more than anything.

He loved to tell me stories about the showings for homes he had listed. He'd lean over the desk, with his face close to mine as he glowed in pride over his place in the real estate world. Sometimes, he had a way of talking down to me while he was teaching me about all things real estate. But I didn't mind. I nodded eagerly and listened to his words. I wanted him to know I supported him. He asked me to babysit his son once while he attended a realtor function and I eagerly agreed. I had dreams of us raising our two kids side by side and creating a future together.

He often stayed at my apartment in Grand Heights. We joked and laughed in bed while the sun shone in from the large window, and I wrapped myself around him. I was intoxicated with everything about him. He was quickly becoming my world. I couldn't imagine how someone as wonderful as him had ended up with someone like me.

He often complained about his ex. He claimed the divorce was all her fault. I staunchly supported him and murmured my agreement when he listed her issues. In the back of my mind, it caused red flags. I wondered if he wasn't over her. He insisted he didn't love her anymore and that their marriage was over, so I pushed those thoughts aside. Besides, he reminded me of how she lost custody of their son because she was unfit. I wondered how bad she truly was, knowing what I knew about fighting for custody over Riley.

Eventually, I told him about my second job. I didn't like hiding that part of me from him. He took it in stride and didn't hold it against me. It was such a relief letting him know. He asked me to dance for him, so I did. I took the secret power I had from my other life and used it on him. I knew how to manipulate men, because that was one of my jobs. I was thankful I didn't have to lie about where I was on the weekends when I needed to make extra money.

I had been cutting down on my club hours, but one weekend, I decided I needed to work because I desperately needed the cash. I had very little money after getting paid, and I knew I couldn't let the weekend slide by without working. We were invited the next day to tailgate for a college football game with Brandon's family. I had never gone tailgating before. I was honored by the invitation and felt like part of the family. When I told him I was working Friday night, he asked me to come over afterward. I agreed, and when I got there, he was waiting for me on the couch, drinking a beer.

I immediately showered as soon as I walked in the door. I hated the smell of the club—cheap body spray and cigarette smoke. There was always a thin layer of sweat and glitter on me whenever I left that job. I always washed away that life as soon as I got home.

We sat on his couch while I unwound from my night. Sheryl Crow's video, "My Favorite Mistake," was playing on MTV. I told him someone once thought I looked like her. I turned around to look at him, and he patted the place next to him on the couch. I climbed up beside him and curled into him. He wrapped his arms around me and held me close. We woke up early for the tailgate. I was exhausted but so happy.

He was everything I ever wanted in a man, and things were going well between us in such a short period of time.

I came into work one morning and saw Brandon and another female agent sitting close together, whispering. When I came around the corner, they backed away from each other, and she looked guilty. A stab of jealousy rushed through me, like when I was at the club and walked up to a girl who was sitting with my regular. I wanted to say something, but it seemed inappropriate. I didn't want to be a nag, and they were professionals. He would have told me I was making it up or being dramatic. She was married, I reasoned with myself. There was no way; it was all in my head.

Brandon's dad, the president of the company, was looking for opportunities to promote Cassie and me, so he offered to pay for us to sit for the real estate exam. Cassie was still working at the west office, and I moved to the Amherst office. Cassie, Becky, the office manager, and I went together for the week of training. I was excited to be given a new opportunity, and it felt good to hang out with Cassie again.

One day, while on a break from training, the three of us were eating lunch at a local bar down the street. I was telling Cassie about Brandon and how things felt off with us lately. I was losing him in a very short period of time. He wasn't answering my calls or returning them unless I called more than once. He sometimes slipped in and out of the office without even telling me he was there.

Suddenly, I looked up and saw Brandon walk through the door with another agent. My heart soared. He glanced my way and came over. Smiling, he asked if it was okay if they joined us for lunch. Maybe it was all in my head. But after they sat down, Brandon's focus was on Cassie. He was engaged in what she was saying. I brushed the thought away and tried to remember we were all professionals. But that creeping fear that something was off came back.

Later, he ended up asking Cassie out for a drink, and she went. She told me it wasn't a big deal, and I believed her because she said she didn't like him in that way. But after that, he actively started avoiding me. We didn't break up, so to speak, but I also knew he didn't like confrontation. He let me get angry enough that I was done talking to him.

I was devastated. He was everything I thought I wanted in a man. I lost him because I wasn't good enough for his world. I was an impostor, someone pretending to be a professional. In my mind, it was because he couldn't have someone like me, a stripper and an office receptionist, as his partner. But he'd allowed me a glimpse of what it looked like to live like him, to live in his world, and it crushed me when we stopped talking.

Looking back, I now realize he had a lot of problems. He drove his mother's car. He was a realtor, but his parents supported him and his son when he didn't sell homes. I had put him on a pedestal, as though he was so much better than me, when in reality, he wasn't. But that was my fault for putting all my hope in him.

I was devastated as though I had done something wrong.

Any Man of Mine

I was approached by my landlord to see if I wanted to move to a larger apartment. I was good at paying my rent and bills. Being offered a larger place was huge for me. I knew I could afford it, since I was still working at Pink Goddess Club and the real estate office. So, Riley and I moved into a larger three-bedroom apartment in Grand Heights.

The president at the real estate office moved me to the main branch, so I didn't have to work with Brandon anymore, but it was painful all the same. After our breakup, my relationship with his family deteriorated. I got into an argument with his brother about my work location. Cassie and I were given more responsibilities after passing our exams, which was great, but I had asked for a raise and was denied. I didn't know how I was ever going to earn enough to quit dancing on the weekends.

Around this time, I learned how to navigate the internet. This was a relatively new experience for everyone in our workplace, and we were learning how to use it for listings and work-related stuff. I quickly discovered chat rooms. It was mind boggling to me that you could get on the computer and talk to someone across the country, or even the world. I didn't have a computer at home, so getting online at work was my only option. As things fell apart in the office, I started going online more often, sometimes logging in as soon as I showed up at work.

One day, I met a guy online from Kalamo named Todd. He was tall, with wavy, light brown hair that hung low over his forehead. He constantly brushed his hair out of his eyes and had a stare that my mom would have called "bedroom eyes." Todd's father was a mortgage officer and had bought him a nice house in a subdivision, with a pool out back.

Todd was extremely immature, even though he was only a couple of years younger than me. This could never possibly go anywhere, but I was still upset about Brandon. Partying with Todd was fun and took my mind off how miserable I was about my previous failed relationship. Todd was not a commitment guy. He had no intention of ever having kids. He didn't mind me having one, but he had no interest in a family, which was fine by me.

Todd invited me to a party in Kalamo. I dragged Brandy with me so that I wouldn't have to go alone. It was a warm, sultry summer evening, and we ended up at a bar with an outdoor patio. Fairy lights were strung up as if it were Christmas, and the band music floated outside. I looked up at the stars in the sky through the twinkling bar lights and wondered where my life had gone—where my dreams from so many years before had disappeared to. It seemed as though once the New System wasn't part of my future; I had given up. I drank so much that night that I puked on the ride back to his house. Todd kept pulling over so that I could vomit.

I wasn't in a good place. I missed Brandon. I was terribly upset and kept coming back to the inner dialogue that told me I wasn't good enough for him. I had failed, and I was looking for love from someone, anyone, who could make me feel better about myself.

So, while I occasionally dated Todd, I also started dating another guy named Ralph from a nearby town, Cotterville. Ralph was recently divorced and had three young children. He was quite a bit older than me. Ralph was quiet and shy, had a great job making good money, and really liked me. I got the sense that he was looking for a replacement mother for his three small children. But I didn't like myself enough to acknowledge someone who truly may have cared about me.

I hadn't put much thought into restrictions for Riley meeting the men in my life. After Brandon and I broke up, she asked about him and reminded me of how sad and lonely I was. One weekend, when she was home, I had Todd over on a Friday night. Todd was immature and fun, and Riley had fun with him when he was there. I sent him home in the morning because I knew I was spending the day with Ralph. When Ralph came over later, Riley accidentally called him Todd. I laughed and made up some excuse about why she would call him that.

But then I realized how my behavior was affecting Riley. My daughter, no longer a toddler, saw different men at our home on different nights of the week. Yes, I was in a lot of pain. I was hurt over Brandon, but it had started way before then. I was coming to grips with who I was as a person—a person I didn't feel was good enough. What was that teaching my daughter? My life was in shambles, but I had to hold it together for her. Yes, I was lonely, and I wanted someone in my life, but I had a responsibility to show my daughter that I could survive on my own and didn't need a man to do that for me. So, I stopped having random men come over when she was there, but I didn't stop my reckless behavior.

I continued working at the real estate company, avoiding Brandon, and getting online to chat with people and learn about other countries. I struck up conversations with people from different parts of the United States, England, and even Australia. I wondered what I was going to do with myself. Who was I meant to be? I knew I couldn't strip forever. What had happened to my dreams for a better life?

Eventually, I lost my job at the real estate company. The president discovered I spent too much time online and not enough time working. I was no longer doing quality work after Brandon and I broke up, and it wasn't a good fit.

I knew I needed a "real" job again. I wasn't in a position to work every single night at a club to make ends meet. I didn't even know if I wanted to return to full-time dancing; it somehow felt like a step back. I had Riley at home during the week attending preschool, and working only on weekends wasn't going to cut it. So, I quickly found a receptionist job at an insurance agency in Johnsonville.

I lost my job on Friday and started a new one on Monday. Meanwhile, I still had dancing to keep me afloat.

Godless

Mic had reservations about Brandy when she first showed up at The Pink Goddess Club. He had a dream to build a strong portfolio of classy women in his club, despite its location and clientele. Brandy was loud, abrasive, and brash—everything Mic didn't want in a club. And Brandy started falling out of love with dancing. She fell hard for a guy who lived near her mother, and she didn't want to dance much longer. Brandy had high hopes that the guy she'd met would sweep her off her feet, and she could stop dancing. But she still showed up occasionally, and we ended up working one Friday night together. Little did I know that it would be our last time.

Brandy sat with two guys and called me over after my set was done. During the course of the conversation, I discovered that one of the men was related to the married realtor whom Brandon had been talking with months prior. I had no problem sharing that I knew her, since I no longer worked there.

At the end of the night, Brandy flashed a wad of cash at me. I couldn't believe she'd made that much money, since I hadn't made nearly as much. I grew bitter, wondering why I couldn't get more dances, or at least tips from dances. I was getting older and had been dancing for nearly four years at this point. The old feeling that maybe I wasn't good enough creeped into my thoughts. A small part of me wondered if I had lost my dream of being a beautiful exotic dancer. The glittery tarnish had worn off and what was left had turned dull and rough.

After our shift, we went downstairs to get dressed. Brandy was in a rush and wanted to get home. She told me to hurry. I figured it was because she wanted to get home to her man, who didn't approve of this job. She was driving that night, so I hurried as fast as I could.

We left the bar and jumped in her truck. It was winter, and her windows needed to be scraped from the frost.

"You start the car; I'll scrape," I said. We made quick work of it to not attract attention.

"Hurry up and get in. It will warm up." She was already in the truck and kept glancing behind her.

Just then, the two guys we were sitting with in the club approached us.

"Shut your door!" she yelled. She slammed hers and put the truck in reverse.

My door swung wide open, and I grappled with it as she squealed out of the parking lot. Her truck engine whined because it didn't have time to warm up. "What are you doing?" I yelled, grabbing my seat belt.

I looked behind us, and the guys were in the parking lot, yelling and shaking their fists in the air.

"Why are they mad? What did you do?"

"Shit! I can't see," she muttered, glancing in the rearview window.

We couldn't see anything out the front or the back. The truck wasn't warmed up, and now the windows were fogged.

"Brandy, we can't see. You can't drive like this."

She glanced behind us again and pulled over in a closed car dealership parking lot. She opened her door, stood on the running board, and wiped the windows with her sleeves. I grabbed the scraper and tried to wipe my own side down. Whatever was happening wasn't good, and I didn't like being in a dark parking lot.

Headlights flashed across our vehicle as a truck pulled in behind us and screeched to a halt. The two men from the club jumped out and started jogging toward us.

Brandy screamed, and we both jumped in the truck again. As we tore out of the parking lot, I struggled to get my seat belt fastened. My hands were shaking and cold from trying to scrape the windows.

They followed us all the way out of town. They pulled alongside our vehicle and shook their hands at us, trying to get us to pull over. They veered toward the truck a couple of times and nearly ran us off the double-lane road.

"What the fuck happened?" I asked, keeping my voice calm. I grabbed my workbag and held it to my chest.

She shrugged her shoulders and lit a cigarette. "Men. They're stupid as fuck."

"What does that mean?"

"I told them I was going to have sex with them."

The wad of cash. All that money. She told them we would meet them after work but took their money instead.

"How much?"

"Three hundred dollars." She hit her cigarette and casually flicked it out the window. "Assholes. Serves them right. Like I would do that for $300 for both of them."

"Brandy, they could have killed us."

"Nothing's going to happen, dude. They're fucking dumb. What are they going to do? Go to the cops and say I stole their money because I was supposed to have sex with them?"

Eventually, they quit following us when we got on the freeway to go home.

I kept glancing in the rearview window the entire way, nervous about every set of headlights.

I got back to my apartment in Grand Heights and let myself in. Riley was at Joey's for the weekend. Just as I climbed into bed, my phone rang.

It was one of them. He had my number from the real estate agent we both knew. She gave him my number.

He swore at me, called me a whore and a slut. He told me he was going to kill me, and he knew where I lived. I hung up on him and refused to answer the phone when he kept calling back. For the rest of the night, I lay in bed in the dark, listening to the noises outside, fearful he would kill me while I slept.

After that stunt, Mic kicked Brandy out. She was officially barred from the Pink Goddess Club. The men had gone back and said she stole money from them, which was true, but they made it sound like she took their wallets. Mic told me he wanted to give her a chance, but he said he'd heard she was trouble, since club managers talk, and he didn't need those sorts of problems for his customers. However, he was going to continue to allow me to work there.

When I told her what Mic said, she shrugged her shoulders. "I don't care, dude. I'm done working at those places."

That was the last time Brandy and I ever ended up working together at a club.

It was the end of an era.

We Belong

I didn't want to drive that distance alone every weekend, so I asked Sheena if she wanted to try it out. She wasn't sure if she would be able to do it, but she wanted to try and caught on immediately. Sheena was naturally a chatty person and loved to talk, so getting paid to do it was right up her alley. She loved the clothes. And she loved dancing.

Eventually, she started getting her own regulars while working. Men loved how she was so friendly and open. One of her regulars ended up being another one of those men who wanted someone to step on his ball sack. She called him a nut-squasher and her formal name for him was Dog Collar Guy because he wanted her to treat him like a dog and smash his balls with her knee. He came in and sat in the corner and silently stared at her until she came to him.

She got along with the other girls in the club, too, which was important. One of the girls at the club was Candy. She was an older lady. And by older, I mean maybe early thirties. I didn't really see myself at thirty still doing this, but I was already in my mid-twenties. More and more, I wondered what else the world held for me after this was done. Candy had a cotton candy pink leather outfit, and she let me wear it for a set once. I danced to Britney Spears "Oops! . . . I Did It Again" and made good stage tips. We also befriended Reya, another dancer who worked there. Reya was straight from the seventies. She had naturally curly dark brown hair and was very pretty, even without a lot of makeup, and she also had large, natural breasts.

The four of us became fast friends at the club.

Sheena's children, Brody and Carmen, were often left with Carmen's grandparents, Martha and Roger, while Sheena worked. Roger was an older, laid-back gentleman who loved smoking weed with us. He was a retired auto industry worker with thin graying hair and a round body. Martha, his wife, was a sweet woman with short curly hair and a gentle smile. She was Roger's second wife and much younger than him. They were open-minded about our jobs and when they weren't watching Carmen and Brody, they liked to visit us at the club.

Roger enjoyed watching us dance more than Martha enjoyed watching him watch us dance. I always felt bad for her, like this wasn't the life she had planned for herself and Roger—a life spent hanging out at strip clubs with her son's ex-girlfriend and practically raising their grandchildren.

One night, Martha and Roger rented a room from the motel at the club. They came to watch us dance and then left for "alone time." Sheena suggested we go over there and get high with them after we got out of work. I agreed but felt like we would be unwanted guests.

We showed up, and Sheena lay on the foot of the bed, regaling them with stories from our night. Martha was covered up with a blanket. I could tell she wasn't happy with our visit. Sheena smoked a joint with Roger, and I sat at the end of the bed, trying to make small talk about our night.

On the way home, I mentioned that it seemed like Martha hadn't wanted us to interrupt their night out. Sheena shrugged. "She knew what she got into when she married Roger," was all she said.

One night, Martha, Roger, and one of their family friends, Trina, came to visit the club when we were working. Trina was younger, with long blonde hair and a boisterous laugh. She reminded me of Brandy. I missed Brandy now that she no longer danced; it wasn't the same without her.

The rounds of shots started flowing, since Roger was buying the drinks. I was woozy, and I tried to remember the last time I had eaten. I didn't necessarily have an eating disorder, but food intake still wasn't high on my list of priorities.

I managed to make my way downstairs to the dressing room and lay on the floor. Sheena came down and brought Trina with her. They tried to get me up.

"Come on, bitch, get up." Sheena kept shaking me and trying to get me to drink water. It was a throwback to the night at Dreamgirls when I was on the bathroom floor and couldn't move, only now I was on some floral carpeting in a renovated motel conference room. I thought to myself, "Something has to change."

Mic freaked out. He would never kick me out of the club but seeing me lying on the floor nearly unconscious made him nervous. He kept asking Sheena what she was going to do about me, his head bobbing like a balloon on a string, as he looked from me to her.

"Don't worry, Mic, this has happened before," I slurred.

This did not, however, make him feel any better.

Eventually, an ambulance was called. They came and took me away. Sheena stayed with me at the hospital, hunched over in a chair. I was in and out of consciousness. There was murmured discussion that perhaps someone had given me something. In my moments of wakefulness, I insisted that wasn't it. I just hadn't eaten in a while.

When I woke up, my mouth was dry. My eyelids were glued shut with dried mascara and my hair was snarled. Someone had thrown a jacket over me, but I was still wearing my club clothes. I was a complete mess.

The doctor came in and stood near the edge of the hospital bed with a clipboard in his hand, looking down at me. "Your bloodwork came back. There's marijuana in your system."

"Yeah, so?" Shame washed over me, and I turned away from him. I was a professional. I worked in an office. This wasn't who I normally was; I had just forgotten to eat.

He quietly stared at me for a moment. "You're going to want to make some lifestyle changes if you want to live longer."

This shocked me. Out of everything he could have said, this struck home.

But still, I looked away and sighed loudly. "So, what, can I go then?"

He didn't answer but exhaled as he gave my file to the nurse and left the room. I gathered my belongings, and Sheena drove me home.

The entire way, I thought about it. Did I even want to live a long life? For so many years, the end of this system was supposed to get here, and I was resigned to dying in Armageddon. But what if it never came? What was the rest of my life in this system going to look like?

The Joker

My younger sister Scarlett was pregnant for the first time by her boyfriend, Peter. Peter was a nice guy but not very responsible. After a brief discussion over drinks, I allowed them to move into our apartment. It was Riley and me in a three-bedroom apartment. I liked the idea of not living alone, especially since that phone call with the men Brandy had ripped off. And I was lonely whenever Riley was at Joey's for the weekend.

Scarlett and Peter moved in, and he brought his animals with him: a flying squirrel, and two ferrets. Riley and I went from having lots of space to no room at all. I had been lonely, and now it was too much.

Sheena lived in an apartment in Lincolnshire and told me her landlord had a vacancy next to her place. Riley and I made the move to a one-bedroom apartment across from Sheena, while my sister and her boyfriend stayed in my old apartment. Riley was starting kindergarten, and Lincolnshire had a good school system. This would be a good move for us.

The bonus was that it was nearer to my job at the insurance agency. It was also closer to the Pink Goddess Club. Despite the recent emergency room visit, I still decided I needed the money from the club and continued working there. Sheena and I carpooled with Reya, and the three of us frequently got stoned before we headed into work on weekends. Typically, after work, we stopped at a Hardee's drive-through as a 3 a.m. treat. Sheena and I always got mushroom Swiss burgers with a side of curly fries. The burgers were huge, dripping with grease and melted cheese. We would get high, devour our fast food on the way back, and share our stories of the night. Those were some of the best evenings when I worked weekends.

Around this same time, I got in touch again with my half-brother, Logan. I met Logan for the first time in high school. He lived with his grandparents in my hometown and attended our school while our biological father was in prison for drugs. After graduation, we periodically talked and kept up with each other.

Logan made it his personal mission to introduce me to our biological father, who had since been released from prison. He bothered me constantly to see if I had changed my mind about wanting to meet him. I hadn't. I was in my mid-twenties, and I'd made it this far without him in my life. Why change that now? I was still upset that our father was a drug dealer who was doing time in prison. My mother told me when he got caught that he had been one of the biggest drug dealers in our county at the time. He drove an IROC-Z sports car, souped up with nitrous. He didn't appear to be legitimately working at a job that could afford his lifestyle, so the authorities had taken notice. After his conviction, he spent quite a few years in prison. As a little girl, I had only wanted him to save me from my childhood.

Logan knew I was a dancer on the weekends and that I worked in Baker at the strip club. He made jokes about it, but sometimes I think he was proud of the fact his big sister was a stripper.

One Friday night, I was working and talking to guys at a table, when Logan and one of my former high school classmates walked into the club.

My stomach dropped to the floor. Did he understand how uncomfortable this would make me? It was bad enough when Martha and Roger visited, since I knew them outside the club, but he was family. He was my brother.

"Hey, sis," he said, opening his arms for a hug. I tugged at my skimpy clothes, trying to cover myself up even more, and hugged him stiffly. Then I waved to my high school classmate, wondering why he hadn't mentioned to my brother that maybe this wasn't a good idea.

Another man had walked in behind them and lingered near the bouncer's podium. I only realized they were all together when Logan stepped aside and introduced us.

"Sis, you refused to set up a time to meet Dad, so I brought him to you." My brother's face shone in excitement. He held his arms open between the two of us, as if to draw us together. His wish came true. Finally, he found a way for us to connect—his father and sister, together at last. My classmate looked away, at least acknowledging how awkward this was for me.

My father smiled benevolently from ear to ear when the introductions were made. Apparently, I was alone in thinking this was the worst possible way to meet a parent for the first time. Of course, it was also awkward because while everyone else was appropriately clothed, I was wearing nearly nothing.

I did not know how to handle this.

I waved feebly in his direction, my body frozen in shock. This was raw exposure in the worst way possible. Over the years, I had built up a persona that was the "club Holly," with a stage name, songs, and clothes that suited that identity. Then there was an "at-home Holly," with family and comfort and the real me. Those worlds didn't mesh well. This was not how this was supposed to happen.

My emotions warred inside me, from the indignant: *I will tell them to leave immediately. They shouldn't have done this.* To the club demeanor: *Make them feel welcome. Embrace it.*

At that point, any decent person would have noticed I was upset and turned around to leave. Logan lost the cheerful expression he'd worn when introductions had been made. Based on my reaction, he appeared to be rethinking his decision about coming to the club.

My biological father was not a tall man; he had a rounded belly, most likely from drinking. I knew from conversations with Logan that he was a truck driver, and he looked like what I thought truck drivers should look like. He wore a flannel shirt, which hung down over loose-fitting blue jeans. His dark brown curly hair sprung up around his head, and he had vivid blue eyes, like mine.

My classmate from school took this opportunity to go to the bar and get a drink. My father ignored my discomfort and lumbered up to the bar with him. They picked up their drinks, then headed over to the pool table, grabbed a pool stick, and cued up to shoot pool.

"Are you crazy, Logan?" I hissed at my brother. "How on earth did you think this was a good idea?"

He looked contrite. "I'm sorry. You wouldn't set up a time. I had to do something. He wanted to meet you." He paused and looked at our father, now playing pool in the strip club where I worked. "Are you mad?"

I didn't know what to say or do. I certainly didn't think it was appropriate that they were here. I found Mic and told him he needed to make them leave. When I explained why to that pallid little weasel, he said he couldn't do anything about it because they weren't causing any problems, and they were paying customers. No one kicks out paying customers, no matter who they are.

"Well, then, I guess take me out of the rotation," I shrugged my shoulders. "I'll go get dressed." If I was fully clothed, it wouldn't be that bad. I just wouldn't be able to make any money that night, unfortunately.

More head nodding, then shaking. "No, Noelle, I can't afford to pull you tonight. I need you to dance. There aren't enough girls as it is."

I stared at him, and he kept nodding his head and looking at me and then away. I was filled with rage, but I told myself I needed this job.

When it was my turn on stage, I kept my back toward the pool tables and refused to remove my top. Then my father approached the stage with money in his hand during my set. I nearly tripped as I backed away from him, a look of horror etched on my face.

He shook his head and threw the money at me. At least he had enough sense to know the depth of how inappropriate it was to approach the stage with cash in his hand.

He yelled to me loudly over the music, "This will help make up for the years I couldn't pay anything."

Somehow, I managed to finish my shift.

When they left, my father gave me a hug. He told me he didn't understand why my mother had married that "no good asshole," and I bristled at his attack. After all, that "no good asshole" raised me and took care of me—maybe he wasn't the best, but he was there a whole hell of a lot more than the current asshole standing in front of me.

He slipped me his phone number and told me he wanted to "be a dad" to me now. I looked at his curly hair and drunken stance, the untucked plaid shirt, and the nearly finished beer in his hand. I recalled my dreams as a young girl of him taking me away to a home with a white picket fence and horses.

A deep, overwhelming sadness consumed me later when I sat with this moment—a profound sadness for the little girl I had been, wondering why he never wanted to see me and if I had done something wrong.

He was a broken man. Just as broken as me.

Slow Ride

I still worked at the insurance agency. Sheena recently finished her medical assistant certification. She didn't want to dance forever, and she had dreams about an education and making money in the medical field. She was a good example of setting goals and reaching them. I became curious about going to school, too. What would it take? Did I have something in me that could help me find a new future and better dreams?

Sheena met a guy named Simon who wanted to go to school to be a cop. Sheena phased out of dancing and decided to go straight and narrow for him. We still went out together on the weekends I wasn't working or didn't have Riley. Even after Sheena met Simon and gave up dancing, she was still talking to other guys in the bars.

We occasionally went out to bars in Baker. Sheena and I were the best dressed. It was a small town, and people knew we were strippers at the local club. I guess I should have been used to the shitty attitudes by then, particularly from women, but it was starting to get old at that point. I used to feel a thrill of excitement when I walked into a bar and knew I looked good. I almost thrived on other women's anxiety and hatred;

I fed off it. I even borrowed a shirt from Sheena once that read "Hold my purse while I kiss your boyfriend."

I met a guy named Brian. He had short dark hair and intense green eyes. There was something quiet and withdrawn about him. His friend was someone Sheena had been trying to hook up with. Brian and his friend lived near each other, and after a night at the bar, we ended up going back to their apartment complex. I hadn't been fond of going, since we barely knew them, but Sheena begged me. I was her alibi for Simon, and she really liked this guy.

I went upstairs with Brian, and we ended up fooling around on his bed. It was as if the night had already been planned in his head. And it had already been decided that we were staying the night so that no one had to drive home drunk. I was stuck here, since Sheena had driven, even though I was mostly sober.

I briefly wondered what would happen if I said I didn't want to have sex. I was getting tired of people thinking that because I was a stripper, I had a lot of sex, or that I was a sure thing. Brian kept pushing, and I eventually gave in. In the middle of it, I realized I wasn't having a good time.

"No. I'm done." I pushed him off me.

But he kept going. "Just a minute," he grunted.

But it lasted longer than a minute.

Eventually, he rolled off me, and I turned away from him. I got the impression he wasn't interested in me for anything further than what had just happened, and it didn't bother me. I wondered if somehow, I was broken, or if life was always going to be a series of one-night stands or nonstarter relationships.

Sheena and I left early, as the sun was coming up. Brian didn't even roll over when I told him I was leaving. I was still numb, and I explained to Sheena what had happened and how it had upset me. She brushed it off, telling me that men could be dicks sometimes. She encouraged me not to say anything about our night. Her focus was on making sure we kept our stories straight so that Simon never found out.

I got quiet and studied the passing scenery outside my car window on the way home and wondered how long my life could last like this. I wanted more. More than just this meager existence. I definitely wanted more out of my relationships. And I wanted out. I dreamt about what it would take to buy a home for Riley and me someday—or go to college and get a good job, maybe even a real career.

Shortly after that, Sheena and her kids moved out of her apartment and into a place in town with Simon. He asked her to marry him. She said yes, and I wondered how good of a fit that would end up being. I didn't dislike Simon, but he was so different from Sheena. And I didn't think he knew who she was.

When Sheena needed to smoke weed or cigarettes, she came to my apartment. Simon didn't like her smoking—not weed, not even cigarettes—and she wanted to comply with that. I had never known Sheena to not be smoking something. Sometimes when I came home, she was waiting for me in the driveway. She couldn't wait for me to get there so that she could have a cigarette or smoke a joint with me.

After we smoked, and before she left my apartment, she pulled out her bag of ammunition. She had Febreze for her vehicle and body spray for her person. She carried Listerine breath strips for her mouth and a wide assortment of breath mints. She went through a huge ritual of spraying, fluffing, spritzing, and sucking before she went home so that Simon wouldn't find out. I thought it was hilarious he had no idea she smoked.

Meanwhile, I still worked the front desk at the insurance agency and mostly enjoyed what I did. Every day we had various packages show up in the mail. The FedEx delivery guy, Jeremy, asked me out on a date. He was tall, with dark brown hair and dark brown eyes that always seemed to be laughing when he looked at me. I could see myself liking him; he reminded me of Brandon.

He took me to a nice restaurant in Williamstown for dinner. It was fancy and not a chain restaurant. The lighting was muted, and there were tablecloths on the table. I got dressed up and so did he. As we shared an appetizer, he told me he liked music and was in a band. Afterward in the car, he asked me if I smoked weed.

"Yeah, I do." I didn't want to start off a relationship on the wrong foot, like Sheena had done. Better that he find out now.

"Really?" he looked shocked. He grinned and opened his glove compartment box.

"You do too?" I asked, equally shocked.

We smoked a joint in the car, and he told me he couldn't tell if I even smoked or not. This was the first time someone had ever assumed I wasn't into some sort of drugs. It felt good to be considered a professional who didn't smoke.

We talked on the phone for a while and things between us progressed in a positive way. I enjoyed spending time with him and found out we had a lot in common. We both liked the same music and reading. He liked writing music, and I enjoyed writing stories.

I eventually told him I danced on the weekends, but I didn't want to do it any longer. It was weird saying that out loud. That was the first time I admitted I didn't like dancing anymore. He said he could understand why.

I was hopeful about finally meeting someone who could help me realize my dreams. He had a good job, was stable, and didn't mind kids.

One evening, after another date night, we started kissing on my couch. I was excited. We were taking it to another level in our relationship, and I was ready. Just as we started reaching the next step, he stopped and pulled back.

"We can't do this."

"Why not? Yes, we can." I giggled and removed more of my clothes, doing a striptease for him. I was a pro at making sure men knew what they wanted. I thought he was playing hard to get.

"No, you don't understand. I can't do this. I thought I could, but I can't."

He was serious.

"You're not married, are you?" I asked, hesitating as I leaned toward him.

"No," he shook his head, and another minute passed, as I waited in front of him with my shirt off. He then explained he had a disease. One that doesn't have a cure. He didn't want to risk exposing me to it.

My heart sank.

Looking back now, I'm so grateful for his honesty with me. But at the time, I was heartbroken and devastated. My dreams of another perfect relationship slipped away.

He apologized and kissed me goodbye, leaving me half-dressed on the couch, alone in my living room.

I cried all night and wondered if I would ever meet someone who was meant for me.

The next morning was Sheena's wedding. Originally, Jeremy was going as my guest, but now, I was going solo. I already had promised her I would do her hair for the wedding, so she showed up bright and early, with her sprays, breath mints, and spritzers, ready to smoke before her big day.

I explained what had happened.

"Hey, babe. I'm so sorry." She hugged me. "But at least he was a good man for being honest about it. There's someone out there for you, just like how I found Simon." She finished rolling the joint, lit it, and handed it to me.

I put on a happy face and did her hair in ringlets, pinned up with baby's breath flowers. I finished her hair and sprayed it to set it. I wanted her to look good for her wedding day. I vaguely wondered if I, too, would ever have a wedding day.

I enjoyed doing updo hair styles. I also liked getting high and doing nails. I constantly asked people if they wanted their toenails painted or their hair pinned up. It reminded me of the old days of cross-stitching with Maggie or making fake sheets of acid. I got high and zoned out.

Eventually, Simon caught on about Sheena smoking, despite her bag of smelly supplies. Somehow, I got dragged into the middle of it. Simon told Sheena he didn't want her hanging out with me any longer because I was a bad influence and clearly the reason she couldn't quit smoking.

After the brief relationship with Jeremy, I was determined not to get involved again. A guy named Paul ended up moving into Sheena's old place across the hallway from me. Paul was a painter and quite a bit older. He smoked weed, and I liked hanging out with him. I started fucking him. I came home for lunch, we fucked, got high, and then I went back to the office.

At that time, one of my school friends, whom I had known since middle school, got a job at the insurance agency where I worked. Shelby and I picked up again like no time had been lost. She even asked me to be in her wedding.

When she came to my apartment one afternoon, I pulled out a joint and lit it up in front of her. I knew she didn't smoke, but I figured she wouldn't mind if I got high before we left. She screamed and ran to my bathroom, shutting the door.

"That's illegal. Don't do that in front of me!" she screeched. She was shocked that I was so different from the girl she'd known from school.

I laughed and poked fun at her. But inside, I was shocked at her response. I hadn't been around anyone who thought it was scary.

I put out the joint, but her reaction made me realize how far I'd drifted from the young, sheltered girl in school I'd once been.

Iris

A tour of bands came to town one year for Oktoberfest, and I had tickets to go. I invited Brandy to join me. We still hung out occasionally, even though she'd left the dance scene. We never talked about what had happened that night, but it had upset me that she put my life in danger, too, when she stole from those men. I put it behind me because we had too much history, and I didn't want to lose her friendship. I had a third ticket, so I decided to take Scarlett, too.

Brandy and I got dressed in our full stripper attire. I wore a black knit halter top with a purple pleather coat and leather pants. Brandy wore her long, shiny black leather coat and her black leather pants. Scarlett wore jeans and a "dude sweater," as she called it. She had just given birth to my niece, and none of her pre-pregnancy clothes fit her yet. This was her first time going out since my niece was born. I'm not sure how comfortable she was with us dressed like we were, complete with glittery eyelids and pleather, but she was happy to get out.

We listened to a couple of the bands play. The crowds were going wild. We couldn't get near the stage with our tickets, so we wandered down the street to get something to drink and smoke a joint.

We came across a fenced-in area with large buses parked behind orange gates. It was somewhat off the main path. Brandy and I stopped to look, and a security guard with his arms crossed in front of him told us to move along.

Just then, one of the bands came off the stage and approached the bus.

"Dude, that's the band," Brandy said. She attempted to make a beeline toward the lead singer, who was surrounded by security and women dressed just like us.

Scarlett and I hung back near the orange dividers. I kept my eyes on the rest of the band members as they walked to one of the buses. The security guard was adamant that we not approach the dividing wall. We loitered near a gay bar called Spiral, until their bouncer came out glancing at my attire and telling us that two women "could not be hanging around the entrance of their bar since we were scaring the men off."

As the band members got nearer, I called to one of them who was mingling a bit with the crowd. He glanced up at me and smiled, then walked over to us. He was tall, at least six foot two and had a shaved head.

"Can you autograph my stomach?" I asked, lifting my shirt and leaning in past the barrels.

"Okay . . . your stomach?" He glanced down at my bared stomach, as I lifted my halter top to show him where he could sign.

Someone handed him a black felt-tip pen.

"Right here?"

I nodded, already mentally figuring out how I could get beyond those orange gates. The security guard watched me closely. He wasn't happy but couldn't say anything.

My sister hung back, glancing around and plucking at her sweater sleeve.

"Can I have a CD?" I asked, using my sweet do-me-a-favor voice.

The guy shook his head and held his hands out. "Sorry, we don't have a lot of them to give away. We had to give some to the radio station."

I must have looked bummed, shocked, surprised. I didn't realize that a band wouldn't have an unlimited supply of CDs hidden away somewhere.

His bandmates called to him. They were getting on the bus. He glanced at me one more time. "You wanna come hang on the bus for a while, though?"

Bingo.

"Sure. My sister can come, too, right?"

There was no way I was getting on that bus alone. I glanced behind me and grabbed my sister's hand. She wasn't happy about this development. Since she was nursing, her breasts were getting full, and she wanted to get back to my niece. I convinced her to come on the bus.

The security guard glared at us. I gracefully tried to climb over the orange divider, but my tight leather pants squeaked in protest. I glanced around for Brandy, who was still fighting to get the attention of the lead singer.

Scarlett and I hesitantly followed the rest of the band members up the steps and on to the bus.

I was so excited to be on the bus of a famous band. It ended up being nothing like I thought it was going to be. It was not like the movies at all. Two of the bandmates plopped down on a couch and started playing a video game, unpausing it and picking up where they left off. Someone asked me if I wanted a drink, and I accepted.

My sister leaned near the door nervously glancing behind her toward the exit, until someone got up to give her a seat. Everyone crammed together to make room.

The band member who asked me to join him on the bus was Adrian, and he really was just a regular guy. He told me he missed home and said being in a band was a lot of work.

"How does it feel to finally make it?" I asked. I was completely starstruck that he got to tour the country and do what he loved.

His answer was profound and has stuck with me to this day.

He asked me, "What does "making it" really mean? I mean, we have a hit. But we're constantly struggling to get airtime. We are always on tour to promote the songs we already did and the new ones we hope are a hit." He then said they always had to be thinking about the next song, the next hit, the next tour. There was no magical place called "it" to make it to; it was always work.

His response gave me a new perspective. All along, I wanted to be the best performer with the nicest costumes, the best shoes, the perfect hair, the most stunning makeup. I wanted to make it as the best dancer, but in the end, there was no measurable way for me to know if I was the best. There was always a struggle.

I would only ever be in competition with myself.

We spent a while talking, and I glanced over at Scarlett. She was deep in conversation with the drummer, whose wife had also recently had a baby. They were discussing their different experiences being first-time parents.

Looking around the bus, I realized this wasn't at all what I thought being famous was about. I was surprised but also grateful for the experience. Maybe "making it" didn't mean something as glamorous as what I thought it did. Maybe making it meant simply being with people who helped you enjoy your life and make the most of your dreams.

The bus door opened, and the lead singer came up the steps. A group of three girls hung off his arms, vying for his attention.

Brandy wasn't one of them.

"I have to find my friend." I stood up. I looked outside the bus windows but didn't see her.

"I'll come with you," Adrian offered. I don't think he wanted me to leave. I was pissed that Brandy hadn't stayed with me and Scarlett, but I felt obligated to find her.

We left the bus and slipped past the security guards. Adrian wore a dark hoodie with his face covered. No one bothered us at first, but I could tell he was uncomfortable. If it were me in a strange town, following a stripper around after dark, I'd also feel nervous.

I couldn't find Brandy.

Some people started noticing Adrian, and he said he needed to get back, so we returned to the bus. He wanted to hang out more, but I had to find Brandy, and Scarlett needed to get back to my niece. I hugged him goodbye, and Scarlett waved goodbye to her new friend and fellow parent, the drummer.

Brandy was standing at the orange barrels, blocked by the security guard who had let my sister and me through.

She was furious she had been left behind, "Dude. What the fuck? Why did you leave me?"

I tried to explain that she left us when she went to hunt down the lead singer and that I had tried to get her to come with us. She kept insisting that I had abandoned her. She was pissed off that she didn't get to go on the bus.

It was a learning experience for me. These guys had a chart-topping hit, played all over the country, and lived part-time on a tour bus. But they still didn't feel like they'd made it.

What was my idea of making it?

I needed to find out. More often than not, I began to wonder if being a stripper wasn't the pinnacle of my success. Maybe there was so much more to me—different parts of me that I needed to learn about.

Men in Black

I worked part-time as a model for Martin Models. Oscar and Harlow Martin ran a model and talent agency out of their home in a subdivision. It wasn't bad work. It was close to fifteen dollars an hour, which was more than what I was making working at the insurance agency.

I did a few gigs with them, mostly for grocery stores. I modeled hair products in the store and handed out samples. If I had to learn a script, it paid more. It was easy money, and I liked the extra cash.

In June of 2000, I worked the Michigan 400 races at the Michigan International Speedway racetrack in Brooklyn, Michigan. There was no script to learn. This job meant smiling, wearing specific clothing, and being nice to the event's attendees. Brandy signed up with me once. We worked at the photo booth where people got their pictures taken with the race cars. It was like old times, hanging out and having fun. We promised to get together again soon after the job was done.

One night, a few weeks later, we decided to go to a bar. While I had outgrown the drugs, parties, and cocaine, Brandy only fell deeper into that lifestyle. I had pulled away from those partying nights, but she still enjoyed them.

At the end of the night, I gave her a hug when we got back to Karen's house where I had parked my car. It was a work night for me, and I had to get up early. Brandy knew how to get some coke because she was still occasionally hanging out with Carl. She suggested we go in on it, but I turned her down since I had to work. No staying out all night for me.

"I miss you, dude," I said. And I did. We'd been partners for so long in the dance world. She was waitressing now, and I had an office job. I remembered how close we were, and I also knew those days were gone.

"Yeah, we could have hung out more, but you *and your job*." She rolled her eyes and laughed.

A couple of days later, I got a call from a police officer while at work.

He asked me if I had a savings bond for Riley in my possession. When I had signed her up for daycare, one of the incentives was a fifty-dollar savings bond in her name.

"Yeah, it's in my purse."

"Would you mind checking for me?" the officer asked.

When I checked, it wasn't there. It had been in my purse, and I hadn't had a chance to put it away in my safe yet.

We eventually discovered that Brandy had stolen the savings bond from my purse after we got back that evening. I hadn't locked my vehicle at Karen's house or brought my purse inside. She had somehow "cashed" it at a gas station, then used the money to buy coke.

"How does someone cash a savings bond?" Karen asked incredulously. "It doesn't even look like a real check."

Brandy was very convincing; I knew this from club days. According to the gas station's security footage, she had filled her truck with twenty-five dollars' worth of gas. Back then, paying at the pump was relatively new. She went in and pleaded with the guy to cash the "check." One, it wasn't even a check. Two, her name wasn't even on it; it was in my daughter's name. The security tapes showed her pleading with the attendant. She somehow convinced this kid to give her change back on a savings bond that wasn't even made out to her. Then, she took the cash and bought cocaine with it.

I knew Brandy was sneaky, but up until that point, it had never been in a harmful way toward me. I didn't want to lose her friendship. But this was my daughter, and I was furious.

She showed up a few days later at my insurance job, twisting her fingers on the strap of her purse. "Dude. Can we talk somewhere?"

I was angry, but I pointed to the conference room. After I shut the door, she spun around and put her hands on my arm.

"I'm sorry. I'll pay it back." There were tears in her dark brown eyes. But I knew her. She only ever considered herself. I realized then that she was probably the most narcissistic person I knew.

I also knew that she stole from customers and her boyfriends. Looking back, I realized I'd misplaced things, and then weeks later, Brandy mysteriously owned the same thing. One time, I bought the CD single "Give Me One Reason" by Tracy Chapman and misplaced it. A few weeks later, she had the same CD in her truck and said it was hers. I had my suspicions, but I never accused her. Something about stealing from Riley made this so much worse.

"Brandy. You stole from me. You stole from Riley. You need help."

"I know. You're right. I do." She stepped away from me and looked down at her clenched hands. "I do need help. I'm sorry." Brandy cried and admitted she had a drug problem and had bought cocaine with the bond. She'd gone to Carl's house after leaving the gas station that night.

"You need help," I repeated. I shuddered when I thought of that creepy old man.

"But will you forgive me? You'll tell the police you forgive me," she breathed out with hope in her eyes.

"What do you mean?"

"You're going to tell them I'm sorry, right? And I'll pay you back?"

"Brandy, it's out of my hands. Even if I forgive you, they're pressing charges on behalf of the gas station. There's nothing I can do."

Her face hardened, and a mask fell over her expression. "K, dude."

And then she left.

Once Brandy realized she was still in trouble no matter what I did, then I became irrelevant—like a man in the strip club who runs out of money.

I made a decision at that point that the relationship between Brandy and me was over.

Stinkfist

The local radio station had a contest for a WCW Thunder wrestling show at the Berlin Center. The contest was open to any female who wanted to sign up to be a ring girl for the WCW wrestlers. The Berlin Center on campus is a huge event facility and holds thousands of people. I decided I wanted to try out for the contest. I knew I was attractive in a club, but I wanted to see if I could win a public contest, too.

The radio station set up a mock runway in the parking lot behind their studio. A small crowd of people gathered. Some were there to support and watch, and a few signed up to walk the runway. I wanted to be a ring girl and knew what I had to do to win. It was no different than the club when I had my sights set on a customer. I had all the right expressions and movements to draw attention. I knew my good sides, I knew how to persuade, and most importantly, I knew how to seduce men, and even most women.

After I signed up, I stood on the sidelines and observed my competition. A few of the women could have been wrestlers themselves. Some of them seemed like they were there because their boyfriends had pressured them. Most showed up in T-shirts and blue jeans. Girls of various sizes and looks congregated like cattle, waiting to be called to walk the runway.

I wore a black jumpsuit, one of my sluttier public outfits. The top consisted of two strips of cloth attached to the waist that covered my breasts and tied in the back of my neck. I wore my stripper heels, which made me quite a bit taller. I applied my full makeup, and my long hair was curled down my back. I gained even more confidence as more people showed up and stared. I channeled my inner Alina and held my head high.

Joey and Riley came with me and supported me from the back of the parking lot. Riley watched me with her big blue eyes. She never saw me wearing clothes like that. And she would only see me with my hair and makeup done for a few minutes before I left the house for the club. She acted shy until I knelt down to her level and gave her a hug.

Joey wanted me to win because there were other perks in the package, including a radio station "Cool Pack" of prizes and fifty dollars in cash. The winners also received free tickets for two people to attend the show with them. There would be a total of three women chosen.

When my name was called, I slowly strutted down the runway and gave my best seductive look. I held eye contact for longer than necessary with those who yelled the loudest. I knew I had the crowd. This was what I did. This was who I was.

The cheers were loud, from both men and women.

I ended up winning one of the three spots.

I immediately knew one of the other winners was a stripper, too. There's something about strippers. They stand out. I don't know if it's the hair, nails, tans, or makeup. I don't know what it is, but there's a glint in the eyes of someone who seduces people for a living. They have a wild look as though nothing and everything scares them at the same time. They have no problem making strong, solid eye contact and studying someone's body language. Most are not haughty, but some are. It was an unspoken code, in the way a woman walked and talked, that made me able to recognize an exotic dancer right away.

When I asked her if she was a dancer, she said yes, at Déjà Vu. Her name was Rebecca. I had no idea if that was her real name or a stage name. Rebecca was loud, with long blonde hair and a raspy voice. She told me my kid was cute but said it in a way that made me think she had no children herself.

The third girl who won was a tomboy named Dana who worked at Subway. She wore jeans and a T-shirt and was sporty and fit. She was the kind of person you knew you could like right away because she was so genuine and kind that she automatically put others at ease.

The three of us won based on the cheering of the small crowd who had gathered.

We got our winning package of goodies, including the free tickets, as well as directions and instructions on who to contact at the Berlin Center when we arrived.

The night of the show, I gave Joey and Riley the extra tickets so that they could come with me. The tickets were for the nosebleeds section. Figured. I came here, showed off my body, and my guests got nosebleeds, watching me from the very top tier. But who was I to argue? It was free.

When the three of us women arrived, a jittery man named Josh greeted us. Josh appeared to be in his mid-to-late thirties. He moved quickly and sweat dampened his thinning hairline. This was hard work, apparently, making sure this wrestling show went off without a hitch. I told Joey and Riley that I'd meet them later, and they left for their seats.

Dana, Rebecca, and I followed Josh into the backstage depths of the Berlin Center. He jogged down the hallway, shouting instructions to us as we struggled to keep up. I dressed in the same outfit I had worn to try out for the contest. Rebecca wore something equally skimpy. Dana had something nice on, but not nearly as revealing as what we wore.

Josh led us through an open area that had sections partitioned off with curtains. There were men in each of the curtained areas, in various stages of costume. I didn't recognize any of them since I wasn't a huge wrestling fan. But as we came through, a few of them hung their heads out and whistled as we walked by.

Most of them looked old to me, complete with missing teeth and combed-over hair. I couldn't believe they made good money, rolling around on a mat with each other and fake fighting.

Eventually, we made our way to a small office. We signed release forms and were given instructions on what our duties entailed. We were supposed to carry the props off set when a wrestler threw them over the ropes and out of the ring. We were to avoid getting hit with the props. We had to stay far enough away so that we wouldn't get struck, but near enough to grab them and make sure no one fell over them.

Josh took our signed release forms and shoved us out the door, still giving us instructions.

When I found out we weren't going to be given sparkly outfits to wear, it became apparent that we were token guests. I thought we would be walking in the ring, holding the numbers up. But there were regular ring girls who did that and traveled with the toothless, older men. Our time ringside was going to be limited as contest winners.

The entrance door opened, and Josh led us onto the mat. As soon as we entered the arena, a deafening roar hit us. We were greeted by thousands of people screaming in the stands.

I looked around, wondering if it had already started and if we'd missed something. I didn't see anyone other than the set-up crew, who had just finished up with the ring and the props. I glanced behind me at Rebecca, who was smiling and waving at the stands.

"Who are they cheering for?" I yelled to Josh.

He winked and leaned into me, "Well, they're not cheering for me . . . wave!"

The crowd was yelling, cheering, standing on its feet.

They were cheering for us.

Dana seemed shell-shocked. Once I knew we were the attraction, my performance persona kicked in. We waved to the crowd on our way toward the ring. Some of the men came out shortly after us, and the crowds went even wilder.

I tried to find where Riley and Joey were sitting, but I couldn't see them anywhere in the stands. They were so far away, and the entire place was packed.

We couldn't have been out there for more than half an hour, picking up chairs, apparel, and other items thrown over the ropes. The real ring girls soon showed up, wearing sparkly outfits, with full-on hair and makeup.

Josh came back and motioned us off the mats and then brought us to the back staging area again.

We were still excited from the adrenaline rush and deafening noise. What a cool job this was! One of the wrestlers walked by and winked at us. He was done up to look like a "real" wrestler with his outfit and greasy body.

"See ya, girls." He waved and headed toward the ring.

"Okay, let's get you back to the office," Josh said, checking his watch.

We followed him to gather our belongings. He and Rebecca led the way to the exit, and Dana and I followed behind, still chatting about our exciting event.

"Okay, you ladies are more than welcome to join your guests in the stands and watch the rest of the show. Thanks for being part of WCW!" Josh motioned to the exit.

There were goodbyes and thank yous all the way around. It truly was a fun evening. Dana left to look for her boyfriend in the stands. I couldn't wait to find Riley and Joey.

As soon as Dana stepped away, Josh leaned in. "Hey, can either of you score some coke?"

Josh hadn't been working hard. He was fucking high. How did I miss that? I guess I assumed that "regular" people with real jobs didn't get high on coke. I drew back from him, instantly more in tune to his nervous, sweaty face.

A tiny part of me wanted to find him some cocaine. I pictured all of us getting stoned, doing lines of coke, and smoking blunts with the toothless men and the road crew. Being part of this world. Hanging out with these people who seemed to have a better, far more exciting life than me. A traveling life of fun, cheering crowds and yelling. This was one more step up from working at a club. This was *traveling* while performing.

And then I thought of Riley and Joey waiting for me in the stands. I imagined meeting up with them—telling them they could leave without me. Little Riley waiting for me, her mama. She was so excited for me when I had left with Josh and told her I would be coming back after I was done and that she was going to see me from the stands. She was so proud to see her mama here, even though she barely understood what it meant for me to win. I thought of Joey, patiently watching her while I did my own thing.

I knew I wasn't leaving them there.

But I hated that man for making me feel bad about my experience. He knew to let Dana leave first before he mentioned the coke. He also knew who he could ask for drugs. I was a person who looked like I could get drugs. He knew we were coke girls, and he knew we could find it. And that pissed me off. I was here with my kid, for God's sake.

"How do you know I'm not a cop?" I asked him with a serious expression on my face. What a dumbass he was to assume it was okay to ask this question without even knowing us. That is what desperation does to a person. All common sense leaves when you're coming down from a high.

"Well, are you?" he asked. He looked me up and down with a flicker of concern.

"No, but you don't know that. Do you?" I took on a cool tone as I looked down at his sweaty face and glistening, balding head. Thankfully, I wore my stilettos.

I instantly went from "potentially cool" to "uncool bitch" in his eyes.

Rebecca laughed to lighten the mood and nodded. "Yeah, I can get it. What are you looking for?"

She had the gleam in her eyes. The wild look. The one that says I can get that for you, but you need to make me part of your world. She didn't have anyone who mattered in the stands waiting for her.

Josh nodded, looking relieved. He found what he wanted. I was useless to him. "Okay, so you're good. You know your way out?" he pointed to the door and barely glanced at me.

Just like that, I was shut out. And I was okay with it. I found myself excited to find Joey and Riley. I wanted to share my experience with them.

I left Rebecca and Josh, who had already forgotten me, and went to the stands.

Don't Come Around Here No More

It was a Friday night at the club, and a couple of guys made a bet on whether I or one of the other dancers could pick up a lighter with our ass cheeks. The other girl giggled. Her name was Athena, and she was new to the club scene—young, with natural breasts and unmarked skin. I was old compared to her, and I was only twenty-six. The guys laughed and then tossed the lighter on the ground between us. I was ready to tell them to spark the lighter and shove it up their asses. But I smiled and laughed and let Athena pick the lighter up.

It was getting harder to fake laugh and pretend to be interested in men who treated us like shit. It wasn't enough money anymore to be worth it. I no longer did cocaine, and smoking weed made me feel indifferent. I didn't know anything else other than this to make ends meet. The modeling gig didn't pay enough and there wasn't enough regular work. I got a promotion at the insurance agency; they made me commercial lines claims. Yet I still felt like I needed this extra money. I didn't know what power I possessed if I wasn't a man's fantasy.

Later that evening, Stormie showed up at the club. Stormie used to work at Jordan's. I hadn't seen her since then, and it had been a while. She was older than me—thin, with short, naturally curly blonde hair. She danced to country music and was a country girl at heart, complete with cowboy boots. Her teeth were messed up if you looked too closely, but she had a good heart.

"Hey, girl. What's up?" I gave her a hug. She felt thin and frail in my arms.

"I just had a baby," she said softly. Her arms fell away from me and clutched around her waist.

"Wow, congrats," I said, trying to remember exactly how many kids she had. She had a lot of them from what I could recall and lived in a trailer park with her husband.

"Yeah, about a week ago."

"You mean," I said, glancing down where her hands rested at her stomach, "you *had a baby* a week ago?"

I was shocked. I couldn't imagine going back to work that soon. Was she even done bleeding? Her stomach was rounded out, not yet flattened after childbirth.

"Yeah, my husband's watching her. We need the money. I've got to work." She shrugged and scoped out the nearly empty club. "Any good ones here tonight?"

"Um, not yet. It's been pretty slow. Well, congratulations. It's so good to see you." But she already wandered off, mentally trying to figure out who to get a dance from.

I grabbed a drink from the bar and made eye contact with potential customers, avoiding lighter ass guys, who had no money for dances. I didn't feel up to it tonight, but maybe I hadn't in a while. Stormie was in her thirties, just had another child, and was already back to work, trying to take her clothes off for men. And she was trying to make money a week after having had a baby—a baby she should be home with right now.

Later in the evening, she was sitting at the bar, crying. I knew she wasn't ready to come back to work yet. The customer she was talking to was trying to be sympathetic, but she was a mess. He held his beer in one hand, and the other awkwardly patted her back. It was clear from his expression that this wasn't the fantasy he had in mind.

Someone told Mic, and I watched as he dragged her from the bar to the back office, apologetically nodding to the customer, like a dashboard bobblehead, the entire time. That was the last time I saw Stormie. She may have decided not to come back, or Mic may have told her not to return until she got her shit together.

The next night, a bachelor party came in. Typical loud and noisy group. One of them shoved me toward a guy and sat me on his lap.

"This man needs a woman." A couple of them jeered and punched his arm.

The guy blushed and laughed.

"I'm Noelle." I shook his hand.

"I'm Jason." He paused. "Is that your real name, Noelle?" he asked, laughing.

I winked and took a sip of my drink, settling into his lap.

He was a little taller than me with medium brown hair, highlighted by the sun. He wore a T-shirt that displayed a Celtic tattoo on his arm. He had "smiling eyes," as my mom would call them. He wasn't the bachelor, but he was a guest they had invited for the night out.

We spent the rest of the evening together, talking. Mic wandered between the tables, nervously nodding in my direction. He hated it when I wasn't working the floor. I didn't make shit for money that night, but I didn't care. I took

Jason's number and said I'd call him. I never gave my number to customers in the club, but for some reason, I decided to take his down. He and his friends were trashed when they left, whistling and yelling all the way out the door.

I ended up calling him, and we talked nearly every night after that. He asked me on a date to the Brownsville County Fair. Brownsville is a small farming community, not much different from Baker, and about half an hour from Lincolnshire.

I picked him up, and we drove to the fair to meet up with a couple of his friends. I had a joint tucked in my cigarette pack and I asked him if he smoked.

"I don't really do that. It just isn't my thing."

I discovered he didn't have a driver's license and had just spent a year in jail. He was still on probation.

After our first date, we started hanging out more often. Since he didn't smoke weed, I slowed way down on it too. I discovered I didn't like being high when I was around other people who weren't high. It made it easier to quit smoking around Riley, now that she was growing up.

I continued working at the club on occasional weekends, but less often now that Jason and I were dating. He didn't mind me working there, and he came with me some nights. I remembered how Joey had ruined my relationship with Jack, my Dreamgirls regular. I told Jason he could come with me but had to stay back and not engage with my customers.

He drank beer and talked with the bouncers and DJ. They enjoyed his company. He held my money and watched my stuff. Mic wasn't happy about him being there, but I reminded him he was a paying customer. What could he say? Particularly since he refused to make my brother and biological father leave for the same reasons.

Jason and I had been dating a few months over the summer. Fall was approaching, and our relationship had become strong. I met his mom, stepdad, his brothers, and his sister. I liked them and they liked me. They adored Riley. Jason had grown up in a household with both of his parents, but his father was emotionally distant, so their relationship wasn't good. I could tell that bothered him. I felt that as long as I loved him and supported him unconditionally, then it would be enough until he learned to love himself. I was falling hard for Jason. He was a good man.

And then my world instantly flipped.

I found out I was pregnant.

Return of the Mack

I was excited to be pregnant; it was different this time, now that I was older. I had a true day job, and I could handle it better. But I was also fearful. How would Jason feel about this? Riley was five years old, in kindergarten. It had been just her and me for a couple of years now, on and off with her dad. How would she feel? And what about my dancing? Alina came to mind; she tried to dance for as long as possible, then had to waitress while she grew rounder. I couldn't do that. What about when the baby was born? Could I go back, or would I even want to? I thought of Stormie, back in the club after a week. I didn't want to be like that.

Jason took it well; he was nervous, but also happy. He signed a lease at an apartment complex in Lincolnshire and told me he wanted Riley and me to move in with him. Relief washed over me. Here was a man who could take care of me, be my partner, and help me. I was overjoyed. I worried about how we would make ends meet, but he promised he would be there for me and our child.

I made the decision to stop dancing. I missed the extra money, but I wasn't making all that much on the weekends, anyway. I lost the spark that initially drove me to want to be a successful dancer. I grew tired of the upkeep it took to be a fantasy—listening to men constantly bitch about their lives had gotten old. There was a whisper in the back of my mind that told me that maybe there was something more out there for me—that maybe being a fantasy was only part of who I was as a person. Maybe I had more to offer.

I left the insurance agency and got a job as a receptionist in a local builder's office. Jason made good money working for a builder full-time in Brownsville. All he was missing was his driver's license. But Joey never had a license either, so that wasn't a deal breaker for me.

We moved into a ground-floor apartment located behind an elementary school. Jason and I had the master bedroom. Riley had her own room, which she would eventually share with the baby.

Riley was happy to learn she was going to be a big sister, and she thrived in kindergarten. She liked Jason, but then again, she liked almost everyone in her own, quiet way. He wasn't used to children, but they had fun together. He sometimes teased her, and she was sensitive about it, but for the most part, they got along.

I started to show after a few months of pregnancy. I weighed around 130 pounds at that point and hadn't been that big in years. I outgrew my size one and three clothes and started to stress about it. But I was still happy; I was pregnant by the man I loved.

One day, when I came home from work, Jason wanted me to go for a ride with him. We drove to a little roadside park. He gave me a ring and asked me to marry him. He was nervous and had been drinking, so he kept repeating himself before he finally got the question out.

I said yes.

He was going to make me so completely happy. This was what I had always wanted. We argued a bit now and then, but it was mostly over small stuff. He drank every night but said he needed to because his construction job was stressful. I grew up with an alcoholic stepfather, but I reconciled it in my mind that at least Jason was providing for our family.

Jason wanted a church wedding since his family was Lutheran. I had a knot of dread in my stomach when I called my mother to tell her I was getting married. We still had a strained relationship after all the years of my drug use and my fall from grace within the Jehovah's Witness religion. But she was still my mother. She wasn't enthusiastic about my upcoming wedding, and even less so when I nervously asked her if she would attend.

She went silent on the phone for a moment, then sighed. "You know I can't go to your wedding. I'm not going to a worldly church."

A reasonable part of me couldn't believe she wouldn't attend her own daughter's wedding. But I knew the rules. She wasn't going to budge. I was still disfellowshipped, and it was unfair of me to ask her. She believed I still had time to repent and save myself and my children from the end of this system of things. But until I went back to the religion, she wasn't changing her mind. It still made me sad that she wouldn't make an exception.

I gave birth to another beautiful daughter, Madison, in May 2001. I had been officially done with dancing for less than a year, but my life had changed so drastically. I no longer smoked weed or did any type of drugs, and I hadn't for a while. I now had a newborn baby girl and a six-year-old daughter to care for, and I was engaged to the man of my dreams.

After Madison was born, Sheena and I got together to go out, like old times. Sheena and Simon had gotten a divorce, and she was ready to party. Jason watched the girls for me so that I could go out. It was the first time I'd been out since Madison had been born. I had fun, but it was somehow different than before. In that moment, I realized how my sister had felt the time we were on that band's tour bus shortly after she'd given birth. Although I had fun with Sheena, I was happy to go home.

Things were stressful for both of us as the wedding date loomed nearer. We had a brand-new baby, which meant more expenses, and without my income, it was a strain on our household and our relationship. Occasionally, we argued, but I chalked it up to normal stress from so many changes in such a short period of time. Jason continued to drink to alleviate the pressure from long work hours and listening to a crying baby all night.

We decided to have our actual wedding at the courthouse—not only to save money, but also so that my mother could still attend. Jason didn't understand my mother's religion, but he understood my pain of not having her there.

I bought a size-large champagne-colored dress from eBay to wear. I hadn't lost all my baby weight, which caused me anxiety. For so long, I had identified as someone in a "fantasy," and now I had turned soft and fluffy in areas that had formerly been sharp and angled. Jason sometimes commented on my weight, chiding me that my stripper attire was useless, since I'd never fit into it again after having Madison.

The day of my wedding, my mom gave in and helped me get ready. I was at my grandparent's house, where my parents now lived, and my mom asked, "Who's up for a screwdriver?" She then poured herself an orange juice and vodka. I was a bit shocked since it was so early in the morning and she rarely drank, but we each had a drink. If she had any reservations about me getting married, she didn't let on about it.

Jason and I were both twenty-eight years old and got married at the courthouse in Fayetteville on a Friday in July 2002. It was right next to the jail where I had spent the night after fighting with Joey. We had been arguing up until the wedding, which I attributed to stress. I figured it would get better once we got on our honeymoon, but we continued to fight over the weekend, and by Monday, I said I wanted an annulment. That should have been a sign, but I hung in there, like a good wife.

Things were stressful for us with a new baby and Jason having no driver's license. He still worked in Brownsville, but we lived in Lincolnshire. I had to drive him back and forth to his job every morning and still get Riley ready for school. Even though I wasn't back at work, I worked hard at getting everyone where they needed to be at any given time.

Despite the constant fighting, we stuck it out. Jason was a good provider in that he worked every day. He paid the bills, even when I couldn't. To me, this was the epitome of a perfect man. I believed I had finally found what I needed and that my dreams were finally coming true.

Closing Time

After living in Lincolnshire for a short time, we moved to Jason's hometown of Brownsville. Riley had already started first grade in Lincolnshire with her friends, but we moved a month into her school year. She cried at the bus stop when I put her on the strange bus to go to her new school.

Jason still worked for the builder, and we struggled to make ends meet. I found a waitressing job, working nights at a nearby bar called Lucky's Bar and Grill. I didn't care for working around drunken men again. It felt like a step back. But there were times when my old personality would slip through. I could tease and laugh and make men feel good about themselves. They'd leave me larger tips. It did not compare to the money I made in the clubs, but it was better than nothing. That part of myself was embedded in me, and I could pull it out and use it anytime I wanted.

The honeymoon phase was over. I realized that just because Jason didn't do drugs and held down a job, it didn't mean that alcohol wasn't a problem. He drank almost immediately when he got off work and continued through the night. He did watch the girls, though, while I worked evenings. Sometimes his sister watched them for me because he complained he needed a night off from "babysitting" all the time.

As our relationship struggled, I found I needed support. Karen and Joseph were still in my life, helping with Riley and now Madison. Karen always told me she would help me in whatever way she could. She treated Madison like her granddaughter too, buying birthday presents for her and wanting to have her for holidays, as well.

Karen also picked Riley up so that she could spend time with Joey. He wasn't angry with me that I had met and married someone else; he also had met another woman and gotten married. We were still mostly friends, except when it came to the occasional child support issues.

As things progressed from okay to worse with my own marriage, I made the decision to move back to Springfield.

When I moved back, it was near the end of Riley's school year. She had gone to three different first grades because of our moves. She looked miserable in her pictures at the end of the year. When Riley was younger, I could move anywhere I wanted and not be concerned with school districts. Once she started elementary school, I couldn't drag her all over the place just because I felt like it or because I was getting out of relationships. This wasn't fair to her.

My grandfather on my stepfather's side had passed away, so his home was vacant. My stepfather temporarily let me move in while I saved money. I started a job at a local insurance agency in Springfield, but Jason couldn't find work as a builder there. He still didn't have a driver's license, so he lived in Brownsville during the week, and I picked him up on the weekends to spend time with us. It was hard on our marriage, living apart during the week, but part of me was fine with the break from keeping him happy.

We tried so hard to make it work. On the weekends, Jason stood in the kitchen and talked about the type of job he really wanted. He wasn't happy working for the builder anymore. I wanted to support him, and I wanted us to reach our dreams together. He was my husband, and this meant something for us to work toward our goals. I asked him about his dream job. We smoked cigarettes, and he drank his beer while he shared his dreams with me. He leaned against the worn countertops with a beer tucked into a koozie in front of him, with an ashtray, cigarettes, and a lighter right next to it. I sat at the table with my feet tucked up beneath me. Sitting there with him reminded me of my stepfather when I was growing up, drinking in the kitchen as he talked about his own dreams of railroad ties and things bigger and brighter than what we were. I imagined my mother also sitting there listening intently as my stepfather talked about their ever-elusive future with fewer problems and less poverty.

I wanted to figure out how to make a better life happen for Jason, and for our family.

At first, Jason wanted to become an airline mechanic. I took the initiative to set an appointment up for him to visit the local community college. I drove him there so he could meet with an advisor and find out what steps he needed to take. We went on a tour and learned about the required classes. I was as excited as he was. I wanted him to be happy. I was willing to stay with the girls and help him get his career going. Then maybe someday, it could be my turn to find my own dreams. I wanted him to be successful, then we could be successful together.

Just before school enrollment, he decided that wasn't what he wanted to do after all. He wanted to learn how to build and fix motorcycles, like they did in West Coast Choppers. It was an abrupt about-face. But he stood at the kitchen counter and discussed those new dreams on the weekend. We drank and smoked cigarettes, and mentally I tried to figure out how to make that dream possible for him instead.

Meanwhile, I hated living in my step-grandfather's old, cold, drafty home. We had running water, but it was frigid cold in the back bedrooms because of inadequate heating in the winter. I saw myself raising my children in the same way I was raised, in poverty. And I didn't want that.

I was grateful for a place to live, but I wanted more. I wanted to raise my girls in a steady environment, not worrying about changing schools or moving. I wanted our own home. I owed them that. When I mentioned a goal of saving for a house, Jason scoffed. "You're crazy. No one's going to sell us a house."

I had been working steadily. I started making small payments on my old debt, including an eviction from many years prior. All the money I had spent on drugs during my dance career would have paid off all my bills and bought me a house outright. But I tried not to think about that. I tried not to think about all the past mistakes, and instead, I focused on moving forward with my dreams. I remembered the daydream I had as a little girl of having a home in the country. I recalled the brick house we never got that my stepfather had pointed out to me on one of our family drives. I continued to make one payment at a time, chiseling off one old debt and then another. Holding a beer in his hand, Jason laughed at me as he stood at the kitchen counter in the cold, drafty house. He insisted I was wasting my time.

One weekend night when he was home, I mentioned that if he didn't have any ideas for going back to school, then perhaps I could return to school first.

"You?" he sneered. "You think you're going to go hang out with college kids now?" Never mind that he had planned on doing the same thing not that long ago.

I began to wonder if he was ever interested in getting better—doing better—for our family. I knew this wasn't all there was for me. I never wanted to go back to dancing; I knew that was in my past. But I longed for more, not just for myself, but also for my children. I knew I had dreams for me and my girls.

I also realized that when it came to going to school, I had always put the interests of the men I was dating before my own. For most of my life, I had taken the back seat and waited for the men I was with to make the better decisions, for themselves and for our family. But I was tired of that. I decided to put myself first.

Eventually, our issues came to a head. I was moving forward, and he wasn't. We decided to go to a marriage counselor, which helped while we were in the room with him. But when we left, everything slid back to normal, and it didn't seem to help anymore.

Jason and I divorced in 2005. It was amicable for the most part. We still got along, but we had different goals in life. Jason had alternate weekend visitations with Madison. I had a great relationship with his family and had reassured his parents they could see Madison whenever they wanted. I had been so close to my grandparents, and I wanted that for my girls, too.

I continued to save and work hard. It took time, but eventually, I paid off my debt and bought a beautiful five-bedroom ranch home on two acres in the country. One of the greatest feelings was standing in the freshly painted home, knowing I had provided for my girls. They each had their own bedroom. We painted their bedrooms in the colors they chose.

I had help along the way. Karen and Joseph watched the girls for me whenever I needed. Karen gave me everything to get my kitchen stocked. She took me shopping to buy furnishings. For my birthday, they bought a microwave for over my stove and Joseph installed it. My stepfather came over and hooked up my kitchen range. When I got home the day of the closing, Joseph was mowing my lawn for me. I found that somewhere along the way, I had forgiven Karen for the times we fought and the times she wouldn't or couldn't defend my actions. I realized there were many times she was concerned not only about Riley but also about me. Ultimately, she was always someone I could count on in a time of need.

I'd had a dream. A dream to own my own home. One that I could raise my family in. I set a goal, and I focused on reaching it no matter how long it took. And when I finally reached it, that feeling was exhilarating. It made me wonder what other goals I could accomplish. What other dreams did I have? I was determined. I had a good job, but I was in my early thirties now, and I wanted more. I wanted to do something else with my life.

I sat on my porch after the closing and smoked a cigarette. The girls were in their rooms, and their quiet chatter drifted from the open window. I contemplated what to cook for dinner that night in my very own kitchen. The sun was setting, and the wood was warm beneath my legs. The crickets chirped in the nature preserve that backed up to my yard, and the mourning doves cooed to each other in the nearby trees. A large bird flew overhead, and I watched as it flew past.

My house.

My own home.

I finally had a sense of peace. For so much of my youth, I had been so terrified of Armageddon and the end of the world that I only focused on surviving day to day, which really wasn't living at all. Somewhere inside me, I found I had hope for the dreams that I still had coming—and for the time I had left to make them come true.

My dreams kept me alive. My hope for something better was what drove me past the drugs, alcohol, and allure of the sex industry. My dreams gave me hope. I had to learn to come clean and forgive myself for the girl I was back then—the girl who was "too good for the club" but still strived to make that her life. I had to forgive myself in order to move forward.

I'm one of the lucky ones. I made it out alive. I'm here. My children are thriving. My life is good. The shame is there, occasionally, but its sting is not as strong, and instead of seduction, I've learned about forgiveness—for myself and others.

And that's the most important thing. That and my dreams.

Epilogue

In the many years since I sat on my new front porch and began striving for a better life, I went back to school and earned a college degree. First, I attended a local community college part-time and got my photography certificate. I bought some equipment and started my own business, photographing weddings, seniors and families. I made many friends and traveled across the country attending After Dark Education conferences as an assistant to the mentors. Eventually, after many years of on-again-off-again attendance, I obtained a Bachelor of Arts degree in Professional Communications from Siena Heights University. I now work in public communications.

I also began writing, trying my hand at a self-published young adult series, romance novel, short stories, and poetry. Writing and journaling helped me work through some painful moments in my life.

I met my current husband, Doug, in 2006. Ironically, Karen introduced us. She told me she "met a wonderful and kind man" at her job and wanted to introduce us. I told her that I was not interested in meeting anyone, but she surreptitiously set it up so we could meet at a bar with a group of her friends. Doug and I hit it off, and we married in June 2008. He actively partnered with me in raising Riley and Madison, supported me throughout college, and we've been married ever since.

Karen and I remain close to this day. She will never be my biological mother, but she has always stepped in and helped me over the years. I'm so thankful for her support and love, even when I wasn't my most loveable. As for my own mother, I do not have a close relationship with her, but we are cordial. She is still a part of the religion, and I respect that she cannot be close to me for those reasons.

Joseph passed away in 2017 due to complications from smoking and drinking. His death was difficult for me, since he had been an instrumental father figure in my life, especially after I became pregnant with Riley and lost my own family.

My stepfather passed away the day after Thanksgiving 2023, and that was also hard to bear. I had left so many words unspoken, and I wish we could have had a better relationship. My sister and I were at his side in the hospital when he died, and I like to think that brought him some peace.

My biological father passed away in 2013 and, while I didn't know him particularly well, I attended his funeral. I didn't speak to any of the family members there other than Logan and Clarice (a sister I met in my forties from my biological father's side) and made a choice not to get to know that side of my family. I do, however, still talk to Logan occasionally and remain friends with him.

Joey and I are not close, but I still have a place in my heart for him. He has made decisions that make it very difficult to live a successful life. Jason and I remain friends to this day, despite our divorce. He works as a welder and is part of Madison's life.

Sheena and I remain close friends. She eventually pursued education in the healthcare business field, works in billing for a private medical company, and occasionally travels the country as a consultant.

I haven't spoken to Brandy in more than ten years. Sometimes people enter our lives for a season, depending on what lessons we need to learn. I feel our friendship had reached a successful ending when we parted ways.

Riley is nearly thirty years old now and a mother herself. She works as a Certified Nursing Assistant in a private nursing home. She has given me three beautiful grandchildren, a four-year-old girl, a two-year-old boy, and a one-year-old girl. They bring me such pride and joy. I love being a grandma.

Madison attended the University of Michigan for her undergraduate degree in psychology and is enrolled in their social work graduate program. She's set to graduate in winter 2024 and looks forward to making a difference for people in their mental health journeys.

While I'm not a religious person, I have found it easier to be a spiritual person. I no longer live in constant fear of Armageddon and the end of this system of things. I have chosen to lead a love-filled life rather than a fear-based life.

And finally, even though I am not actively engaged in the sex industry today, I will always advocate for sex worker rights. I support legislation that will offer protection and rights to people who are engaged in sex work, and I firmly believe that as long as there are people working in those industries, they deserve respect and workers' rights. Shutting down clubs and criminalizing workers is not a solution and will only lead to more dangerous working environments. Sex work is work.

Acknowledgments

Thanks to John from Koehler Books—for taking a chance on me and on this story, for listening to me talk about my doubts and worries, and most importantly, for making me laugh and pulling me out of the dumps when I only felt like crying.

My amazing editor, Nina Correa White. What would I do without you helping to guide me on this path to publication and making my story the best it could be? You saw my vision and helped me shape this into a true reflection of my beautiful life. Thank you.

Thanks to Catherine "Cat" Herold, my awesome cover designer. From our very first discussion, you already started forming the vision of my story in your mind. It's a true gift to be able to take a story and shape a visual concept for it. Thanks for sharing your talent with me.

My therapist, Matt, who started out as my couples therapist for my first marriage and ended up guiding me through some of the toughest moments of my life. I hope you're enjoying some of the best years in your retirement. I know you said that my recovery and eventual path to wellness was all my doing, but I never would have known that path if it weren't for you.

My Babes 'N Beer crew. Thanks for being my first readers and my biggest cheerleaders.

Thanks to the Screaming Peens. I hope you know how much your support and writing guidance drives me to be a better writer, and I am so happy for all of you in my life.

To my sister, thank you for being there for me and coming back to my life. I love you.

To my daughters. Thank you for being my beautiful saviors. I know there were times when I felt I shouldn't be a mom, but being a mom to you both saved me in so many ways.

And mostly, thank you to my husband for his support during the darkest hours of writing and editing this book. I couldn't have done it without you.

I want to acknowledge the many women currently working in the sex industry who I developed close virtual friendships with over the years. I also want to acknowledge the hard work from organizations such as www.swopusa.org, www.nswp.org, and www.swopbehindbars.org who work tirelessly to ensure that sex workers' rights are considered human rights. Please consider donating to them to show your support.

www.ingramcontent.com/pod-product-compliance
Lightning Source LLC
LaVergne TN
LVHW042250070526
838201LV00089B/102